THE **NROTC** GUIDE

THE **NROTC GUIDE**

VADM Peter H. Daly, USN (Ret.), CDR Micah D. Murphy, USN,
and LT Brendan E. Cordial, USN

NAVAL INSTITUTE PRESS

Annapolis, Maryland

Naval Institute Press
291 Wood Road
Annapolis, MD 21402

Library of Congress Cataloging-in-Publication Data
Names: Daly, Peter H., VADM, author. | Murphy, Micah D., author. | Cordial, Brendan E., author.
Title: The NROTC guide / VADM Peter H. Daly, USN (Ret.), CDR Micah D. Murphy, USN,
    and LT Brendan E. Cordial, USN.
Other titles: Naval Reserve Officers' Training Corps guide
Description: Annapolis, Maryland : Naval Institute Press, [2020] | Includes index.
Identifiers: LCCN 2020002126 | ISBN 9781682475003 (paperback)
Subjects: LCSH: United States. Naval Reserve Officers Training Corps—Handbooks,
    manuals, etc. | Naval education—United States—Handbooks, manuals, etc.
Classification: LCC V426 .N765 2020 | DDC 359.2/232071173—dc23
LC record available at https://lccn.loc.gov/2020002126

♾ Print editions meet the requirements of ANSI/NISO z39.48-1992
(Permanence of Paper).
Printed in the United States of America.

28 27 26 25 24 23 22 21 20   9 8 7 6 5 4 3 2 1
First printing

I applied for a Navy Reserve Officers Training Corps scholarship because, quite candidly, I was not sure when I was a senior in high school that I really wanted to enter the Navy. I also applied to the Naval Academy and was accepted, so I had a difficult choice, though it was a choice between two excellent options. I accepted the scholarship because, while I knew I could easily leave the NROTC program, I would never quit the Academy, even if I was unhappy there. I also knew I had a lot of growing up to do, and wasn't sure I wanted to do it in front of a host of people I might be serving with for many years!

"It turns out that I quickly decided during my freshman year in college that, after watching F-14s flying around the landing pattern at Oceana Naval Air Station in Virginia Beach, I would commit myself to the program. It also turns out that I couldn't have gone wrong either way. I remain to this day a staunch supporter of the U.S. Naval Academy, but I'm also extremely grateful for the education and experiences I had while attending Georgia Tech.

"Many will wonder whether one is at a disadvantage going the NROTC route rather than the Naval Academy. I can answer with a resounding 'no.' Over the past four decades, the Navy has transitioned into what I believe is a true meritocracy. . . . [W]e want to promote the best regardless of their commissioning source or, for that matter, gender, race, or other personally defining characteristic. An airplane doesn't care what you look like when you're landing it at the back of the ship at night, nor does a submarine when you're navigating under the ice, a surface ship when conducting a challenging underway replenishment, nor a Marine platoon when it is being led into battle. What matters is competence and character. Moreover, there are things you may experience on your chosen path that are advantageous. If you look around, you will find many successful naval officers who did not attend the Academy.

"In any case, I would urge anyone entering NROTC to make the extra effort to learn as much as possible about the naval services and their various communities. This means making the most of your summer cruises, and undertaking extra reading about the services when you find the time on the margins of your studies. It also means keeping up with the latest news through resources like Naval Institute *Proceedings* magazine, *Naval History* magazine, and the Institute's various online products.

"I also suggest you work as hard as you can to develop yourself. The most important thing you can do other than learning about how leaders lead— through observation, reading, and your own experience in college—is to develop yourself as a writer. You can think well and not write well, but you cannot write well and not think well. So learn about writing by asking yourself, when you read something that is well written, how the author approached his or her craft. Learn by reading about writing. And then learn by actually writing—a lot. I wrote my first article for *Proceedings* (about ROTC recruiting, of all things!) when I was a midshipman. It wasn't an especially important article, but it was precious experience to expose myself to the discipline required to write for a real publication. You will learn something every time you write at this level, and I encourage you to do it!"

—ADM JAMES WINNEFELD, USN (RET.),
former Vice Chairman of the Joint Chiefs of Staff,
Georgia Institute of Technology NROTC Class of 1978

"In my senior year in high school, I was headed to the Navy recruiter to enlist. My dad, a twenty-three-year Navy veteran, put a stop to that and 'recommended' I take the exam for an NROTC scholarship. As it turned out, I was accepted and sent to Miami University in Oxford, Ohio. My first choice was The Ohio State University as I wanted to obtain an aerospace engineering degree. The Navy knew best. My years at Miami passed quickly and I gained a great appreciation for their academic excellence and the caliber of the student body.

"I developed great friendships within and outside the NROTC unit. Additionally, the summer cruises opened the door for experiencing new activities and cultures. I experienced my first flight in an aircraft and even fired a rocket. I stormed the beach from a 'Mike' boat and experienced the cultures and nightlife in Lisbon, Cherbourg, Paris, Barcelona and Belfast. I even had a turn as helmsman aboard USS *Missouri* (BB 63).

"Upon commissioning I was sent to Pensacola, Florida, for flight training and thus began my thirty-eight years of active duty.

"When I look back, I would not have changed a thing. I felt that my time at Miami provided me with a solid education and a grand opportunity to meet people who had a much different background than I. As for the aerospace engineering degree, the Navy sent me to the Naval Postgraduate School after my first fleet assignment. Later on in my career, I was provided the opportunity to obtain a master's degree from George Washington University.

"I believe that naval officers need to have a very broad education and also exposure to alternative outlooks. The NROTC program offers that opportunity. Just remember, once you are commissioned, it is performance, not your source of commissioning, that is the key to future success."

—ADM STANLEY ARTHUR, USN (RET.),
former Vice Chief of Naval Operations, recipient of 11
Distinguished Flying Crosses and 51 Air Medals for Combat
Actions over Vietnam, University of Miami NROTC Class of 1957

Contents

APPENDICES

Preface

THE STRENGTH of the officer corps is in its diversity, and in that diversity the NROTC program plays a key role. Officers come from different ethnic, religious, and socioeconomic backgrounds. They also come from different colleges and universities from around the United States. Those factors produce a diversity of thinking, and that is all-important. You will face many difficult challenges as a leader. The best leaders don't just rely on their own experience and skills—they take input from others. Always remember to learn from the different viewpoints and solutions that are right there in your wardroom and ready room.

This approach fully extends to your enlisted Sailors and Marines, whose diverse backgrounds, technical skills, and ideas can make the difference between success and failure at sea and in combat. Make it a point to know your Sailors or Marines and their backgrounds. If you know your stuff, maintain high standards for yourself and for them, take care of your people, and have the courage to do the right thing, success will surely follow.

You never know where the best innovation and solution may come from, so you need to create an environment that rewards critical thinking and a culture of positive critique. The best value of your NROTC experience may be the special viewpoint and way of thinking you bring to the mix and what you learn from others.

—VADM Peter H. Daly, USN (Ret.)

Acknowledgments

THE AUTHORS are grateful for the generous assistance of the many naval professionals who helped bring this book to life. While we are unable to thank specifically everyone concerned, we are particularly appreciative of ADM James Winnefeld, USN (Ret.); ADM Stanley Arthur, USN (Ret.); ADM Christopher Grady, USN; RADM Michael Bernacchi, USN; and CDR Thomas Singleton, USN, for their review and input. Additionally, we are grateful to the officers and staff of the Naval Service Training Command, Officer Development; the commanding officers and staffs of the dozens of NROTC units across the nation who assisted in this book; and the active-duty NROTC alumni who shared their experiences in the fleet and in NROTC.

Next, the staff of the Naval Institute Press professional books series, headed by LCDR Tom Cutler, USN (Ret.), provided incredible support and advice to this group of first-time authors—we thank you for your guidance and encouragement.

Last, we thank the hundreds of NROTC midshipmen who volunteered their time to supply us with the stories that truly bring the spirit of the NROTC program to life throughout the text.

Authors' Note

THE TRANSITION from high school to college to professional life is a rapid, critical stage of a young person's life. Thus, as perspectives change so quickly—from, say, the high school senior to a college sophomore—different sections of this book speak more directly to different audiences. The first six chapters are directed primarily toward high school students interested in applying and preparing for NROTC. Chapters 7–15 are tailored toward midshipmen already within the program. After that, chapters 16 and 17 speak particularly to senior midshipmen preparing for commissioning. The penultimate chapter is for the parents and loved ones of young persons interested in or already participating in NROTC, and it can be viewed almost as a stand-alone primer for the engaged parent.

1 Introduction to the Naval Reserve Officers Training Corps

WELCOME ABOARD! This is the standard greeting for new shipmates or visitors embarking a naval vessel. Although we will not literally be taking in all lines and getting under way on board one of our Navy's powerful warships, we are beginning a voyage of sorts to detail a critical first step in the careers of many U.S. Navy and Marine Corps officers. This book is a guide to the Naval Reserve Officers Training Corps (NROTC) program, and we are very happy to have you on board.

NROTC is one of the primary means of commissioning eligible American citizens as officers in the U.S. Navy and Marine Corps. Since the early part of the twentieth century, the Department of the Navy has partnered with civilian undergraduate institutions to train and commission officers in the naval services. This guide is designed to discuss in depth the NROTC program, answer many of the most common questions surrounding it, and highlight some of the many reasons why the NROTC program may be right for you or someone you know.

This book is primarily written for high school or early college students (and their parents or guidance counselors) interested in learning more about service as a commissioned officer in either the U.S. Navy or U.S. Marine Corps. Each branch of service has its own ROTC program; this book specifically addresses the NROTC, but there are enough similarities that this book can also provide some insight into the Army and Air Force versions, too. The U.S. military operates on an exclusively "closed" accession and advancement model—all admirals and generals have started off as brand-new ensigns or second lieutenants. As compared to the civilian world, there are very few possibilities—mostly in the medical or cyber field—of immediately joining the mid- or high-level leadership without having worked your way up through the ranks. Thus, to replenish the ranks of their officer corps, the naval services work diligently to attract young men and women with demonstrated abilities, leadership potential, and a sincere desire to serve in the armed forces.

This book is also designed to be helpful for the parents, guardians, guidance counselors, and recruiters of young men and women interested in serving in the U.S. Navy or Marine Corps. Further, for naval officers assigned as staff officers at NROTC units, the information in this book may help prepare them for, and offer guidance to succeed in, a rewarding but challenging position. The U.S. Naval Institute offers a catalog of outstanding professional books for all stages of a naval officer's career. For officers just beginning their journey, one of them, *The Newly Commissioned Naval Officer's Guide,* is an excellent complement to this text.

All of the authors of this guide had the great fortune to participate in the NROTC program as students, and one later as an instructor. Our paths to entering the NROTC were fairly typical and may be analogous to your own journey.

NROTC Midshipman Chris Robinson stands watch on the bridge wing of the *Arleigh Burke*–class guided-missile destroyer USS *Carney* during a replenishment at sea with the fleet replenishment oiler USNS *Leroy Grumman* in the Mediterranean Sea. *U.S. Navy photo by Ryan U. Kledzik*

This guide's writing team spans the Navy's leadership spectrum—one is a retired three-star admiral who held command at the highest levels within the Navy. As of this writing, another is the commanding officer of one of the world's premier surface combatants, an *Arleigh Burke*–class guided-missile destroyer. The third member of the writing team served at sea after commissioning through the NROTC program and then as an instructor during his first shore duty. We are very pleased indeed to share with you our knowledge and experience (and that of many others) of the NROTC program and follow-on service.

Why a Guide on the NROTC Program?

One of the primary means by which the Navy attracts potential officers is offering scholarships that fund undergraduate education at either the U.S. Naval Academy in Annapolis, Md., or one of the NROTC-affiliated universities and colleges around the country. Approximately 25 percent of an average year's officer accessions will come from those two sources, the remaining 50 percent through the Navy's Officer Candidate School in Newport, R.I. The Naval Academy, and its Brigade of Midshipmen, enjoys a justly deserved renown. Myriad books, guides, and movies chronicle various aspects of life as a Naval Academy midshipman. Each December much of the country enjoys watching the nationally televised, and often presidentially attended, Army/Navy football game between the U.S. Military and Naval Academies. There is much less public awareness of or knowledge about an equally important commissioning source, the NROTC.

"In high school, I participated in my school's Junior ROTC program and had a general desire to earn my undergraduate degree and to serve in the military. The local Navy recruiter visited our high school and a teacher who knew my plans mentioned my name to him. His timing was fortuitous as the application deadline for the upcoming NROTC scholarship was quickly approaching. I agreed to visit the recruiter's office and became enamored with a poster on the wall of a battleship firing a broadside. I went through the application process, completed the physical examination, and conducted an officer interview all in rapid succession. A few months later I learned that I had been offered a scholarship. That was over ten years ago now and I am grateful for the concern those individuals showed in me that helped me to get where I am today."

—LIEUTENANT CORDIAL

"I chose to be part of the NROTC program in order to fulfill the calling I felt to serve my country as part of our Navy combat team, while also developing myself as a college student. I was attracted to the idea of going to college as a real student and getting to live all of those experiences, while at the same time going on afterwards to serve."

—MIDSHIPMAN 1ST CLASS CLOW, Georgetown University, The George Washington University NROTC

This guide aims to fill that gap. It will describe the NROTC program in sufficient detail to help young men and women, and the parents and guardians who love them, to learn about the incredible opportunity that the NROTC program can represent for those with sufficient academic credentials, physical aptitude, potential for leadership ability, and desire to serve as a commissioned naval officer. This guide will help you make informed decisions about pursuing, applying for, and participating in the NROTC program.

History of the NROTC

From the time of the American Revolution, the United States has boasted a strong heritage of citizen soldiers mobilizing in times of national crisis. However, the development of the officer corps remained largely the purview of the military and naval academies at West Point, N.Y., and Annapolis. While American armed forces remained relatively small after the end of the Civil War, the growing industrialization and mass mobilization of warfare required more officers than the academies could produce. In 1916, as World War I raged in Europe, the U.S. Army established the first Reserve Officer Training Corps as a means to train rapidly the additional officers that would be needed were America to mobilize. In 1924 the Navy began its own effort, by founding an NROTC program at St. John's College, in Annapolis, also home to the U.S. Naval Academy. Congress established the Naval Reserve Officers Training Corps in 1926 as a means of both increasing the numbers of officers trained to man a growing fleet and broadening the body of citizens knowledgeable in the art and science of naval warfare. Prior to the establishment of NROTC, nearly all officers in the Navy and Marine Corps had been commissioned after having attended the Naval Academy. Initially, only six universities (the University of California at Berkeley, the Georgia Institute of Technology, Northwestern University, the University of Washington, Harvard University, and Yale University) partnered with the Navy; in 1930 they collectively commissioned 126 naval officers, of whom three would rise to flag rank.

During World War II, the NROTC program rapidly expanded as a means to meet the increased demand for officers in the U.S. Navy and Marine Corps. Wartime ROTC programs focused on rapidly training and commissioning reserve officers who would serve their country during the emergency but demobilize and return to civilian life after the war had been won. After the end of World War II, the Army and Army Air Corps sought a return to the prewar officer-training model that emphasized the military academy. The Navy, under the leadership of RADM James Holloway, recognized the benefits of a more diverse officer corps comprising not only Annapolis graduates. Of the development of the so-called Holloway Plan, which first implemented such staples of ROTC programs as tuition scholarships and monthly stipends, Admiral Holloway claimed:

> Those who evolved this plan believe that the integration of the best type of college and university man from the outstanding institutions associated with the NROTC will be of positive benefit to the Navy; benefit in that there will be associated, in the permanent and career officers, outstanding young college men of diverse and superior educational background representing a wide and catholic range of interest, imposing an introduction of a critical set of values, frankly unregimented in the professional sense, but so equipped withal by practical experience on summer cruises and a modicum of essential nomenclature (that is, the language of naval equipment, method, and custom) as to permit their immediate and reasonable usefulness as junior officers in the Fleet and their development into capable senior officers as well.

Since the end of World War II, the size of the NROTC has fluctuated along with the national emphasis on military strength, but overall it has greatly expanded. From the initial six schools there are now over seventy affiliated host institutions, some among the most prestigious and best-known universities and colleges around the country. From the Ivy League to Southern California, from the Midwest to the Gulf Coast, and the Great Northwest to Dixieland, fine schools across the country either host NROTC programs themselves or have "cross-town agreements" with neighboring schools that do.

For a full listing of currently affiliated NROTC or cross-town universities, please take a look at appendix I.

Naval Terminology

Before going further, it is necessary to define briefly some terms unique to the naval services and NROTC. First, a student participating in the NROTC program is a "midshipman." In the U.S. Navy "midshipman" is not technically a rank as it is in other navies; the term originated in the Britain's Royal Navy to refer to the most junior young officers. Consider a midshipman as similar to a cadet in a nonnaval service.

Second, although NROTC is the Naval *Reserve* Officers Training Corps, all Navy-Option midshipmen are commissioned as "regular" active-duty naval officers. If you are interested in joining the Navy Reserves, then, unintuitively enough, NROTC is *not* the program for you. Opportunities do exist, however, for young men and women to earn commissions in the Marine Corps Reserve through NROTC. Contact your local officer recruiter for more information on how to join the Reserves. (You will find that naval life is full of apparent contradictions in terminology; soon enough, you will take it all in stride.)

Next, an "NROTC unit" is simply the military organization that runs the NROTC program at the school with which it is affiliated. Each NROTC unit is led by a Professor of Naval Science (PNS), typically a senior Navy captain or Marine colonel, assisted by a staff of midgrade and junior officers, senior enlisted, and government civilians. Each NROTC unit is formally, "Naval Reserve Officers Training Corps Unit, *Name of Institution*." For example, two of the authors are Fighting Irish alumni, and the Navy component at their alma mater is known as Naval Reserve Officers Training Corps Unit, University of Notre Dame. Academically, the Professor of Naval Science is head of the Department of Naval Science within an appropriate academic school within the college or university. Thus, the PNS serves in both formal military and academic roles, with responsibilities to both the Navy and the university's administration, as specified in federal law.

All of the midshipmen assigned to a particular NROTC unit are organized into its Battalion of Midshipmen. The structure of battalions varies based on each school's particular situation, but in general the battalion will be composed of a number of companies, which comprise platoons, which are composed of squads. We will discuss in detail the structure and function of the NROTC unit in chapter 2, but for now you need only to understand that when talking about the "unit," we mean the office and active-duty naval staff who run the NROTC program at a particular university.

By "host institution," we mean a university that both maintains its own NROTC program and allows students from nearby schools to take classes on its campus and participate in its program. One of our authors served as an instructor at George Washington University (GWU) in Washington, D.C. Other Washington-area schools partner with GWU and the Navy so that their students are eligible for the NROTC program. The "Capital Battalion" thus trains students from GWU, Georgetown University, Howard University, and the Catholic University of America. In general, students at "cross-town" schools (in this case students in a D.C.-area school who did not attend GWU) would take their required naval science classes "across town" at the "host institution." Many host institutions are partnered with nearby schools. Some of these group partnerships, known as "consortiums," are large networks of affiliated schools within close geographic proximity; they have a single PNS and executive officer, but classes are taught at multiple universities. An example is the Boston Consortium, composed of Harvard, the Massachusetts Institute of Technology (MIT), Boston University, Tufts, Northeastern, and Boston College.

Finally, administratively speaking, all NROTC units are organized under the N9 NROTC Operations (part of the "N code" of the Naval Service Training Command [NSTC]), which is itself subordinate to the Chief of Naval Education and Training, in Pensacola, Fla. NSTC, headquartered in Great Lakes, Ill., is the naval command primarily responsible for the Navy's enlisted Recruit Training Command ("boot camp") in Great Lakes; the Officer Candidate School, in Newport, R.I.; and all of the NROTC units across the country. NSTC is led by a one-star Navy admiral (that is, a rear admiral) and, through N9, exercises centralized control of general NROTC regulations and processes.

The Mission of NROTC

From modest beginnings, NROTC has grown and become one of the primary means of commissioning officers into the U.S. Navy and Marine Corps. Toward this end, the mission of the NROTC is:

> To develop future officers mentally, morally, and physically, and to instill in them the highest ideals of duty, loyalty, and the core values of Honor, Courage, and Commitment in order to commission college graduates as Naval officers who possess a basic professional background, are motivated toward careers in the Naval Service, and have a potential for future development in mind and character so as to assume the highest responsibilities of command, citizenship, and government.

This mission statement encompasses why the NROTC exists. Critical to the health of the future officer's corps is the holistic development of midshipmen—that is, morally, mentally, and physically. The NROTC program seeks, through both academic and practical training, to cultivate leaders with strong moral compasses, outstanding mental abilities, and the physical strength and courage to lead Sailors and Marines in combat. Within the NROTC program are various "options" for midshipmen interested in different types of service within the Navy or Marine Corps.

Within each option are various "communities," which will be discussed in detail later. At this point, however, we would like to make clear that references to "service assignment" are constrained to service within a given NROTC option. For example, the service-assignment process for a Navy-Option midshipman has nothing to do with the military service (Army, Navy, Marines, Air Force) the midshipman will belong to. Rather, by "service assignment" is meant the warfighting community, such as naval aviation or undersea warfare, within the U.S. Navy to which the young officer will be detailed upon commissioning.

The Navy Option

The "Navy Option" is the largest component of NROTC. Midshipmen in the Navy Option will train for and ultimately commission as active-duty officers in the U.S. Navy. Navy-Option midshipmen must complete New Student Indoctrination, Sea Trials, first-class summer cruise, their baccalaureate degree curriculum, naval science courses, physical requirements, and medical requirements in order to be commissioned as naval officers. Specifics regarding all of these requirements will be discussed in subsequent chapters. In return for meeting and completing these standards and agreeing to serve in the U.S. Navy for a period of at least eight years (five of which must be on active duty), the Navy will provide, to qualifying students, a full-tuition scholarship, fee reimbursement, a book allowance, and a monthly stipend.

The overwhelming majority of these midshipmen will commission into an unrestricted line (URL) officer community. A URL officer is a commissioned officer "in line" for command at sea. That means that their career paths lead to command of a Navy combatant unit, such as a warship, submarine, aviation squadron, or SEAL team. The primary URL communities are Surface Warfare Officer (SWO), Submarine Officer, Naval Aviator, Naval Flight Officer (NFO), Special Warfare

(SEAL) Officer, and Explosive Ordnance Disposal (EOD) Officer. Restricted Line (RL) Officers and Staff Corps Officers are not eligible for command of combatant units; they serve rather in "support" roles. Examples of Restricted Line Officers are Intelligence Officers, Public Affairs Officers, and Engineering Duty Officers. The Navy Staff Corps comprise the Supply Corps, the Judge Advocate General (JAG) Corps, Medical Corps, Medical Service Corps, Dental Corps, and Civil Engineer Corps. For more about the various officer communities in the U.S. Navy, check out the online resources in appendix IV.

In addition to the NROTC program requirements during the academic year, each summer midshipmen attend "summer cruises," where they have an opportunity to explore the different URL communities, get under way on a surface ship or submarine, fly with an aviation squadron, or participate in a Special Warfare screening experience with SEALs. These summer training sessions are notionally

Naval Reserve Officers Training Corps (NROTC) midshipman candidates fight a fire in a simulated shipboard compartment in the USS *Chief* Recruit Fire Fighter Trainer at Recruit Training Command (RTC), Great Lakes, Illinois. *U.S. Navy photo by Scott A. Thornbloom*

three to six weeks in length and are collectively an integral part of the NROTC experience. Summer cruises will be covered in depth in chapters 13 and 14. An example of a summer cruise training period is "Sea Trials," where rising junior midshipmen must complete realistic fleet training in firefighting, damage control wet trainers, weapons, and ship navigation. These and related efforts will be explored throughout the text.

When determining whether or not you are interested in the Navy-Option NROTC program, it is critical to keep in mind that NROTC exists primarily to commission URL officers. If your long-term career goals are to become a supply officer, lawyer, or medical doctor, then NROTC may not be the commissioning program for you. Only an extremely small number of midshipmen may commission into an RL or Staff Corps community each year, and such quotas are subject to annual reapportionment and the needs of the service at the time. If you are primarily interested in serving in a RL or Staff Corps community, contact your nearest Navy Officer Recruiter. General contact information can be found in appendix IV.

Marine Option

As part of the Department of the Navy, which contains both the Navy and the Marine Corps, NROTC also serves as a commissioning source for active-duty Marine officers. Marine-Option midshipmen are integral members of each NROTC unit and are held to most of the same basic academic and training standards as are Navy-Option midshipmen. However, there are some significant differences in naval science, training, and physical requirements for Marine-Option midshipmen that distinctly flavor the Marine-Option midshipmen NROTC experience.

The biggest difference between Marine- and Navy-Option midshipmen stem from differences in the service screening and assignment processes. Marine-Option midshipmen must attend and pass the demanding Officer Candidates School (OCS) course in Quantico, Va., before being eligible for commissions as Marine officers. Typically, this will occur in the summer prior to a midshipman's senior year. After successfully completing OCS and earning an undergraduate degree, a Marine officer attends The Basic School (TBS) in Quantico for additional training and evaluation. Based on academic record, TBS performance, and needs of the service, an officer will then be assigned a primary Military Occupational Specialty (MOS). Examples of MOS include Infantry Officer (0302), Logistics Officer

(0402), and Intelligence Officer (0602). An exception exists by which qualified and interested applicants serve as Marine aviators. Approved Marine-Option midshipmen may be awarded a guaranteed flight contract that secures them training as a naval aviator after completion of TBS.

This different process for screening and assigning officers influences the focus of training for Marine-Option midshipmen during their time in NROTC. Each NROTC unit is assigned an experienced Marine Officer Instructor (MOI), typically a Marine captain or major with significant fleet experience. The MOI will be assisted by a senior enlisted Assistant Marine Officer Instructor (AMOI), typically a staff sergeant or a gunnery sergeant. Marine-Option midshipmen typically have more physical, tactical, and practical leadership training and development than their Navy-Option peers to help them prepare themselves for OCS and TBS. However, Marine-Option midshipmen have fewer naval science course requirements and fewer academic requirements. Additional information will be covered in chapter 8.

Nurse Option

The Nurse Option prepares NROTC graduates for a career in the Navy Nursing Corps. The Nurse Option is by far the smallest portion of NROTC graduates and is available only to students who attend NROTC units where the Nurse Option is offered. Since not all host institutions have nursing programs or are affiliated with cross-town schools that have nursing programs, school limitations for Nurse-Option midshipmen are relatively stringent.

As in the case of Marine-Option midshipmen, most of the basic training and professional development requirements for Nurse-Option midshipmen are the same as for their URL counterparts. What distinguishes Nurse-Option midshipmen is the necessary focus on completing their nursing curriculum and earning regionally recognized credentials so as to become eligible for assignment to a military medical facility. Instead of receiving summer training on a naval combatant, a Nurse-Option midshipman may be assigned to a naval hospital or other medical facility to help develop the skills necessary to serve as a Navy Nurse.

Scholarship Opportunities

A significant benefit of participating in the NROTC program is the opportunity to earn a valuable full-tuition scholarship to a participating university of your choice.

NROTC NATIONAL SCHOLARSHIP

Full-tuition scholarship at an NROTC-affiliated civilian institution (> $200,000 value)
All mandatory fees
$750 annual textbook stipend
Uniforms and Naval Science textbooks
Three paid summer training periods
Subsistence Allowance paid each academic month:
- Freshman $250/month
- Sophomore $300/month
- Junior $350/month
- Senior $400/month

There are multiple types of NROTC scholarships available, and each has different application, screening, and selection processes. The types of scholarships available will be briefly discussed here as an introduction and more fully in chapter 3.

The first and most prevalent NROTC scholarship is the National Scholarship. Application for the National Scholarship is open to high school juniors and seniors and college students who have completed no more than thirty credit hours of undergraduate work. The National Scholarship pays the full cost of tuition and fees at an NROTC-affiliated university. The National Scholarship also provides for a book allowance and a monthly stipend. With the rapidly growing cost of a college education, this assistance can be valued in excess of $50,000 annually. As its name suggests, the National Scholarship is nationally competitive, with applications screened by a selection board in NSTC N9. The National Scholarship is available to Navy-, Marine-, and Nurse-Option midshipmen, with the numbers of each option offered determined by the individual service or community. These numbers fluctuate from year to year, but overall, approximately one thousand NROTC scholarships are offered annually.

For midshipmen not on the National Scholarship, there is the College Program, which exists to allow students interested in a career in the naval services to participate with their university's NROTC unit and compete for "sideload" scholarships. For instance, if you have already exceeded the thirty-credit limit and are ineligible for the National Scholarship, the College Program makes other scholarships available, in three- and two-year increments, to college sophomores and juniors. Requirements for College Program midshipmen are identical to those for individuals already on scholarship, and the College Program is available to all options of midshipmen. Scholarship boards meet on a recurrent basis and take into account completed undergraduate grades. Students who are offered and accept a two- or three-year scholarship receive the same benefits as do those on the National Scholarship—full tuition, fees, book allowance, and a monthly stipend. If you are interested in participating in the College Program and competing for a scholarship and are attending an NROTC-affiliated university, visit the local NROTC unit staff to inquire on local application processes.

Conclusion

In this chapter we introduced the Naval Reserve Officers Training Corps program as one of the primary commissioning sources for commissioned officers in the U.S. Navy and Marine Corps. We discussed the different "options" available to NROTC midshipmen, along with the various scholarship opportunities available to both high school and undergraduate students. In the next chapter we will explore in detail the structure and organization of an NROTC unit.

2 The NROTC Unit

WITH OUR INTRODUCTION out of the way, we will now begin to describe in fuller detail the organization and working of the NROTC unit. In this chapter, we will discuss the notional organization of an NROTC unit, the serving staff members, and the unit's role as an academic department within the hosting institution. We will also delve into the notional organization and running of the midshipmen battalion within each NROTC unit. Finally, we will address the variety that exists from NROTC unit to NROTC unit as many take on the flavors and cultures of the host institutions.

By convention, each unit takes the name of the host institution. For example, the NROTC unit at the University of South Carolina is the Naval Reserve Officers Training Corps Unit, University of South Carolina. As noted previously, although the unit resides at the host institution, one NROTC unit may contain students from a few different "cross-town" affiliated universities or colleges. NROTCU Boston University trains midshipmen from Boston University, Boston College, and Northeastern University. However, no matter the academic institution, all these midshipmen are members of NROTCU Boston University.

NROTC Chain of Command

The U.S. military is a marvel of organization and training. Each NROTC unit, as a military organization, has a formally defined chain of command. Each level of the chain of command has distinct roles and responsibilities to ensure mission accomplishment.

If you are still in high school, most of your communication and correspondence will be with the N9 (NROTC Operations) office of the Naval Service

Training Command (NSTC). This office handles the application screening, selection, and scholarship award process. Medical screening too is handled centrally from NSTC N9. You are encouraged to reach out to the staff of the NROTC unit you hope to join upon entering college, but they will only be able to answer general questions concerning life in the unit, its size, etc.

Once officially enrolled in the NROTC program as a midshipman, however, you will have very little or no meaningful contact with Navy echelons above your individual NROTC unit. As you would expect in a hierarchical organization, any personal administration that requires action beyond your NROTC unit chain of command will almost certainly be handled by the appropriate staff officer within the unit. However, in the military it is always important to understand the chain of command, and in the rare circumstance that direct communication above and beyond your unit staff is necessary, it is critical that you realize that even your seemingly daunting NROTC unit commander has a boss as well.

NROTC Unit Structure and Staffing

The NROTC unit is the fundamental organization of the NROTC program. Each unit is manned and resourced to complete its assigned mission: to develop

Iowa State University NROTC midshipmen conduct endurance training around campus.
U.S. Navy photo by Scott A. Thornbloom

midshipmen morally, mentally, and physically so as to commission them as naval officers ready to assume positions of incredible responsibility—leading Sailors and Marines in combat. In this section we will discuss the organizational construct of an NROTC unit and examine the roles and responsibilities of staff members.

The NROTC unit is unique in that it is both a military and an academic organization. The commanding officer of the NROTC unit reports both to NSTC N9 and to the appropriate academic office (perhaps a deanery) within the host college or university. Particular reporting responsibilities and relationships vary from unit to unit, but every NROTC commanding officer is both the military commander of an organized military unit (as commanding officer) and the head of an academic department (as Professor of Naval Science) within a larger academic institution. This last point is really important. Both the Navy and the academic institution recognize that NROTC generally and NROTC courses must meet the school's standards of quality for academic credit.

NROTC UNIT CHAIN OF COMMAND

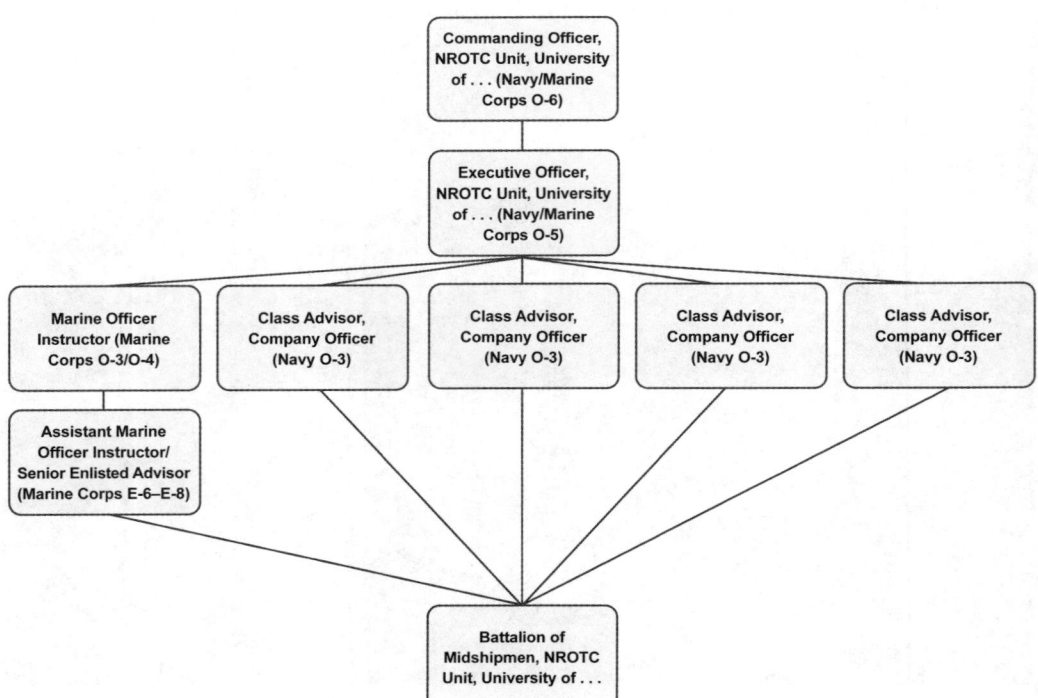

THE COMMANDING OFFICER

The most senior officer of the NROTC unit is the unit's commander. Per Navy Regulations, a commanding officer (CO) is ultimately responsible for all personnel, events, and equipment within a command. The tradition of the accountability and responsibility of the commanding officer is particularly strong within the naval services. Commanding officers of NROTC units are typically either Navy captains or Marine Corps colonels, both of which are at the military grade O-6. Certain NROTC units may be led by a more junior officer, known as the officer-in-charge (OIC), who has most but not all of the roles and responsibilities as a commanding officer. For all practical purposes, however, at the unit level the most senior naval officer is both responsible and accountable for all matters pertaining to the unit.

The unit's commanding officer is an extremely important resource to prospective naval officers. Both the Navy and Marine Corps are particularly selective in assigning officers to command NROTC units, due to the importance of that role in developing and training the future cadre of naval officers. Those selected will have already successfully exercised command of a naval warfighting unit (a ship, submarine, squadron, Marine battalion, etc.) and thus bring invaluable experience and practical knowledge of the naval profession.

As Professor of Naval Science, the senior naval officer at the NROTC unit is also an integral member of the institution's academic structure, as head of the Department of Naval Science. All other staff members assigned to the NROTC unit are assistant or associate professors of naval science and perform their instructional duties by the authority and under the oversight of the Professor of Naval Science. As head of an academic department, the CO is responsible for maintaining the academic rigor of naval science courses and for meeting accreditation requirements.

Last, the commanding officer will serve as instructor in the capstone Leadership and Ethics course, which culminates a midshipman's naval science curriculum. Explored more fully in chapter 8, this seminar course serves to calibrate and refine a prospective naval officer's ethical leadership practice immediately prior to joining the fleet.

THE EXECUTIVE OFFICER

The executive officer (XO) is the second-most-senior naval officer (both Navy and Marine officers are, properly, "naval officers," because they all serve within the

Department of the Navy) assigned to an NROTC unit. The officer serving as XO is typically a Navy or Marine Corps officer in the grade of O-5 (commander or lieutenant colonel, respectively) from a different warfare community than the commanding officer. The XO has significant influence on the day-to-day operations of any naval command, and this holds true for the NROTC unit.

The XO's primary duty is to ensure that the commanding officer's overall vision for the assigned mission and his plan to accomplish it are professionally and promptly carried out. Toward this goal, executive officers ensure that rigid standards of military professionalism and decorum are maintained by all in the unit. Minor infractions and disciplinary matters not requiring the attention of the commanding officer are handled by the executive officer.

Just as with commanding officers, officers assigned to serve as XO of an NROTC unit will bring nearly two decades of fleet experience, or more, to their leadership role and so are a great resource for future naval officers. XOs may have more recent experience than their COs as immediate superiors of junior officers and can discuss best practices and potential pitfalls. These officers are intimately concerned with helping develop, train, and commission the best midshipmen possible and will be happy to counsel and guide them.

XOs primarily focus on the details and planning of unit operations and serve as immediate supervisor for other unit staff members. While everyone within the unit works "for" the commanding officer, in reality they work "through" the executive officer in nearly all of their duties. The executive officer is the final quality-assurance check and filter before matters are elevated to the CO.

Finally, the executive officer is also tasked, appropriately, with teaching Leadership and Management, a course typically taught to spring-semester sophomores. This course, discussed more in depth in chapter 8, deals with the practical challenges involved in directing and leading Sailors and Marines.

THE CLASS ADVISOR

Class advisors are the "workhorses" of the unit, and at least one will oversee and supervise at every official battalion event. Advisors are successful junior officers selected to teach, mentor, and, of course, advise midshipmen. As a midshipman, you will have the most frequent staff contact and interaction with your assigned class advisor. For Navy-Option midshipmen, your class advisor will be one of the Navy lieutenants assigned to the NROTC unit. For Marine-Option midshipmen, your class advisor will be the Marine Officer Instructor (MOI). MOIs have specific Marine-related responsibilities that will be discussed in their own section. Let's look at the Navy-Option class advisors first.

For Navy midshipmen, NROTC Class Advisors are Unrestricted Line Officers from one of the Navy's warfighting communities (Surface Warfare Officer, Submarine Officer, Naval Aviator, Naval Flight Officer, SEAL, EOD). For them, assignment to NROTC units typically comes upon successful completion of initial operational sea assignments. These officers typically have anywhere from four to seven years in the service, aside, of course, from those with prior enlisted experience. These commissioned officers may seem intimidating; however, they relate well to the midshipmen. They have the perfect combination of fleet experience and recent recollections of their own undergraduate education experience and officer training.

Class advisors are assigned on "shore duty," a naval term denoting an assignment to a nonoperational (nondeployable) command. Shore-duty assignments typically offer a more relaxed working environment and less demanding work schedule than operational sea tours. Your class advisors are coming off operational tours that demanded significant investments in time and effort in stressful settings to accomplish real-world operational tasking. Like your civilian college instructors, your advisor may have established "office hours" to meet with midshipmen. However, your advisor will always be available in emergency situations or if special circumstances arise.

Typically, NROTC units are organized such that a Navy lieutenant advises all midshipmen in a given year—that is, one lieutenant for the freshmen, another lieutenant for the sophomores, and so on. Since midshipmen of a given year tend to have similar problems (freshman typically have college adjustment or scheduling issues, while sophomores may be planning to study abroad during their junior year), an advisor may become the unit "expert" on particular issues and have unit and institutional resources ready to call on. Another construct is to mirror the battalion organization, such that a lieutenant serves as an advisor for a company of midshipmen of various year groups. Other arrangements may be made in accordance with the desires of the Professor of Naval Science. Regardless of the arrangement, each midshipman will have a staff professional and academic advisor.

The class advisor is your first point of contact for nearly any matter relating to NROTC and your professional/academic development. Regulations dictate that every class advisor conduct a formal counseling session with each midshipman at least twice a semester. However, advisors are to make themselves available for more frequent consultation as necessary.

A positive relationship with your class advisor can be critical to success in NROTC. If you are acing your courses, excelling within the battalion, and behaving yourself during free time, you may not feel the need for frequent meet-ups. However, at the first sign of potential trouble, whether it be a poor quiz or test grade, personal issues, or any other matter that could affect your professional or academic performance, it is essential that you inform your class advisor. Your class advisor is first and foremost your advocate to the commanding officer (and Professor of Naval Science)—the advisor's job is to help prepare you to serve as commissioned officers. If they don't know of potentially troubling issues, they cannot help you thoughtfully address them.

Additionally, all advisors will teach naval science courses in their areas of professional background and experience. For example, the staff Surface Warfare Officer is likely to teach courses dealing with navigation and seamanship, while the staff nuclear officer probably teaches courses dealing with naval engineering. In addition to the naval training and professional development earned through their own careers, staff members attend a seminar focused on educational theory, best practices, and available resources to help improve their teaching abilities. Not all advisors teach every semester; in the "off" semesters, considerable effort and time goes into preparing upcoming curricula and materials.

In many cases, class advisors chose orders to an NROTC unit for the opportunity to earn graduate degrees at the schools where they are assigned. The Navy places emphasis on graduate education when considering officers for promotion and career-milestone screening. Thus your class advisor may have to balance a considerable academic workload with duties within the unit.

Finally, class advisors will be assigned additional "collateral duties" that they must perform in addition to their primary responsibilities. Collateral duties may include command fitness leader, summer cruise coordinator, Trident Naval Society sponsor, etc.

THE MARINE OFFICER INSTRUCTOR

Marine Officer Instructors are the senior Marine Corps officers assigned to NROTC units. They are tasked by Marine Corps Recruiting Command with the professional development and training of assigned Marine Corps–Option midshipmen. Coming from a different career path, MOIs are typically more senior and experienced than other class advisors on staff. All Marine-Option midshipmen will have the MOI as their class advisor. In addition to all the duties and responsibilities of Navy-class advisors, MOIs lead and instruct Marine-Option midshipmen in additional physical training, field exercises, and leadership development to prepare them for the demanding Officer Candidates School all potential Marine officers must complete to earn their commissions. The MOI will also serve as the primary unit instructor in close-order drill and military ceremony.

The unit MOI also is typically the command operations officer, responsible to the commanding officer for short- and long-term plans for the unit and the battalion. The battalion operations officer and battalion staff assist the MOI in these duties.

Supporting the MOI as necessary is the Assistant Marine Officer Instructor (AMOI), the senior Marine Corps enlisted staff member. While the AMOI's primary duty is to train Marine-Option midshipmen, the AMOI usually serves as the unit Senior Enlisted Leader (SEL) to the NROTC unit commanding officer and to the entire midshipmen battalion. In most cases, the AMOI is the only active-duty enlisted member on the NROTC unit staff. As a senior enlisted Marine staff sergeant or gunnery sergeant, the AMOI has extensive and valuable fleet experience. In the fleet, senior enlisteds have the critical duty and responsibility of helping to assist, mentor, and develop their junior officer leadership—the AMOI plays this role within the NROTC unit.

Collectively, the NROTC unit staff's primary responsibility is to develop midshipmen morally, mentally, and physically in preparation for service as commissioned naval officers. Unit staff are deeply invested in your professional development and academic success. The U.S. naval services must be continually replenished by talented, patriotic, and motivated young men and women who will grow and may one day reach the highest levels of leadership. Take advantage of their experience and their interest in your growth to succeed in the NROTC program.

Now that we have explored the various roles and responsibilities of unit staff members, we will examine the Battalion of Midshipmen, which is the primary organizational vehicle for accomplishing the training necessary to develop future naval officers.

The Battalion of Midshipmen

Collectively, the midshipmen making up an NROTC unit constitute the "battalion." The Battalion of Midshipmen is organized as a framework for professional development, leadership opportunities, and effective training. The particular organization, structure, and relationships between various levels of the Battalion of Midshipmen are determined by the NROTC unit CO, but below is a typical organization.

Periodically, usually each semester, the PNS will assign midshipmen to designated "billets" (jobs) within the battalion. The midshipman designated by the PNS to lead the battalion is the battalion commanding officer (BCO). Typically, this is an accomplished senior midshipman who already serves as a model for junior midshipmen to emulate. The BCO is assisted by the battalion executive officer (BXO), who acts as directed by the BCO. While arrangements may differ by unit, the BCO outlines priorities and goals, and the BXO ensures that steps are taken to meet them. The BCO/BXO similarly coordinate extensively with the PNS and unit staff to ensure the proper and effective conduct of the battalion.

Under the BXO it is typical to have some manner of battalion staff to assist in running the battalion efficiently and effectively. Billets such as battalion operations officer (BOPS); battalion administrative officer; battalion physical fitness officer; battalion morale, welfare, and recreation officer; and battalion recruitment officer are supporting staff roles assigned as necessary. They are often filled by fairly senior midshipmen but may themselves have more junior midshipmen to assist. While these billets are not primarily concerned with leadership development, they provide valuable opportunities to increase administrative and managerial skills vital to success as a junior naval officer. An effective headquarters staff will have a positive effect on the quality of midshipmen training events and increase the overall smoothness and cohesion of the Battalion of Midshipmen.

Next, the battalion is subdivided into companies, platoons, and squads, depending on the number of midshipmen in the battalion. Companies are composed of several platoons, each of which is composed of squads, in each of which are a number of midshipmen. Squads are led by squad leaders, platoons by platoon leaders, and companies by company commanders. Company commanders report to the BCO through the BXO. New midshipmen tend to begin as squad members and gradually are entrusted with increasing levels of leadership and responsibility.

NROTC UNIT BATTALION OF
MIDSHIPMEN CHAIN OF COMMAND

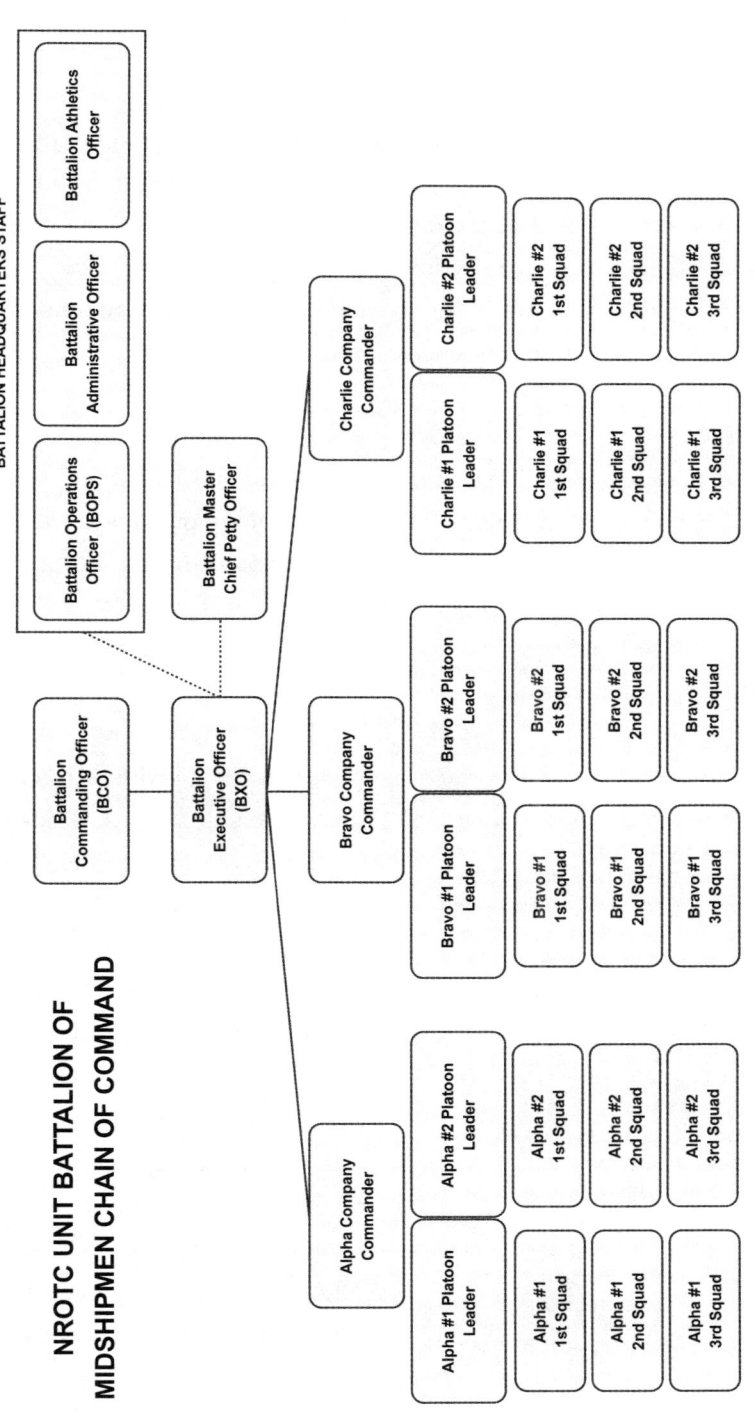

Most NROTC training events are accomplished within the battalion structure. In addition to serving as a leadership-development opportunity for those in appropriate billets, the framework has the effect of pitting platoons or companies against one another, which increases midshipmen buy-in and motivation. For example, instead of holding a battalion-wide physical fitness training event, the unit may hold a series of competitive physical training events (races, tugs-of-war, etc.) that meet the objective of improving midshipmen's physical fitness while also promoting platoon/company camaraderie and teamwork.

Variations

Recall that each NROTC unit takes on the flavor and identity of its host institution. Although fundamentally similar in organization, individual units vary considerably in practical structure and organization. A host-institution NROTC unit may include cross-town schools; an institution may have its own military traditions—these and various other factors can influence the character of the particular NROTC unit.

> "My NROTC unit at the University of Washington is the best in the country because of how well we work together. Our student staff members are given varying roles that are responsible for everything from our weekly schedules, to organizing major events, and to coming up with physical training plans. All of UW's NROTC activities are student led and student run to varying degrees with our unit staff standing as mentors and support if needed. Everyone works together and takes their positions, from 4/C MIDN to Commanding Officer, seriously, so that everything we do is professional and something we can be proud of."
>
> —MIDSHIPMAN 2ND CLASS SELTMANN, University of Washington NROTC

In addition, different constructs are present at schools with their own military traditions and customs. Schools such as Virginia Tech, The Citadel, Texas A&M University, Norwich University, and the Virginia Military Institute all have Corps of Cadets that support ROTC programs but are not formally affiliated with the military services. The Corps of Cadet curricula are integral to these institutions and in many cases are more demanding of time and effort than NROTC. Students at these institutions will have to meet all NROTC program requirements in addition to whatever demands the Corp of Cadets places on them.

"I am the product of a straightforward NROTC unit at the University of Notre Dame. NROTCU Notre Dame has a single cross-town agreement with St. Mary's College. St. Mary's University is only a short walk away from Notre Dame's campus and has a long tradition of being a partner institution stemming from a history of Notre Dame being all-male and St. Mary's being all-female. The Midshipmen Battalion included three companies (Alpha, Bravo, and Charlie), each comprising two platoons. Marine-Option midshipmen were integrated within the platoons and all midshipmen participated in the few battalion-wide events held weekly. With all midshipmen on essentially the same campus, members of the battalion would hang out regularly in the unit wardroom to study or relax. Unit staff and battalion leadership had a fairly straightforward time promoting camaraderie and battalion cohesion.

"I experienced a significantly different challenge while serving as an instructor at the George Washington University in Washington, D.C. When I first reported, in addition to GWU, Georgetown University, Howard University, Catholic University, and University of Maryland College Park were all members of the Capital Battalion. With GWU being in the heart of metro Washington, D.C., and with five different institution schedules to balance, getting the entire midshipmen battalion together was a challenge. Unit and battalion leadership had to balance the desire to promote battalion cohesion by intermixing students from different universities with the realities of public transit and potentially long travel times. Certain training events might be held at each cross-town school which made it easier on those students but stressed the staff to accommodate."

—LIEUTENANT CORDIAL

In each circumstance, it is worthwhile, when exploring your potential options for college and NROTC, to reach out to the unit directly and inquire about the organization, culture, and traditions of its battalion. If you intend to visit the campus, the NROTC unit will schedule a campus and battalion tour led by one of the stellar midshipmen already enrolled. You should also be afforded an opportunity to observe scheduled midshipmen training events and a naval science course. Unit staff and enrolled midshipmen will be happy to answer any questions you might have to help you make an informed decision.

As mentioned previously, one of the prime advantages of the NROTC program as a commissioning source is the choice of schools available to prospective students. The Naval Academy is an outstanding commissioning source for many naval officers, but it cannot provide a true college experience or the diversity of academic and cultural environments that marks NROTC. Whether you hope to attend school in the Great Northwest, Big Sky Country, the Sun Belt, or the cold Northeast, there is an NROTC-affiliated school for you.

Conclusion

In this chapter we discussed the military chain of command for an NROTC unit, the roles and responsibilities of military and civilian staff members assigned, and the organization of the Battalion of Midshipmen. Above all else, the NROTC unit is organized to accomplish efficiently and effectively its mission to develop midshipmen morally, mentally, and physically in preparation for commissioning as naval officers. With awareness now of how NROTC is organized and the duties various staff and battalion members perform, we will next expand upon the different types of NROTC scholarships mentioned in chapter 1.

"The Battalion is essentially midshipmen-led in every aspect. There is very little staff involvement unless needed. This develops critical-thinking and decision-making skills better than any other method. During my summer cruises, I have consistently noticed that midshipmen from my unit have been a cut above those from other units and even the Naval Academy."

—MIDSHIPMAN 1ST CLASS McNEAL, University of South Carolina NROTC

3 NROTC Scholarship Opportunities

WITH A WORKING KNOWLEDGE of what NROTC is, how an NROTC unit is organized and staffed, and the role of the Battalion of Midshipmen, we will now explore the specifics of the NROTC scholarship.

Aside from the honor and privilege of serving your country, perhaps the greatest benefit of participating in the NROTC program is the full-tuition scholarship that it offers to cover your undergraduate education. Student-loan debt is a growing problem for many young people in the United States; an NROTC scholarship can help alleviate this potentially large financial burden and provide as well a pathway to earn a commission as an officer in the naval service.

While the scholarship is important, it is most important to keep in mind that the purpose of the scholarship is to attract, develop, and retain officers for the Navy and Marine Corps. If being a leader and commissioned officer in the Navy and Marine Corps is not your goal, NROTC is not the right path for you.

In this chapter, we will discuss in depth the types of scholarships available within the NROTC program for Navy-Option, Nurse Corps–Option, and Marine Corps–Option midshipmen. In chapter 5, specifics regarding the mechanics of filling out and submitting an NROTC scholarship application will be covered.

The National Scholarship

The premier NROTC academic scholarship is the National Scholarship. The National Scholarship is a nationally competitive scholarship for applicants for the NROTC program. The National Scholarship provides a full-tuition scholarship, book/fee allowances, and a monthly stipend to students for a total of no more than forty academic months (waiverable to fifty months for selected curricula) in preparation for service in the U.S. Navy or Marine Corps. In practice this covers the months you are at school during the fall and spring semesters. For the time spent on summer cruise, midshipmen earn a third of O-1 pay for the active-duty period (summer cruise dates). During the summer months when you are not on cruise, you will not earn a stipend. The majority of NROTC midshipmen enter the program after having been awarded a National Scholarship during their senior year of high school.

Further, obligation to serve in the armed forces is incurred only after formally signing a commitment upon returning to your institution to begin your sophomore year. You have your entire first academic year and summer cruise training period to decide whether or not you would like to continue in the NROTC program. Your first year of tuition does not require an obligation.

"You'll be part of monumental world events. In my career, I've been there from the end of the Cold War to the destruction of Daesh. Because you'll have a hand in similar events, you'll care deeply about how history views them. When you go back home for a visit, you'll see how much your perspective has changed from those who chose to stay. However, you'll also realize just how wonderful and sheltered Hometown, U.S.A., is! I think the most important lesson of my career has been gaining an even deeper appreciation for how lucky I was to be born into this amazing experiment with the lofty goal of a Perfect Union."

—CDR T. SINGLETON, USN

Applicants for the National Scholarship must meet the following requirements:

1. Be American citizens, naturalized U.S. citizens, or have submitted naturalization papers.
   a. Scholarship selectees must be American citizens in order to "activate" the scholarship.
   b. Scholarship selectees must obtain their American citizenship and activate their scholarships within the first academic year after the stated scholarship offer's beginning date listed in their scholarship notification letters, or their scholarship offers will be rescinded.
   c. Retroactive benefits will not be approved for selectees who delayed activating their scholarship because they had not obtained U.S. citizenship.
   d. Applicants with dual citizenship may apply and, if selected, activate their scholarships but must renounce their citizenship to the other countries and surrender passports for those countries in order to continue in the NROTC program.

2. Have no moral obligations or personal convictions that will prevent bearing of arms and supporting and defending the Constitution of the United States against all enemies, foreign and domestic, or to taking an oath to perform such acts.

3. Be at least seventeen years of age and not yet twenty-three on or before 1 September of the year of enrollment and less than twenty-seven years of age upon commissioning. Those with prior or current active duty in the armed forces may be granted age waivers equal to the number of months served; at the maximum, they must not have reached their twenty-ninth birthday upon commissioning. Note that waivers may be granted for designators that allow commissioning after the age of twenty-nine (e.g., Naval Flight Officer [NFO], thirty-one years old; Surface Warfare Officer [SWO], thirty-five; Nuclear, thirty-one; Sea-Air-Land/Explosive Ordnance Disposal [SEAL/EOD], forty-two).

4. Meet physical requirements for the NROTC program.

5. Possess a high school diploma or equivalent certificate.

6. Be accepted for admission as a full-time student at a participating NROTC college or university.

7. Successfully complete NROTC New Student Indoctrination at Great Lakes, Illinois, prior to the start of the first academic semester.

In addition to these requirements, because the naval services have become increasingly technologically sophisticated, the vast majority of NROTC midshipmen pursue degrees in engineering or other "hard sciences." We will cover this matter in detail in chapter 5, but be aware that approximately 85 percent of each incoming NROTC class will be committed to earning an engineering or hard-science degree. These are termed "Tier 1" (engineering) and "Tier 2" (math/science) majors. Students are by no means precluded from pursuing liberal arts degrees, but they should be aware that the program prioritizes engineering and hard-science students. You can participate in a liberal arts education, but mathematics and science majors, for instance, have an edge over, say, political science and English majors in the competition for full scholarships.

To give an example on what a terrific benefit a four-year full-tuition scholarship is, consider the example of a recently affiliated NROTC institution, Brown University in Providence, R.I. For the 2018–19 academic year, full-time undergraduate tuition and fees totaled $55,556. Over the course of a four-year undergraduate degree program, that would come to over $220,000. Compare that figure to the median home price in the United States in 2017, approximately $200,000. Earning a National Scholarship is the financial equivalent of being given a paid-off house! In 2017, statistics show, 70 percent of college students graduated with outstanding student-loan debt, on the average $37,172. Securing a full-tuition scholarship and having a well-paying, career-oriented profession immediately upon graduation are incredibly valuable and increasingly rare propositions.

To be clear, the National Scholarship does not provide any funds toward room and board. At Brown University during the 2018–19 academic year, expected costs of room and board were $14,670. To live on campus for four years at Brown would run approximately $60,000. An NROTC midshipman would be responsible for these costs—on the other hand, per federal regulations, financial aid departments at institutions receiving federal funding (which includes all schools with NROTC programs) cannot factor your full-tuition scholarship into their calculations of your demonstrated financial need.

However, certain institutions offer full or partial grants to students on NROTC scholarships. At the time of this writing, an example is the University of San Diego (USD), which offers a full-room-and-board grant to USD NROTC scholarship students who participate in a work-study program. Similarly, George Washington University (GWU) recently began to offer a partial room-and-board grant to GWU NROTC scholarship students. These are only two examples, but later in this book we will highlight other unique benefits some units offer. It is critical to remember that such agreements are solely the purview of the academic institutions involved and are subject to change at the sole discretion of their administrations. Be sure to speak directly to the NROTC unit and the institution's financial aid department to determine precisely what additional scholarship funds or grants are available to NROTC students at the school.

The first step in applying for the National Scholarship is to visit the Navy's official NROTC website, at http://www.nrotc.navy.mil/, and to click on the "Apply" tab toward the top of the screen. The website will have the most up-to-date information concerning specific application instructions. If you have questions while working through the application, get help by using the contact information also available on the site. Chapter 5 will cover the application process in greater detail.

Other Scholarship Opportunities

In addition to the National Scholarship, the NROTC program offers a few other four-year scholarship opportunities at particular institutions. Also, for students who have already completed more than thirty credits toward an undergraduate degree, the NROTC program offers three- and two-year scholarships.

Both the Navy and Marine Corps offer special scholarship opportunities for students either currently attending or intending to attend Historically Black Colleges and Universities (HBCUs) or Hispanic Serving Institutions (HSIs). It is essential to note that these opportunities are open to applicants of any race or ethnicity—the scholarship opportunities are tied to the institution, not the applicant.

The Navy offers the Minority Serving Institution Scholarship Reservation (MSISR) to qualified students attending NROTC-affiliated "Minority Serving Institutions." A couple of examples are Howard University in Washington, D.C., and Morehouse College in Atlanta, Georgia. The application process is nearly identical to the National Scholarship but requires an additional interview, either in person or over the phone, with the NROTC unit's PNS. Additionally, some of the minimum application requirements, such as high school GPA and SAT/ACT scores, are slightly lower than for the National Scholarship. However, upon entrance into the NROTC program, all midshipmen are held to exactly the same standards as far as completing required coursework and maintaining undergraduate GPAs. If you indicate a desire to be considered for an MSISR scholarship, so indicate on your National Scholarship application. Your application will first be considered in the running for the National Scholarship and, if not selected for that, will be competed against other applications for MSISR scholarships. Since an MSISR application requires the recommendation of the MSI-affiliated NROTC unit, it is critical that you make early contact with the unit to set up the required interview well before application deadlines.

There is also an Alternate Scholarship Reservation (ASR) through the Navy Junior Reserve Officer Training Corps (NJROTC) program. This allows NJROTC area managers to nominate candidates for scholarships in a manner similar to other scholarship reservations. Normally, those receiving these nominations are from NJROTC units at high schools across the country. Like other reservations, there are still minimum application standards to meet and a board process to work through.

The Marine Corps offers the Frederick C. Branch Marine Leadership Scholarship and the Pedro Del Valle Marine Leadership Scholarship programs for students attending HBCUs and HSIs, respectively. These scholarships are made available to qualified and interested students already attending affiliated schools. Benefits are the same as other scholarships offered through the NROTC program. These scholarships are made available on an annual, as-needed basis, so if you are interested, you must contact the Marine Officer Instructor at the affiliated NROTC unit.

"Walking On": The College Program

For students who either failed to apply in time for a four-year scholarship or were not offered one, the NROTC offers a robust "walk-on" program to screen current undergraduate students at affiliated universities for opportunities to compete for and earn scholarships or commissions in the naval services. Each NROTC unit must make it possible for non-scholarship students to apply for admission to its "College Program," whereby students who meet the basic academic and physical requirements of the NROTC program participate fully within the battalion, take the necessary naval science courses, and compete to earn three- or two-year scholarships or "Advanced Standing" (discussed later in the chapter) leading to a commission in either the Navy or Marine Corps.

Much like university varsity athletic teams, the Navy and Marine Corps recruit and offer scholarships to a sufficient number of freshman students to meet

Embry-Riddle Aeronautical University NROTC midshipmen run along a campus trail during a morning physical training session. *U.S. Navy photo by Scott A. Thornbloom*

expected future commissioning demands (analogous to team needs in athletics) for the naval services. However, just like the few highly recruited players who fail to excel at a higher level of competitions, a small portion of NROTC midshipmen either fail to meet NROTC standards or decide that a commission as a naval officer is no longer their career goal. The gaps this attrition will open up are filled by offering scholarships to students participating in the College Programs of various NROTC units.

Introduction into an NROTC unit's College Program is at the discretion of the unit's commanding officer. If you are interested in participating in the College Program and, ideally, earning a scholarship, you must contact the NROTC unit to inquire about the local screening and application process. Only two- and three-year scholarships are offered through the College Program, and thus it is open only to current college freshmen and sophomores. Again, contact your local NROTC unit to inquire about timelines and discuss your particular situation.

While, in general, acceptance standards for the College Program are less than those for the National Scholarship, competition for College Program scholarships is fierce. Just as walk-on players often must greatly exceed the performance of the average scholarship player if they are to see significant playing time, College Program midshipmen desiring to be competitive for a scholarship must have excellent grades, high levels of physical performance, and leadership potential if they are to be selected for a sideload scholarship. In addition, annual scholarship availability is a function of scholarship-midshipmen attrition. If all scholarship midshipmen met academic and aptitude standards and continued to desire commissions, there would be no sideload scholarships available at all. In reality this is never the case, but the number of spots available varies, and annual competitiveness can depend on that. Just as in the National Scholarship, the Navy desires high percentages of Tier 1 or Tier 2 majors, so some preference may be shown to students pursuing science, technology, engineering, or math (STEM) degrees or who have, at the minimum, completed college-level calculus or physics courses.

A final option available to students in the College Program is "Advanced Standing." For students meeting program standards, in good standing within the Battalion of Midshipmen, and receiving the recommendation of the unit's commanding officer, the NROTC program offers the promise of a commission as an active-duty naval officer upon graduation but without an undergraduate scholarship. College Program juniors not offered two-year scholarships may be offered Advanced Standing as a secure path to a commission. Advanced Standing midshipmen continue to be integral members of the battalion but receive only a monthly stipend until graduation and commissioning. They attend precommissioning summer cruise training prior to their senior year and continue the normal NROTC curriculum. College Program midshipmen not offered scholarships by the beginning of their junior years who choose to disenroll from the NROTC program but still wish to earn a commission would have to apply directly to OCS upon graduation. If you are committed to earning a commission regardless of the scholarship benefit, Advanced Standing is an achievable path.

Finally, NROTC GPA and physical fitness requirements, along with service obligations, are exactly the same, whatever your scholarship status.

Conclusion

In this chapter, we discussed in depth the different types of NROTC scholarships available, the general application process and timelines, the basic academic and physical requirements, and the College Program. For all application processes, it is essential that you start as soon as practicable, to allow time to deal with any complications and avoid adding to the stress of the application process. Your local Navy/Marine Corps officer recruiter or NROTC unit are your go-to sources for information and assistance.

The scholarship application process may seem overwhelming but is in fact easily managed if you give yourself adequate time, take your college entrance exams early, and systematically work your way through the steps. In the next chapter, we will discuss in depth the unique benefits of the NROTC program as a means to earn a commission as a naval officer.

"Being a college student and an NROTC midshipman is tough. It's not easy, no matter what anyone else tells you. You have the challenge of developing yourself as a leader, getting your service selection, maintaining fitness standards and battalion leadership positions all on top of your academics and other extracurriculars. It can be hard to focus on the end goal. But remember why you're in the program. You have the privilege of being trained to lead some of the best men and women this nation has to offer, and our country is relying on you to defend it. Don't take that lightly. Tackle this challenge head-on and give it all you've got!"

—MIDSHIPMAN 2ND CLASS
SHAFFER,
University of South Florida NROTC

4 Why NROTC?

AS AN ACCOMPLISHED high school or college student, you may find yourself asking, "Why NROTC? I am getting all kinds of information booklets, scholarship offers, and recruitment materials from tons of different schools, organizations, companies, even from recruiters. What makes NROTC so special?" We hope to help explain why NROTC might be a great fit for you—particularly if you are already interested in serving in the military.

To clarify before continuing: we will make references throughout this chapter and the rest of the book to different "service cultures." The culture of any organization is difficult to define and is influenced by differing individual perceptions. By "culture," we mean the accepted standards of social and professional behavior, often unwritten and unofficial, of a given community. Individuals within a community may align their personal behavior more or less with cultural norms. Thus, we would like to make clear that we do not intend stereotyping either the naval or other military services but rather share what are commonly held understandings throughout the military of the various service "norms." As an example, it is a safe assumption that the average Marine infantry officer is more interested in physical fitness than the average nuclear submarine officer. However, were you to select an individual Marine and a submariner, there is absolutely no reason why that submariner might not happen to be in better shape than that Marine. In an all-volunteer force, people tend to choose communities within the military that are in alignment with their natural interests and talents. This is useful to keep in mind as you make decisions about serving in the military.

Students who are competitive for an NROTC scholarship or are already studying at an NROTC-affiliated institution are qualified for myriad career and life opportunities. It is not uncommon for a student applying for an NROTC scholarship also to have nomination packages submitted to one of the service academies or applications for Army or Air Force ROTC programs as well. Others, and many whose anecdotes are shared throughout the text, count themselves as among those rising high school seniors who simply had a general desire to serve briefly in the military until maturing and then figuring out their long-term career aspirations. No matter the underlying reasons for seeking to serve, the mere act of putting oneself forward as a volunteer for the armed services is laudable.

In this chapter, we will examine the remarkable benefits of participating in the NROTC program and compare and contrast aspects of NROTC to and with other commissioning sources. As you make, or your loved one makes, fundamental choices for the future, you should feel confident that you have all information necessary to make those choices informed and deliberate.

Military Service

The first and primary benefit of participating in any ROTC program is that it provides a pathway to serve your country as a member of the armed services. The United States is a great nation, with varied interests around the world in promoting stability, democracy, and rule of law. To promote these interests and to defend our homeland and allies from aggression, the United States maintains and supports the most capable military forces in the world. The military is a dynamic, fast-paced, and mission-focused organization of teams that work together to accomplish astonishing feats. The friendships, camaraderie, and skills gained through any period of military service are life-changing. Less than 0.5 percent of Americans are active-duty service members—and of that number, only about 10 percent are officers—so you are joining an exclusive group of passionate, patriotic, and motivated Americans who work together to provide a vital service to the nation and world.

While many paths exist to service with noble and worthwhile institutions—international organizations; civil service at the federal, state, or local level; charitable organizations and religious missions; and so on—we feel that military, and specifically naval, service offers a unique opportunity, unique in terms of the scope of responsibility and accountability. How many of your civilian peers will be traveling to far-off places, accompanied by a team of competent professionals united in purpose to accomplish missions of vital importance to your nation? Few other organizations can make such an offer to recent high school graduates or college students.

Service as a Commissioned Officer

Like nearly all military organizations throughout history, the U.S. military has a hierarchical structure, with the commander in chief (the President of the United States) at the top and reporting chains and links down to the newest enlisted recruit at the bottom. Within the active-duty and reserve components, the military is broken, broadly speaking, into two groups, enlisted service members and commissioned officers. Enlisted service members enter the military through their services' recruit training ("boot camp") and other initial military training commands, usually shortly after high school. Although an increasing proportion of enlisted service members hold undergraduate or even graduate degrees, there is no requirement for advanced education for enlistment. Enlisted Sailors, Marines, Coast Guardsmen, soldiers, and airmen serve for defined periods and then must reenlist if offered the opportunity and if they have the desire to continue their military careers. Enlisted service members tend to specialize in specific warfighting or support areas—infantryman, radar technician, logistics specialist, etc. They tend to stay within their specialties throughout their careers, rising to positions of increased responsibility and influence but always focused on improving their capabilities and leadership potential within their military specialties. For example, a seaman recruit (E-1) assigned in the deck department on a U.S. Navy warship may aspire to serve one day as a boatswain's mate master chief petty officer (E-9) or even as the Master Chief Petty Officer of the Navy (MCPON), the most senior enlisted Sailor in the Navy.

Ensign standing watch on board the amphibious assault ship USS *Iwo Jima* (LHD 7). *U.S. Navy photo by Kevin Leitner*

Commissioned military officers are charged with commanding or preparing to command subordinate officers and enlisted service members. Commissioned officers serve at the pleasure of the President of the United States and have the responsibility to lead and command forces apportioned to them by higher authority in order to accomplish assigned missions. Officers tend to have broader professional purviews than their enlisted counterparts; a Marine infantry officer may hold any of the various leadership positions within a battalion, and a Navy submarine officer is likely to lead Sailors in a number of departments of a submarine or on the staff of a squadron of submarines. The general career path for an unrestricted line officer (from chapter 1, and more below) is designed to culminate in command and potentially in general- or flag (admiral)-level positions of leadership. Both officers and enlisted service members are bound to follow the legal orders of officers appointed over them, and officers are further bound to exercise their authority justly and with a focus on mission accomplishment.

All ROTC programs provide paths to service as commissioned military officers. Service as an officer means a remarkable and immediate opportunity to lead some of the finest young men and women in the United States. Immediately upon commissioning and completing required introductory community-tailored training, you will be entrusted with the well-being and fighting effectiveness of those under your charge. While your peers in the civilian world may be starting out at the first or second rung of the corporate ladder, you will be handling highly sophisticated warships, flying the most advanced aircraft in existence, or leading a team of lethal, dedicated Marines to accomplish vital objectives in our nation's defense. The scope of responsibility and authority entrusted to a twenty-two-year-old ensign or second lieutenant has very few counterparts in the civilian world.

So Why NROTC? The Army Recruiter Seems to Have a Good Deal . . .

Given the attraction of service in the military, and specifically as a commissioned officer, what is special about being a *naval* officer? To be clear, once again, the term "naval officer" includes commissioned officers of both U.S. Navy and U.S. Marine Corps, as both the Navy and Marine Corps are within the Department of the Navy. So, this is a book about *Naval* ROTC, as opposed to similar Army and Air Force ROTC programs.

NROTC has some systemic advantages over its counterpart programs. First, NROTC offers high school students only four-year scholarships. If you are awarded a National Scholarship as a high school senior, you can be confident that as long as you meet program requirements you will have your full tuition scholarship all the way to graduation. Both the Army and Air Force do offer four-year scholarships, but their systems are tiered and may award two- or three-year scholarships instead, based on your expected field of study or academic record. With the Navy, you either have a scholarship or you don't. While we encourage you to speak with recruitment officers from other services, we would want you to be aware that when they speak of offering a scholarship to help pay for your undergraduate degree, they may not be speaking of the full-tuition, four-year scholarship that NROTC is guaranteed to offer. It is important to understand all the fine print before committing to *any* military program.

Second, the NROTC overwhelmingly commissions officers into the unrestricted line of the Navy and Marine Corps. You can think of unrestricted line officers as "in the line" for command. Broadly speaking, URL officers are those concerned with leading combat units: infantry officers, artillery officers, submarine officers, naval aviators, Surface Warfare Officers, Special Warfare Officers, etc. In the restricted line are commissioned officers who are focused on supporting, nonwarfighting specialties: intelligence, public affairs, information warfare, and so on. There are also staff corps officers who are doctors, lawyers, chaplains, civil engineers, and the like. These distinctions may seem pedantic, as all members of the military contribute to the mission, but only unrestricted line (URL) officers can serve as commanding officers of warships, submarines, aviation squadrons, battalions, etc. Further, only URL officers can ascend to the highest levels of leadership within the uniformed military. The overwhelming majority of flag and general officers within each service are unrestricted line (or "combat arms," to use an Army term) officers.

Things are different for Army and Air Force ROTC programs. Those services, which rely on the Reserve Component as integral parts of their overall organizational structures, must continually replenish their cadre of officers that can be mobilized in case of war or other national emergency. The naval services, in contrast, being expeditionary in nature, are essentially "perpetually mobilized." Our aircraft carriers, submarines, ships, embarked Marines, and aircraft are forward deployed by design—to be in position to respond rapidly in times of crisis, provide deterrence, and train with allies and partners. While the Navy does maintain a fleet of inactive ships that can be called upon in time of great need, there is no "reserve" fleet in the same sense that there are reserve Army, Air Force, and National Guard units that can be activated as needed. Navy Reserve personnel are often activated on an individual basis to supplement or help a "regular" unit; also, some categories of inactive ships take time to put into service.

If you are interested in the truly amazing opportunity and responsibility that come with direct leadership right away, a guaranteed commission into the active-duty URL is a significant benefit of participating in the NROTC program specifically. If, on the other hand, you might prefer service in the Reserves or in a staff corps community, then the Air Force or Army ROTC programs may be for you. As for NROTC, as long as you meet program requirements, it offers you a commission as a URL officer and with it the potential to go as far as your talent and circumstances allow. NROTC may be the very start of a career culminating as the Chairman of the Joint Chiefs of Staff.

In comparison to the other services' programs, Navy ROTC units are fewer in number but larger in size and are led by more senior officers (Navy captains and Marine colonels). They have larger, more experienced staffs to instruct and mentor midshipmen. On the other hand, there are many more Army- and Air Force–affiliated schools from which to choose. Aside from factors of size, staff, resources, and experience, there are also some cultural differences. More than the other services, the Navy and Marines embrace the concept of decentralized command. Historically, owing to constraints on communications between headquarters and ships at sea, substantial trust had to be placed in the decisions and initiative of ships' commanding officers. Although nearly instantaneous worldwide communications are now possible, the service retains a cultural paradigm of allowing subordinate commanders substantial leeway in how they accomplish their tasks. This philosophy, for other services a distinct approach they term "mission command," seeks to empower subordinate leaders to solve problems creatively within the framework of a higher commander's expressed "intent" without waiting for specific orders. In other words, the system would rather have you solve—within bounds set by a commander—a problem than have you wait to be ordered exactly how to do it.

Third, the Navy has some of the best duty stations of all the military services. Naval bases are, unsurprisingly, close to major bodies of water. Whether San Diego, Virginia Beach, Seattle, Pearl Harbor, or Jacksonville, major fleet concentration areas are in some of the best locales in the country—not to mention Spain and Japan! Further, just as the old commercials said, once you join the Navy you can

Sailors talk on the bridge wing of the *Independence*-class littoral combat ship USS *Coronado* (LCS 4) as the ship transits the San Diego Bay. *U.S. Navy photo by Marcus Stanley*

"see the world." Ships pull into foreign ports as part of an American commitment to "show the flag," and you as a naval officer are an unofficial ambassador. Port visits are some of the most memorable parts of naval service.

Last, and this may be subjective, the naval services have the best uniforms. You are sure to turn heads in a smart set of Navy service dress whites (or "choker whites") or Marine Corps blue dress alphas, like what you see in the movies— though, of course, daily and working uniforms might be less striking. Basing your choice of career on seemingly superficial matters may not be what your parents or guidance counselor hope for, but if you need a tiebreaker between the naval and other services, consider that you could be wearing the uniform for five or twenty-five years . . . you may as well look as sharp as you can!

Comparisons of Commissioning Sources

Now that we have made a persuasive (we hope) case that military service is best accomplished in the Navy or Marine Corps, we now delve into why NROTC specifically is the best path toward a commission in those services. As stated in earlier chapters, there are options. You may desire to rise through the ranks, first serving as an enlisted Sailor or Marine before applying to Officer Candidate School. You may be considering the U.S. Naval Academy (USNA) in Annapolis, Maryland. You may simply want to complete your undergraduate degree at a civilian college before directly applying to OCS. So let's briefly look at the chief benefits of the NROTC program compared to other commissioning sources.

First, the primary benefit of the NROTC program is the full-tuition scholarship available to qualified students at a diverse choice of the best civilian institutions in the country. To have your undergraduate education paid for is an incredible leg up on your peers, who will likely have substantial loan debt, and it can ease your way into the other responsibilities of adulthood. The financial incentive is a considerable advantage over paying for your own education and seeking a commission through OCS.

Second, the NROTC program is significantly more flexible than USNA. Whatever your desires for undergraduate education, it is likely there is an NROTC program affiliated with a college fitting your wishes. Whether you are a Californian hoping to cross the country and attend an "Ivy" or a Midwesterner looking to stay close to home and attend a parent's alma mater, there are options open to you. USNA offers a great financial incentive too, but with NROTC you retain significant flexibility as to where you will earn your degree and what you study.

Third, in addition to offering a wide variety of schools to choose from, the "touch time" of NROTC is significantly less than at the Naval Academy. While specifics may vary from school to school, in general your NROTC obligations will consist of a few additional physical training sessions, an additional academic class per semester, and the wearing of your uniform once or twice per week. By and large—with the exceptions of military schools like The Citadel, Virginia Military Institute, etc.—you have a "normal" undergraduate experience at your university.

Based on your perspective, there may be meaningful attraction in other commissioning sources. As we will repeat throughout the text, and although we feel strongly about the benefits of NROTC, it is not necessarily the perfect fit for every young person considering a career in

> "I wanted to be a part of something bigger than myself. I also knew I wanted to go to college and join the military, so this seemed like a natural choice. There was some debate between NROTC and the Naval Academy, but I ultimately decided that NROTC fit my desired college/life experience expectations better."
>
> —MIDSHIPMAN 1ST CLASS HNATKO, University of Minnesota NROTC

the naval services. Both the Naval Academy and OCS commission outstanding naval officers and, together with NROTC, field a naval officer corps with intellectual and experiential diversity that helps make our services stronger. It is critical to understand fully the differences between the various commissioning programs.

First, while more demanding, the Naval Academy does offer a more structured and organized holistic naval training environment. If you desire the more regimented training setting that a service academy offers, then the Naval Academy may be a better option for you.

Second, while NROTC offers a full-tuition scholarship, NROTC does *not* cover room and board. In some high-cost-of-living areas, room and board at a private institution may be more expensive than the total annual cost of attending an in-state public school. Some institutions offer special incentives to NROTC students and may cover some or all room-and-board costs. These incentives are completely separate from the U.S. Navy and the NROTC program, so please check with individual NROTC units to see if any such benefits exist at their particular schools.

Finally, the Naval Academy does enjoy, in general and with respect to naval careers, superior resources and opportunities not available to NROTC midshipmen. While all midshipmen participate in a form of summer training, Naval Academy midshipmen attend multiple "blocks" of training throughout the summer. The

	NAVAL ACADEMY	NROTC	OCS
Scholarship	100% tuition, room and board, monthly stipend	Full tuition and fees, book allowance, monthly stipend	No scholarship
Location	Annapolis, Md.	Over 70 affiliated civilian institutions across the nation	Newport, R.I. (Navy) Quantico, Va. (USMC)
Type of Experience	Regimented, disciplined service-academy environment	Civilian undergraduate experience at your school with some NROTC courses and faculty	Civilian undergraduate experience—no obligations until reporting to OCS
Minimum Service Obligation	At least 5 years active duty, 8 years total	At least 5 years active duty, 8 years total	For active-duty and reserve officers, at least 4 years
Designators Available	Mostly Navy Unrestricted Line (SWO, subs, aviation, Special Warfare), USMC, and a small number of restricted line and staff corps	Navy Unrestricted Line (SWO, subs, aviation, Special Warfare), USMC *Note*: Very limited other options, such as Nursing, Medical, Strategic Sealift	All URL, RL, and staff corps designators

Naval Academy has unique training facilities, such as a full-mission shiphandling simulator, small naval training "ships," sailing teams, dedicated Special Warfare training teams, etc. Because of its history and status as a service academy, the USNA is the best with respect to resources, facilities, and staff experience of the commissioning choices. The small cadre of an NROTC unit's staff may be the only naval personnel at the university. None of this is to say that the training offered by NROTC is inadequate—again, we are all proud graduates of the NROTC program and would not trade our experiences for anything. It simply means that there are substantive differences between a service academy dedicated solely to commissioning naval officers and a civilian institution that has agreed to affiliate itself with the naval services.

For a brief comparison and contrast of the three primary commissioning sources as related to the college experience, see the below table.

How Much Does It Matter?

No matter their commissioning sources, all officers are judged by their performance—there are no special provisions for officers from the Naval Academy, NROTC, or OCS. Fine officers from all commissioning sources have been promoted to the highest levels of Navy and Marine Corps leadership. The officer corps of the Navy and Marine Corps are stronger because their officers come from a variety of backgrounds and academic disciplines. Diversity of thinking and background make them better, and the services recognize this. Much more important than your commissioning source is your motivation and energy in learning your profession and how to lead Sailors or Marines. Any minor disparities in the quality of training offered at the various commissioning sources quickly work themselves out in the fleet. We encourage you to focus primarily on where you think you can best develop morally, mentally, and physically during your college years. We are confident that for many young people a quality civilian education coupled with participation in the NROTC program makes them invaluable assets to the naval services and does so in ways entirely compatible with other potential life goals.

5 The National Scholarship Application Process

IF YOU HAVE DECIDED you are genuinely interested in participating in the NROTC program, this chapter is more practical than the previous, introductory section—we will help you with the mechanics of applying for the competitive NROTC National Scholarship.

In this chapter we will cover in detail (we've mentioned some of it before) the application process and timeline for the NROTC National Scholarship from the perspective of a high school student interested in participating in NROTC. If you are a college student with fewer than thirty undergraduate semester hours you too are eligible to apply for the National Scholarship. If you have questions concerning your eligibility, please be sure to discuss the matter with an officer recruiter or the NROTC unit at the school you are interested in attending. You can find contact information for your nearest officer recruiter on the official Navy recruiting website, https://www.navy.com/local, or Marine Corps Officer Selection Officer (OSO) at https://www.marines.com/becoming-a-marine/officer.html.

The National Scholarship application resides on the official Navy NROTC website, http://www.nrotc.navy.mil/apply.html. This website is updated regularly to reflect administrative and programmatic changes, so be sure to refer to it frequently when considering your application. The information in this chapter, which is current and correct as of this writing, is designed to supplement the official NROTC website.

Applicants must meet a series of application requirements, be selected by a board of senior naval officers, gain admission into an affiliated college or university, and pass a Department of Defense medical screening to be awarded a National

Scholarship. The typical applicant is still in high school, but, again, college students who have completed fewer than thirty credit hours of their undergraduate curriculum are eligible to apply as well. The scholarship application process can be started as soon as the second semester of your junior year of high school or as late as the first semester of your freshman year of college. We strongly recommend that if you are indeed interested, you submit your application as early as possible. The selection board that chooses whom to offer scholarships to meets on a rotating basis and each time reconsiders applications not accepted in previous sessions. The earliest National Scholarship offers are actually made in September of the year prior to school start, so there is no need to wait for the application deadline later in the year.

Application Requirements

Before going further, ensure that you meet the basic requirements to be eligible for an NROTC National Scholarship. It will do you little good to have an outstanding application and go through the hours of work necessary to prepare it only to be deemed ineligible. Applicants for the National Scholarship must meet the application requirements listed in chapter 3.

Selecting the Right School

Choosing the right school is a challenge for many high school students. As mentioned previously, NROTC is unique in offering a variety of school types and academic environments that all lead to a commission in the Navy or Marine Corps. In your application you must select five different schools, each with its own NROTC unit. For example, you may not list both Boston College and Boston University, as they both use the Boston University NROTC unit. Further, you must be eligible for in-state tuition at one of the schools, at a minimum. Typically, this means being a resident of the state, but check the eligibility requirements for public schools in which you may be interested; they may offer in-state pricing to military dependents or have regional agreements with residents of neighboring states.

It is possible to be awarded a scholarship but not at the school you most desire. If this is the case, contact both your desired and assigned NROTC units; the roster of students assigned to each unit is fluid, as some students offered NROTC scholarship at particular schools either decline the offers or choose to attend different schools. In practice, you should be able to activate your NROTC scholarship at the school of your choice, but beware: individual NROTC units are constrained in the total number of midshipmen they can effectively train and scholarships they can host. But again: while it is technically possible for your desired school to be "too full" for all the prospective NROTC students who were both admitted and offered scholarships there, in practice the numbers tend to work themselves out.

The major hurdles are the first two: to gain admittance to your university of choice and to earn a National Scholarship. Once you have achieved these two initial steps, Naval Service Training Command and individual NROTC units will work with you to help you attend college where you most want to—if that can be done within the limits of unit availability and the needs of the service.

Our recommendation is to consider strongly the four-year graduation rate at schools you are interested in attending that host NROTC units. NROTC program requirements are based upon completing your degree within four years. Only with special permission or in special five-year programs will you be allowed to take more than four years to complete your studies. However, a growing plurality of academic institutions are allowing or planning for their students to take up to six years to complete their degrees. If this culture is particularly strong at your school, you may have trouble convincing your university academic counselor of the necessity of completing your degree requirements within a traditional four-year time frame. This could well spell trouble for your success in NROTC.

Application Process and Timeline

An important factor to keep in mind is that your desired college or university admissions process is *completely distinct* from the NROTC National Scholarship process. For the latter, applications close at

> "The Navy initially assigned my scholarship to the University of South Carolina, a school I had not applied to but put down as the in-state option, as required. Although I was initially freaked out that I would need to apply late to South Carolina, I reached out to the point of contact listed in my scholarship award and was able to transfer my scholarship without issues. While it worked out in my case, I would encourage you to actually apply to all of the schools you put on your NROTC application!"
>
> —LIEUTENANT CORDIAL

> "Start and finish the application process as early as possible. If you have all the information ready and you are on top of it, filling out the online application and performing the physical assessment can be done in less than two weeks. That way by the time your officer interview comes around you're already finished and can enjoy the rest of your senior year in high school."
>
> —MIDSHIPMAN 3RD CLASS HURST, University of Utah NROTC

the end of the year prior to the beginning of the freshman fall semester of the incoming NROTC class. For example, applications for college freshman beginning studies in the fall 2021 academic semester are due 31 December 2020. The application window opens some eighteen months before the beginning of the fall semester, and you are encouraged to apply early; but unless you are admitted early to your desired school, you may not know your school's admission decision before hearing if you have been accepted into the NROTC program. Be sure to gather required information, prepare your application, and submit well ahead of the due date so that any issues with your application can be discovered and corrected well before the selection boards.

Again, be sure to not confuse the NROTC scholarship application process with the application process at the colleges or universities to which you are applying. The Navy will not communicate its intent to offer an NROTC scholarship to your desired school's admissions committee. The NROTC National Scholarship Board and the school's admissions board are completely separate and distinct entities. Your earning an NROTC scholarship is unlikely to have any effect on the decision of the institution's admissions board. It is therefore prudent to apply to all of the schools where you can activate your scholarship in case (as we suggested above) you do not know if you will be accepted to your top school until after the deadline for the NROTC scholarship application. The National Scholarship Board meets several times per year and notifies applicants to whom it makes scholarship offers, but even students who submit their applications early may not be awarded scholarships until well along in the application cycle. As mentioned above, applicants not selected will be rolled into subsequent competitive selection pools until they are sent either offers or denials, sometime in late winter/early spring preceding their high school graduation.

Completing a High-Quality Application

Now that you understand the basic application review and scholarship award process, we will work through the major steps involved in completing an NROTC application. It's worth your time: be mindful that though answering the specific questions on the application may be accomplished in a few hours, the rest of the task—providing required test scores, high school transcripts, and letters of recommendation, as well as completing your physical fitness assessment—will take considerable time and coordination. Keeping all of what follows in mind and

The commanding officer of Navy Recruiting District San Diego presents a high school senior a ceremonial check for an NROTC college scholarship worth $180,000.
U.S. Navy photo by Anastasia Puscian

dealing with them well before the NROTC application is due will pay dividends and help you generate a high-quality application.

The first step is simply accessing the online application site. In order to get on the NROTC Scholarship Application system you must register for a NETFOCUS gateway account at https://netfocus.netc.navy.mil/nrotc/candidate_app/Login .aspx, using your personal information and e-mail address. If you do not have a modest, professional e-mail address (such as, firstname.lastname@email.com) we recommend securing one from any of the various free e-mail hosting sites. That's not a requirement, but your NETFOCUS e-mail address will be used for official communication—better if correspondence back and forth with an organization you are asking to commission you as a naval officer doesn't carry an e-mail address like soccer_starz_yolo1337@. . . . Once your account is created be sure to log in regularly, to prevent the system from locking and then disabling your account.

Once you have completed the registration process and have successfully logged in, select the "NSRA" (NROTC Scholarship Application) link to access the online application. At that point, take advantage of the comprehensive online checklist that NSTC N9 maintains (at http://www.nrotc.navy.mil/apply.html) to assist you in completing the application, item by item. Much of the application consists of straightforward, self-explanatory data entry—name, birthdate, parent's education, etc. There follow, however, aspects of the application that are not quite as straightforward, and we invite your attention to them.

STANDARDIZED TEST SCORES

As part of your application you must submit scores from either the SAT or ACT taken within the previous three years. Standards for the NROTC program are:

- *Navy and Nurse application.* Applicants with the minimum individual Math and Verbal scores but not the minimum combined score, and who respond positively to the MSISR interest question (discussed below) in the application, are eligible to apply and will be considered on the MSISR selection board (Navy Option only).
  –SAT: 540 Math; 550 Evidence Based Reading and Writing *and* 1200 Combined (Math plus Evidence Based Reading and Writing)
  –ACT: 21 Math; 22 English *and* 47 Combined (Math plus English)
- *Marine Corps application.*
  –SAT minimum combined score of 1000 on the Math and Evidence Based Reading and Writing portions of the test
  –ACT minimum composite score of 22
  –Armed Forces Qualification Test (AFQT) minimum score of 74.

You are allowed to combine scores from different iterations of the test and put the highest composite score on your application. As an example, say you score 720 Math and 660 Evidence Based Reading and Writing on your first attempt of the SAT and then on your second, 680 Math and 700 Evidence Based Reading and Writing. You would pick your highest score for each section from either test, for a combined score of 720 Math + 700 Evidence Based Reading and Writing = 1420 composite score. NSTC does not publicize class profiles, as do many colleges, of average standardized test scores. However, it is safe to assume that the majority of successful candidates score above the minimum requirements.

We strongly encourage you to register and take both the SAT and ACT at least a year before your National Scholarship application is due. Some students prefer the testing format of one test over another and correspondingly do better on that one. Again, either test is perfectly acceptable, and a poor score on the SAT, say, will have no negative effect on a high score on the ACT in your application. Once you have taken both tests, unless you score well above both the minimum requirements for the NROTC National Scholarship and the average scores for the schools you intend to apply to, we recommend you take the test you scored higher on at least once more. (However, don't be discouraged by some false information out there that you need almost a 1600 to compete.) It may also be prudent to take a test preparation course such as is offered at many schools, online (live-streamed), and via self-study. Your test scores can be forwarded directly from the test organization to NSTC, or you can provide a hard copy score sheet to your officer recruiter.

ACADEMIC TRANSCRIPTS

You must provide verified academic transcripts from all high schools, junior/community colleges, and undergraduate colleges where you have earned academic credit. In most cases these should be mailed directly from the school to the NROTC National Scholarship Board, at the address found on its application website. Securing these transcripts could involve some administrative effort, time, and nominal fees, so do be sure to fill out any required paperwork well ahead of final application deadlines. If you submit your application early, you should forward an additional transcript once your senior fall semester grades are officially registered. In addition, you will be required to provide a list of courses you intend to take during your senior spring semester.

REFERENCES

As part of the application process, you must provide references, as you would for a job interview. NSTC will contact them directly to assess their opinions of your performance and character, relative to your peers. You must provide full contact information for a guidance counselor/school administrator (such as a principal, dean, etc.), a math/science teacher, and an athletic coach/music instructor/scoutmaster/ additional teacher, etc. It is proper etiquette to ask for the references' permission before listing them. You should also discuss the importance of the NROTC application with them and let them know how much you appreciate their assistance. Obviously, you should choose teachers or coaches with whom you have good relationships and who are likely to portray your qualities in a positive light.

EXTRACURRICULAR ACTIVITIES

You will have an opportunity as part of your NROTC application to list your extra-curricular activities and leadership positions. Success as a military officer requires a combination of mental acuity, physical prowess, and leadership ability. While we encourage you to participate in a variety of athletic, musical, school government, charitable, and religious activities according to your interests, we would like to stress that demonstrated commitment to and leadership positions within a single activity may be more worthwhile for your NROTC application than being simply a member of a dozen different clubs and teams. Athletic teams are particularly worthwhile in developing the teamwork, physical fitness, and competitive spirit that are applicable to service in the military.

MINORITY SERVING INSTITUTION SCHOLARSHIP INTEREST

The NROTC program grants scholarships to Minority Serving Institutions (MSIs) at NROTC-affiliated Historically Black Colleges and Universities, Minority Institutions (MIs), and institutions with High Hispanic Enrollment (HHEs). Please indicate your interest in the MSI scholarship program by checking the appropriate box. Your response indicates interest only: you must still contact the NROTC unit at the Minority Serving Institution you wish to attend in order to begin the application process for the MSISR scholarship.

During the NROTC application itself, you will be afforded an opportunity to express interest for other specific programs as well within the overall NROTC framework. Expression of interest in a program does not oblige you participate in it; but if your application is not accepted for a National Scholarship but you expressed interest in one, you will be considered for it by a subsequent scholarship board.

ESSAYS

Included in the application are a series of short essay prompts that should be answered in one or two paragraphs totaling 250–500 words. We encourage you to think deeply and write carefully in your responses. These will be your only direct statements to the National Scholarship Board, and they are your opportunity to convey your sincerity in seeking to serve your country. It may be prudent to have a peer or teacher whom you respect review and edit to lessen the possibility of grammatical or syntactical errors. In a perfect world, you would have a mentor or friend who has served in the military also review it. Answer the prompts concisely, completely, and honestly.

PHYSICAL FITNESS

You will have to complete and document an NROTC Applicant Fitness Assessment (AFA) with your high school's physical education instructor, athletic coach, JROTC staff, or Navy or Marine Corps recruiting personnel, E-7 or senior. The AFA is composed of three events: crunches, push-ups, and a one-mile run. You will have two minutes to complete both crunches and push-ups and ten minutes for the mile run. You are afforded brief rest periods between each event. Upon completion, your testing officer will document your scores, sign the AFA, and then forward it to NSTC for inclusion in your application.

Once you are in the naval service, it will be essential that you attain and remain in proper physical condition. It is especially critical at this juncture: failure to report in shape to your assigned NROTC unit in the fall of your freshman year will result in your scholarship offer being rescinded.

The College of the Holy Cross and Yale University Naval Reserve Officers Training Corps incoming freshman midshipmen candidates participate in their initial baseline Physical Fitness Assessment (PFA) run on the William C. McCool Memorial Track at Naval Station Newport, Rhode Island. *U.S. Navy photo by Scott A. Thornbloom*

APPLICATION TOP 5

1. *Excel at your passion.* The Navy and Marine Corps are looking for young men and women who have demonstrated excellence and passion in their pursuits. A young person who has excelled in a few areas in high school is more attractive than someone who has simply participated in a laundry list of activities. Make sure your essays and statements within your application reflect this.

2. *Seek leadership positions.* Demonstrated leadership ability is a difference maker. Team captain, class president, scout troop senior patrol leader, model UN chair—taking the initiative and seeking leadership positions within your peer group are great indicators of potential suitability to a career leading Sailors and Marines.

3. *Take the tough classes.* Whether you seek to join the Navy or Marine Corps, taking the toughest classes available to you, even if you earn a slightly lower grade, will look better on your application than straight As in less demanding courses. Advanced Placement, International Baccalaureate, Community College, or other high-level classes, particularly in calculus and physics, will play very well on your application.

4. *Have a mentor review your application.* Be deliberate in preparing and reviewing your application, particularly your written statements. Have a trusted mentor offer feedback. Your application will be the primary means of communicating with the selection board—it should be the best representation of your performance and potential.

5. *Submit early!* With the rolling selection board, you are losing out on potential opportunities for selection if you wait until just before the final deadline to submit your application. There are *no* downsides to submitting your application early. A final grade not yet received in a demanding class that would boost your application's attractiveness can be forwarded to a subsequent selection board, if necessary. Submitting early also demonstrates to the board the priority you place on a potential career in the Navy or Marine Corps.

ACADEMIC MAJORS

The National Scholarship Board also considers projected academic majors for its scholarship classes; accordingly, during the application process you must state your intended major. The selection board is seeking to offer scholarships to students in such a way that the incoming class will have at least 85 percent technical majors (either Tier 1 or Tier 2). A reason for this is that NROTC is a major supplier of entry-level officers into the Navy Nuclear Propulsion Program, which has a technically demanding training pipeline in which, history has shown, those with technical majors are more likely to succeed.

For Navy-Option midshipmen, the NROTC program breaks prospective majors into "tiers." The tier system generally breaks down into engineering, hard sciences, and liberal arts/other.

Tier 1

Aerospace, Aeronautical, Astronautical Engineering
Chemical Engineering
Electrical Engineering
Mechanical Engineering
Naval Architecture and Marine/Naval Engineering
Nuclear Engineering
Ocean Engineering
Systems Engineering

Tier 2

Agriculture/Biological Engineering and Bioengineering
Architectural Engineering/Architectural Engineering Technologies
Astrophysics
Biochemistry, Biophysics, and Molecular Biology
Biomathematics and Bioinformatics
Biomedical/Medical Engineering
Cell/Cellular Biology and Anatomical Sciences
Ceramic Sciences and Engineering
Chemistry
Civil Engineering/Civil Engineering Technologies
Computer Engineering
Computer Programming
Computer Science/Information Technology
Construction Engineering
Electronics and Communications Engineering
Engineering Mechanics
Engineering Physics
Engineering Science
General Engineering
General Science
Industrial Engineering

Manufacturing Engineering
Materials Engineering
Mathematics
Metallurgical Engineering
Microbiological Sciences and Immunology
Mining and Mineral Engineering
Nuclear and Industrial Radiologic Technology
Oceanography
Petroleum Engineering
Pharmacology and Toxicology
Physics
Physiology, Pathology, and Related Sciences
Polymer/Plastics Engineering
Quantitative Economics
Statistics
Textile Sciences and Engineering

Tier 3 comprises all other academic majors, anything not listed as Tier 1 or Tier 2. If you have a question concerning a specific major that is not listed above, you should contact the NROTC unit where you intend to apply. If the major being questioned is not one in which a midshipman is currently enrolled, it may take a few days to get a good answer. The major will have to be assessed to determine its appropriate tier.

Given the clear preference for technical majors, you might think it would be a good idea to declare yourself as an engineer for the application process and then simply switch upon beginning your studies. While technically possible, it is very difficult to move down in tiers. If you have an authentic change of heart upon entering college and desire to change your major from, for example, electrical engineering to history, you must first get a recommendation from your Professor of Naval Science and approval from a selection board at NSTC N9. Your scholarship depends on it. For the reasons we've explained, the selection board cannot entertain all requests for tier switches.

If from the beginning you are interested in history as an undergraduate major—put history on your application! One of the best indicators of undergraduate success is genuine interest in the chosen curriculum. Simply putting down a Tier 1 major because it "looks better" will do you little good in the long run if you cannot get through your engineering curriculum on time and with sufficiently high grades. It is in the best interest of the naval service, and of yourself as a young professional, to study a subject in which you are genuinely interested.

Just like those for most competitive universities, the best candidates for NROTC scholarships are well rounded and have a sincere desire to excel in their chosen fields—and yours is leading Sailors or Marines. Those students who have demonstrated academic, athletic, and leadership abilities and show potential for further growth are the most attractive—students not at the top of their classes but who perform well academically and serve as captains of varsity football teams, say, may beat out a straight-A student who is weak physically. In any case, demonstrating sincere motivation to serve your country and effectively lead Sailors and Marines is ultimately the best indicator of success in the NROTC program.

THE INTERVIEW

A significant aspect of your application's overall quality is the officer interview. You will need to sit down (or schedule a voice/video call) with an officer from either a local NROTC unit or the one you hope to attend. This is the only formal opportunity you will have to make clear in person your poise, character, and commitment to leading Sailors or Marines. In many ways, it is similar to a job interview; you are likely to be asked questions about your interests, strengths, and weaknesses. It is critical that you be candid and forthright with the interviewer. It may be prudent to practice beforehand with a parent, guidance counselor, mentor, or friend to ensure you can speak confidently and coherently, presenting the best version of yourself as part of your application. Particularly try to impress upon the officer conducting the interview your sincere desire to serve and become a commissioned officer.

To set up your interview, contact your local NROTC unit or Navy Officer Recruiter. If you happen to live near an NROTC-affiliated college or university, we recommend simply giving its office a call, asking to speak to the unit's recruitment officer, and stating your intention to apply for the NROTC National Scholarship. A list of NROTC-affiliated schools can be found in appendix I or online. If you are not near an NROTC-affiliated school, reach out to your regional Navy Officer Recruiter or Marine Corps Officer Selection Officer, perform an Internet search for "Local Navy Officer Recruiter," or visit https://www.navy.com/local. Marine Corps information can be found at https://www.marines.com/becoming-a-marine /officer.html.

In either case, when you reach a recruitment officer, your opening should sound something along the lines of,

> Good Morning/Afternoon Sir/Ma'am, my name is John Doe, and I am a rising senior at George Washington High School in Springville, Ohio. I am very interested in attending State University and earning a commission in the Navy through the NROTC program. I understand that I need to fill out the online application, but I had a question about setting up the required application interview. Could you assist me with this, please?

Such a mature, proactive approach will portray you in a positive light and lay the groundwork for good working relationships as you complete and submit your application. The application interview is an important component of the overall application package, and it can only be to your benefit to establish a rapport with your local recruiter or NROTC unit staff as you schedule and conduct it.

Conclusion

We would like to stress three critical points about your application. First, submitting and accepting a scholarship does not commit you to *any* service in the U.S. Navy or Marine Corps. The first year is a sort of trial, and only after the beginning of your sophomore year will you be obligated to serve for a period on active duty.

Second, in general, when you do incur a commitment, it will be for eight years from the day you are commissioned, five years of which must be on active duty. (The remaining three years can be also be served on active duty, reserve duty, or Individual Ready Reserve [IRR] status.) Your service commitment is also dependent on the warfighting community to which you are assigned upon commissioning. Naval aviators incur an eight-year commitment from the date of "winging"—a ceremony in recognition of a student aviator's having completed the arduous flight-training curriculum and earning the coveted "Wings of Gold." Naval Flight Officers incur a six-year commitment from the date of winging. For submariners and Surface Warfare Officers, a five-year commitment is essentially a matter of completing the first afloat tour. For Naval Special Warfare and Explosive Ordnance Disposal officers, there is a five-year commitment. Again: recipients of the National Scholarship become obligated to serve out their post-commissioning commitments upon returning to their NROTC unit in the fall of their sophomore year.

Third and last, don't just dive into the application itself: give yourself adequate time to fill in the required information to the best of your ability. Be concise, professional, and honest. Use NSTC's preapplication checklist, which we discussed previously, to facilitate the gathering of required information and to ensure you have your thoughts in order. At the end of the application, as the last step, the online system will run an electronic audit of the application information to ensure data are complete and properly entered. After making any necessary corrections or additions to the application, you can electronically submit it. From then on, any supplements or alterations will require direct contact with NSTC.

We wish you the best of luck in completing your application. We understand that this can be a stressful period—work diligently, and ask questions if you are unclear about anything. We are confident that you will present "your best self" if you follow the advice in this chapter.

6 Making the Most of Your "Last" Summer

WE WILL ASSUME NOW that you have successfully worked your way through both the National Scholarship and college admissions processes. Congratulations on graduating from high school and earning acceptance into college! Your final summer at home before college marks an important transition period, one that should be taken advantage of to put yourself in the best possible position to excel in your undergraduate studies from the beginning. For those either on an NROTC scholarship or hoping to compete for one in their freshman year, a swift start is critical to success. All college students hope to carry over their academic success from high school, but the stakes may be higher for students who, like you, are held to standards typically higher than those for civilian students at most institutions. In this chapter, we will discuss the typical stumbling blocks for new midshipmen and offer some advice on ways to prepare for an outstanding first year.

Broadly speaking, issues that present problems for new freshmen are much the same as for college students generally: trouble adapting to the increased academic rigor of the collegiate level, homesickness, difficulty adjusting to a new social environment, and sleep-related issues. Each individual will have to overcome their particular difficulties in ways that work for them, but we feel sure you will find some of these tips helpful.

Academic Preparation

Academic excellence is vital to success in the NROTC program. While a comprehensive guide to excelling as an undergraduate is beyond the scope of this book, it is worth noting the unique challenges that NROTC will place upon you relative

An instructor at Surface Warfare Officers School (SWOS) discusses pier work and shiphandling with an NROTC University of Michigan midshipman 2nd class during the 2018 NROTC National Shiphandler of the Year competition at SWOS. *U.S. Navy photo by Nardel Gervacio*

to civilian college students. The mere fact that you are taking a look at a guidebook like this as a high school student is a clear indication of your maturity, foresight, and proactiveness. Your academic success will largely depend on your ability to manage your time effectively to complete assigned work.

Academic hardship within the NROTC program stems overwhelmingly from calculus and physics. You will save yourself, and your NROTC staff, headache and disciplinary paperwork if you do well in these classes. All midshipmen, regardless of major, must take at least two semesters of undergraduate level calculus and calculus-based physics while maintaining a 2.5 GPA. The calculus requirement must be met by no later than the end of the sophomore year and physics by the end of the junior year. We strongly encourage you to dive right in and take at least precalculus during your first semester. In order to have been accepted into the NROTC program, you likely demonstrated a high level of mathematical ability in high school. Letting those skills atrophy for a year will not help you.

During the summer, try to get ahead of the expected coursework by studying and practicing the skills that will be necessary for success. For many courses, you can find old syllabi or course requirements on department websites. Many institutions use a standard textbook for introductory courses that you should also be able to find out about on their websites or by e-mailing department chairs. Once you identify the textbook, you can order or rent it early and work through the opening chapters to get ahead of the material.

Many online, interactive teaching tools exist to help make your studying more efficient and effective. Popular "apps" and sites like the Khan Academy or IXL offer free math lessons and practice problems with solutions to improve your fundamentals. Open courseware is offered increasingly commonly by many of the best schools in the world. The Massachusetts Institute of Technology, Stanford University, and many others publish videos of lectures, syllabi, assignments, notes, and tests online with which anyone interested can essentially teach themselves. Many introductory calculus courses cover similar material, so listening to lectures and working through practice problems even from another university's course may help improve your performance come the fall.

> "Take AP Calculus and Physics in high school and do well. Having your calculus and physics requirements done with before you report to your unit is an enormous advantage, though if you have to choose, get calculus done first; college physics isn't nearly as bad as college calculus in terms of the increase in difficulty. You'll have more time in your schedule to take the courses you really want to take and have more opportunities to explore as well. Arrive fit—academics and PT are the two hardest things to master and maintain as a new midshipman. Plenty of opportunities in other areas will present themselves, but make sure those two areas don't fall short."
>
> —MIDSHIPMAN 3RD CLASS GREENHILL, The George Washington University NROTC

Some students find it a helpful preparation to take an introductory calculus course at a local community college. You will be financially liable for it, and any credit you earn is unlikely to transfer to your full-time college. Still, a summer course will give you access to a qualified instructor to help you work through any weakness you may have, and you should be taking it more as practice than for credit.

We cannot impress upon you enough the importance for success in NROTC of a solid foundation in mathematics. The calculus and physics requirements are far and away the biggest academic stumbling blocks for midshipmen. To put it another way, we have never seen a midshipman fail out of the program because he or she could not write a good enough history essay. We all know of the otherwise bright student who had difficulty with calculus and ultimately was disenrolled.

Unless you are supremely confident in your mathematical and technical abilities, and if your degree plan allows, we would encourage you not to take both calculus and physics during your first semester. You have until the end of your junior year to complete your physics requirements, so there is no need to overburden yourself during your first semester. Physics courses are often taught in sequence— say, physics I in the fall semester, physics II in the spring semester—so it typically makes the most sense to complete your calculus requirements during your freshman year and then physics during your sophomore year. For some Tier 1 and Tier 2 majors, your degree plans may indeed require you to complete both calculus and physics during your first year, in which case you will have to study and practice diligently during the summer to ensure you do well.

Regardless of major, you will have to succeed in calculus and physics in order to be commissioned. Like any other skill in life, proficiency in these courses is the product of consistent, effective, and determined effort. Do yourself a favor: be humble and work diligently to improve upon your math skills now, no matter how successful you were in high school. Building upon or laying a strong foundation in math by practice and study during the summer prior to your freshman year will pay dividends for your success in the NROTC program.

Physical Preparations

Another primary obstacle to midshipman success in the NROTC program is a failure to meet physical readiness standards. Physical readiness means both meeting established height/weight standards and demonstrating performance standards in running, push-ups, and sit-ups (called curl-ups by the Navy; the Marine Corps uses crunches). To have been offered an NROTC scholarship you will have met a certain standard, but the bar is moved higher when you enter the program. A consistent physical fitness regimen is vital for everybody for health and happiness, but unlike the average student, you must always maintain your fitness to Navy or Marine Corps standards.

If your body composition may be an issue, be proactive about learning the standards and recognizing trouble signs. Transitioning to college presents many challenges for effective weight management. If you are used to your family's well-balanced, healthy dinners, you may now find yourself in a buffet-style dining hall with many less-healthy options. Peers may be quick to order pizza every night, but you may not be as able to afford a "freshman fifteen."

One of the first hurdles you will encounter upon reporting for the fall semester is a Physical Readiness Test (PRT). With the advent of standardized New Student

NROTC midshipman candidates run to their next event during New Student Indoctrination (NSI). *U.S. Navy photo by Scott A. Thornbloom*

Indoctrination at NSTC, in Great Lakes, you *must* pass your initial PRT in order to activate your scholarship. That is, your scholarship cannot be activated until you are fully medically qualified, and that in turn requires success on the initial PRT. For Navy-Option midshipman the PRT is a three-event test: you must complete curl-ups, push-ups, and a 1.5-mile run (the Navy will transition curl-ups to plank holds in fall 2020). Marine-Option midshipmen must perform crunches, pull-ups, and a three-mile run. Be sure to check the standards listed in appendix V or online resources to make sure you are on track to succeed.

An effective plan and consistent effort are critical to long-term physical readiness. First, recognize your physical weaknesses and work steadily to improve yourself in that area. The great thing about physical fitness is that if you work consistently and intelligently toward a goal,

> "The most challenging aspect of the NROTC program for me was maintaining physical fitness. For most of my classmates, I think learning to live independently was a challenge, but I had already been doing that and working a job, making car payments, renting an apartment, etc., so it was really just getting into a habit of physical fitness."
>
> —MIDSHIPMAN 1ST CLASS BURGESS, University of Washington NROTC

you can't help but improve. Doing lots of push-ups will almost certainly make you better at push-ups. The best way to get better at running is—running!

This book is not the place for a detailed workout plan, but an easy and effective approach is simply to perform as many push-ups and curl-ups as you can a few days a week. You should feel some muscle soreness the day after exercise, so allow your body sufficient time to rest and recover before attempting to improve your performance. A balanced diet is also vital to recovery from exercise.

Midshipmen most commonly struggle with the running portion of the test. The good news—or the bad news, depending on how much you love running—is that improving your running performance is almost entirely a function of time spent running. Before beginning a running regimen, understand that the largest impediment to success in running is injury. It will do you absolutely no good to cause a stress injury by trying to do too much too quickly. Building an aerobic foundation takes time, patience, and diligence. Again, your scholarship cannot be activated without passing the Physical Readiness Test upon reporting to your NROTC unit—showing up injured is not a good idea.

A 1.5-mile run is a test of your aerobic capacity, not your overall running speed. For most novice runners, the most effective way to improve aerobic capacity is to run at a conversational pace for at least thirty minutes a few days per week. If you are completely new to running, you may need to alternate between periods of running and walking. Do not take it so easy that you do not challenge yourself, but you should not be wiped out after a training run. For beginning runners, the good news is that your body will rapidly respond to moderate increases in aerobic stress. Unless you are naturally athletic, running is a skill that must be consistently worked at in order to succeed. Most high schools support cross-country and track teams; participating in either may be an excellent way to improve your running ability.

Sleep

One of the biggest adjustments many new college students have to make concerns their sleep schedules. College students tend to be night owls, staying up later and sleeping in much longer than they did in high school. Some students are able to avoid early morning classes and are free to maintain a "night-walking" schedule with relative ease. Many colleges recognize that a large portion of their student body is at peak performance later in the day and have begun to offer undergraduate courses in the late afternoon or early evening to accommodate. As an NROTC midshipman, however, you are unlikely to have the luxury of sleeping in until noon.

While the specific timing of mandatory NROTC events, such as naval science courses, physical training, and leadership lab, will depend on the schedule developed by the NROTC unit staff, these events are typically held early in the morning to minimize conflicts with degree curricula and extracurricular activities. Given the schedule requirements of potentially hundreds of students, the only feasible option is often to meet before "normal" classes begin. Although this practice may seem to put a damper on your social life, the reality is that the ability to wake and perform early in the day is a necessary skill for a career in the military.

Lack of sleep can have a devastating effect on your academic and physical performance. Your body needs sufficient rest in order to perform at its best. Attempting to study or perform physically while overly fatigued owing to lack of rest is like attempting those same activities while intoxicated. High levels of caffeine or other stimulants can be dangerous to rely on and will never be as effective as a proper sleep regimen. We have all had to "power through" periods when rest was hard to come by, but such instances should be the exception and not the norm. We strongly encourage you to treat sufficient sleep as seriously as you do proper nutrition, study habits, and exercise.

Communicate with your freshman class advisor during the summer to identify the earliest event you will be required to attend. For example, your host unit may conduct physical training (PT) sessions beginning at 0630 (6:30 a.m.) on Monday and Wednesday mornings. Say that your dorm is across campus and that you will need to "muster" (physically show up) for accountability purposes ten to fifteen minutes ahead of event; that means you should plan on being out of your dorm twenty to thirty minutes ahead of time. Allowing for time to wake up, eat a small snack, and perform necessary hygiene, etc., you may be waking up an hour before PT begins. In this case, to ensure you are not late you should be prepared to wake up around 0530 (5:30 a.m.).

"Don't overload yourself at the beginning of your college career; sacrificing sleep in order to fit more stuff into your day is a recipe for disaster. I have seen it lead to bad grades, a poor social life, physical injury or sickness, and general unhappiness."

—MIDSHIPMAN 4TH CLASS CAMPEAU, The George Washington University NROTC

For many, the most effective way of adjusting your biological clock is simply to be disciplined about waking up at a designated time. You can begin to train your body for this during the summer. In the previous example, you should simply set an alarm for 0530 all the time and, even though you do not really have a mandatory PT training event to attend, go ahead and start your day. Go for a run, head to your local YMCA to work out, or get a head start on your day's work, but train yourself to be up and functional at the time you will need to be upon reporting to school. While your peers are sleeping away their last summer before college, you will be disciplining yourself to excel as soon as you get there.

Now, here comes the difficult part, particularly when you are just beginning your transition to earlier mornings—do not let yourself take long naps during the day to "catch up." Many college students, unfortunately, binge-nap and also try to offset the effects of their late nights with two-to-four-hour afternoon naps. These naps do nothing more than further distort their biological clocks and prevent them from going to sleep earlier in the evening as they should. The most reliable way to keep yourself from sabotaging your biological clock this summer with long naps is to eliminate opportunities to take any. Plan to be out of the house for the afternoons and early evenings so that you will not have the temptation to curl up on the couch and pass out for a few hours. Your body will feel much less tired if you are engaged in a physical activity you enjoy, such as sports, hiking, walking, or volunteering, or in a job. All the hard work required to get out of bed in the morning will be wasted if you do not also stay up during the day so that you can fall asleep earlier.

You should plan on consistently getting at least seven hours of sleep each night, maybe more, to feel your best on a daily basis. Effective, healthy sleep habits are the product of consistent amounts of quality sleep, not of going without during the week and "catching up" by sleeping through the weekend. In the example, if you know you need to wake up at 0530, you should plan on being asleep no later than 2230 (10:30 p.m.), to allow for seven hours of rest. If you are able to get to sleep earlier, that is even better.

Do not worry particularly about going to sleep at a certain time; once adjusted, your body should naturally become tired and prepared for sleep at about the time you should be heading to bed anyway. You should try to develop an evening routine that helps your body fall asleep quickly. Try to avoid bright lights or excessive screen time in the hour preceding your bedtime. A chief culprit is your phone—browsing social media, texting, or viewing online videos. The bright lights of digital screens "trick" your body into thinking it is daylight and hinder its ability to fall asleep. You will save yourself many restless hours if you can discipline yourself to put down your phone and stop playing video games or watching movies earlier in the evening. Other relaxed activities, such as reading a physical book, listening to low-volume music, or having a conversation with a friend or family member can help pass the time without waking your body up.

Last, have a good sleep environment: a comfortable pillow and quality sheets and blankets. Most dorm rooms will come with a standard mattress, so you may have to adjust to it, but having a familiar pillow and comforter/blanket combination may ease the transition. Try to make the room as dark as possible. If you are used to sleeping in near silence, you may find the dorm environment jarringly loud. You may want to try sleeping with a "white noise" machine or a fan for background noise to get you used to sleeping in a noisier environment. As an added reinforcement, consider that you will one day find that there is constant noise on board ship, whether from aircraft landing or launching, fluids moving through pipes, machinery coming on line, or large ventilation fans being started—you will absolutely need to be able to sleep with background noise. After a while, you may find yourself less able to sleep in perfect quiet than with noise you have come to expect—in fact, nothing will bring you wide awake more quickly than all that noise suddenly replaced by perfect quiet.

Be prepared for some surprises on reporting to school. Many freshmen are randomly assigned roommates. Depending on your dorm room layout, you may not have any private space and so may have to accommodate your roommate's schedule and lifestyle. As a midshipman, you are much more likely to have early morning commitments than your roommate. The likelihood is that your roommate will stay up and wake up later than you will be able to. With luck, your roommate will be respectful of your need to sleep and your early morning commitments and keep noise and light levels low so as not to disturb you, but if you were used to a perfectly dark, quiet, and empty bedroom back home, you may have trouble adjusting. If you find that you and your roommate's study or personal habits clash, the two of you should respectfully discuss these issues. They might not even have been aware they were disturbing you and appreciate your bringing the issue to their attention. If you are unable to reconcile your living habits, try talking the matter over with your Resident Assistant (RA) or other dorm authority.

Unfortunately, bad roommates are a fact of life for many college students, and you may simply have to cope. If this is the case, set yourself up as best you can for success. Some students find eye masks and earplugs (or noise-canceling headphones) helpful. You may want to try these during the summer to get used to wearing them.

Conclusion

For college students, summer break is an opportunity to rest and come back reinvigorated to excel during the upcoming semester. For students beginning their freshman year, that is especially true, and all the more for you, facing the demands of both college and NROTC—you should use the summer as a time to discipline for it. Success in the military is largely a product of consistent discipline; developing effective habits early on can pay important dividends as you progress through NROTC and your naval career.

7 New Student Indoctrination

WHAT AN EXCITING TIME! The beginning of your college years is quickly approaching. You should be motivated, rested, and enthusiastic to start this tough but critical part of your life. If you are reading this book well in advance of your departure for college and the beginning of your NROTC career, we are confident that you have energetically acted upon the recommendations in the previous chapter. In fact, if you are the type of person to read our book, you are probably already ahead of the game. However, if you are still developing your discipline and mental toughness, you will need to come up to speed quickly to excel during your NROTC New Student Indoctrination (NSI).

In this chapter, we will discuss what NROTC midshipmen joining the program immediately after high school undergo—the NROTC New Student Indoctrination. NSI is a foundational event that will set the tone for both your freshman year and your overall NROTC experience. It marks a distinct transition from your status as a civilian high school graduate to an NROTC midshipman and college student.

A brief note before going further: We are writing mostly in terms of the standardized initial NROTC midshipmen training program, "New Student Indoctrination," which has been recently established. Where all prospective NROTC midshipmen previously attended a week of introductory training, known as "New Student Orientation" (NSO), at their NROTC units, freshmen now complete this training at Naval Station Great Lakes, just north of Chicago, Illinois, home of the U.S. Navy's Recruit Training Command for enlisted Sailors. Students offered scholarships must attend and complete NSI, to include meeting Navy or Marine Corps physical requirements, in order to activate their scholarships.

NROTC midshipman candidates participate in an abandon-ship exercise in the USS *Indianapolis* Combat Training Pool at Recruit Training Command (RTC). *U.S. Navy photo by Scott A. Thornbloom*

What Is New Student Indoctrination?

NSI is a training period prior to the commencement of the academic year designed to introduce new midshipmen to the objectives, standards, and procedures of the NROTC program. While the term military "indoctrination" can invoke images of ruthless drill instructors berating helpless enlistees, the reality is that NSI is designed to be challenging but by no means brutal. In no sense is NSI structured as a "weeding out" event. You should feel confident in your ability to excel at NSI as long as you kept in shape over the summer, maintain a positive attitude in challenging circumstances, and report ready to learn and contribute to your new NROTC team.

Your assigned NROTC unit staff should have been in regular contact with you over the summer concerning logistics of the NSI. Typically, your prospective freshman class advisor will communicate such necessary details as reporting date, time, location, and uniform. You will work with your assigned NROTC unit to arrange for (official, government-paid) travel to and from NSI in Great Lakes. It is usual for NROTC units to send "Welcome Aboard" packages to all prospective midshipmen assigned to them, with all necessary information on the NSI. Ensure that you understand fully where you should be, when you should be there, and what you should be wearing.

Another key point is to have early and open communication with your institution's (that is, the school's, not the unit's) freshman advisor concerning its freshman orientation requirements. Nearly all academic institutions have an obligatory freshman orientation program that you will need to attend in addition to your NROTC NSI. Fortunately, most offer more than one freshman orientation session, which should allow you to meet your school's requirements without conflicting with the NSI. Ensure that your freshman class advisor is aware of potential conflicts—particularly if you are attending a cross-town affiliate. If you are unable to reconcile scheduling conflicts between the NSI and "normal" college orientation, your NROTC unit staff may give priority to your academic institution's orientation. That would be reasonable, as the primary purpose of your being at school is to earn your degree. However, do not start off on the wrong foot with your unit leadership by making such a decision on your own. Your unit staff will work with you and the institution's administration to make possible attendance at

"My NSO experience taught me so much and I am appreciative. There was one time when we were not putting on our uniforms at a quick enough pace. So we were ordered to take apart our meticulously organized racks and redo them several times, bringing all components (sheets, pillow, etc.) into the passageway each time. That was done at too slow of a pace, and we needed to now bring out our whole mattress into the passageway in addition to the rest of our bed gear. Fast-forward through ten minutes or so of this and we are standing in formation outside with our mattress at our side. Although this seems ridiculous, it helped teach us the need for strict attention to detail and timeliness."

—MIDSHIPMAN 2ND CLASS McAVOY, College of the Holy Cross NROTC

"I vividly and fondly remember my first week and recall with some pride how dramatic an effect such a short period of time can have on implementing the foundations of military smartness and camaraderie. Although at the time I felt stressed with the marching, drilling, PT'ing, standing fire watch, and immediately reacting to the 'firm' direction of the midshipmen staff members, the overall experience did an excellent job of indoctrinating me into the NROTC program. I can honestly say that I only vaguely remember what happened during my university orientation, but I can distinctly bring to mind my NROTC new student orientation."

—LIEUTENANT CORDIAL

Midshipmen from the Vanderbilt University NROTC unit observe and judge Junior NROTC cadets competing. *U.S. Navy photo by Scott A. Thornbloom*

both orientations if there is any way to do it. If it can't be done after all, you may think that means you "skate out of" an unnecessary week of drill, PT, and inspections. But the fact is that you will certainly come to regret the loss of a significant bonding experience with your peers.

New Student Indoctrination also serves as an effective leadership-development opportunity for upper-class NROTC midshipmen, who will serve as the orientation staff for NSI as they did for NSO. While an established military organization exists within the Battalion of Midshipmen throughout the academic year, NSI is one of the few times during the year in which all midshipmen can focus 100 percent on midshipmen professional training. Even as a freshman, take advantage of the opportunity to learn from your instructors, both midshipman and active-duty, in order to prepare yourself for potential duty as an instructor a couple of years in the future.

You may be skeptical that upper-class midshipmen are capable of providing an appropriate level of training—after all, they are only young men and women, slightly older than you. Is there really that much of a difference between college freshmen and college juniors? Rest assured that considerable planning, preparation, and rehearsal went into your NSI period. With the centralization and standardization that NSI brings to this training, each midshipman, regardless of school, will receive the same high level of military indoctrination. In addition, active-duty

NROTC unit staff will serve as "duty officers" and directly oversee all NSI training evolutions to ensure the safety of all involved and to rein in "overeager" upperclass midshipmen.

The components of NSI for new NROTC students typically include:

1. Administrative enrollment processing
2. Issuance of uniforms and basic instruction in their proper wear
3. Introduction to basics of military customs, courtesies, and traditions
4. Introduction to the NROTC unit's organization, regulations, and chain of command
5. Instruction in basic military drill and ceremony procedures
6. Instruction in basic physical fitness per NROTC program requirements
7. Assessment in both physical fitness and swimming
8. Instruction in the benefits of participation in the NROTC program
9. Instruction on individual responsibilities for participation in the NROTC program
10. The centrality of teamwork to the naval services.

The NSI period is designed to introduce the NROTC unit and begin the process of professional development that will continue throughout the four years until commissioning. The initial stages of the NSI period may be more stressful than your academic institution's welcome-aboard, but again, the NROTC NSI is by no means a "boot camp" experience designed to rid the program of those unsuited for naval service. You should have no qualms about not "surviving" your NSI. You will be just fine as long as you listen attentively, respond enthusiastically to direction, and have an open mind concerning the beginning of your naval career.

A Navy Physical Readiness Test (PRT) or Marine Corps Physical Fitness Test (PFT) is typically one of the first events held during New Student Indoctrination. As we have several times emphasized, the Professor of Naval Science is unable to activate your scholarship

"NSO was extremely important for building class cohesion. Without it, I wouldn't have gotten to know the people in my class as well as I have. My favorite memory of NSO was when we were field-daying (cleaning) the barracks in which we were staying. The troop handler in charge of the area was loudly singing the 'Clean Up Song' and we had to try and sing along without laughing or smiling."

—MIDSHIPMAN 1ST CLASS HENNIE-ROED, Georgia Institute of Technology NROTC until you have met the Navy's or Marine Corps' physical readiness standards. In layman's terms, the Navy or Marine Corps will not pay your tuition until you can prove your physical readiness. That's why we've said that it is critical to start off your NSI and NROTC career positively by reporting in good shape and able to perform to standards. Please see the preceding chapter for tips concerning preparations for excelling on the PRT or PFT.

Another large element of NSI is introduction to the basics of military drill. Although to the novice military drill seems to be nothing more than walking in a straight line and turning when told, smart and coordinated drill requires instruction, practice, and meticulous attention to detail. A significant portion of your time during NSI will be devoted to learning, practicing, and executing basic drill evolutions so that you and your classmates can rapidly join the rest of the battalion in unit-wide formations and parades.

A rapid indoctrination to the naval services also occurs, through instruction in "Naval Knowledge." Typically, NROTC units prepare and distribute "gouge" books—small bound books that contain various facts and historical events concerning the naval services. You will be called on to study and remember the contents of the gouge and demonstrate your knowledge to NSI staff. A Naval Knowledge check is integral to all uniform and drill inspections, so you will be well served by studying diligently. You may not have access to the gouge prior to reporting to NSI—part of the training value resides in compressing the time available to learn the information—but researching and remembering some basic facts about the naval services and your host institution could help ease your learning curve. It is standard for questions such as these to be asked, "What is the Navy's birthday?"; "When was the battle of Midway?"; "Who is the most decorated Marine in history?"; "Where does the Mameluke Sword come from?"; "Where are the Halls of Montezuma?"—and so on.

NSI will also likely be your introduction to mandatory "General Military Training" (GMT), which is a staple of the modern military career. GMT covers such topics as sexual assault prevention and response (SAPR), fraternization, hazing, and other general aspects of promoting a healthy command climate. Particularly for new members of the military family, GMT is an opportunity to learn about the vast resources available to you specifically designed to help maintain your personal wellness. The quality of GMT instruction can vary from speakers reading in a monotone from a PowerPoint slide deck to an inattentive audience struggling to stay awake to a vibrant, interactive lesson that acts out relevant college-environment situations, proper responses, and available resources. We encourage you, above all else, to take fully on board that your personal well-being is critical to contributing to the Navy and Marine Corps team—it is never a bad thing to seek legitimate help when in need. As an NROTC midshipman on a civilian academic campus, you are in a unique circumstance: you will have access to the services and counseling provided through the school's office of student affairs (or equivalent), but except on active duty during your summer cruise you are not typically authorized to use services designed for active-duty service members.

A note on the term "fire watch." You can expect a fire watch (stood by midshipmen) to be set all night in the building you are in to ensure that it doesn't suddenly catch fire. As ridiculous as that may sound to you now, the military principle is quite sound—obviously, a constant watch must be set at sea, particularly at night when visibility is low, and below decks a "sounding and security" watch roves continually, looking for fire and flooding. While bivouacked, an infantry platoon will set sentries to sound the alarm in case enemies approach. Granted, it is extremely unlikely that your building will experience a spontaneous conflagration; nevertheless, there will be a watch rotation each night of midshipmen required to march vigilantly throughout the halls ensuring that no issues arise. Thus, at least one night you should plan on your sleep being interrupted. Specific procedures on properly standing a fire watch will be part of the training curriculum before anyone actually assumes the watch.

Sample Notional Schedule

With the establishment of the centralized New Student Indoctrination, each midshipman will experience the same rigorous training schedule. The following sample schedule is given only to suggest the tight scheduling and illustrate how busy you are likely to be during NSI.

"Our NSO was the most valuable seven weeks of my training in ROTC. My favorite memory from our NSO was when our Unit XO wanted to give everyone a practice medical emergency scenario. He instructed a 4/C MIDN in our NSO to lie on the ground to feign an injury to see how everyone would respond and assess the situation. The 4/C MIDN was so locked-on from our training that he laid down on the ground at attention. When asked by an NSO instructor what he was doing, he replied with something along the lines of 'This MIDN is not supposed to tell you.' Needless to say, the scenario did not play out as expected."

—MIDSHIPMAN 1ST CLASS GRABIS, University of Michigan NROTC

Monday

    0700—Report to Great Lakes, Illinois, for Administrative In-Processing/
            Uniform Issue

    1000—Parent's Introduction Brief/MIDN Welcome Aboard/MIDN Oath

    1100—Parent's Goodbye/MIDNs Depart to Training Area

    1130—Introduction to Drill

    1230—Lunch

    1300—Classroom GMT

    1500—Drill

    1700—Dinner

    1800—Classroom GMT

    1900—Room/Rack (bunk) Inspection Preparation

    2100—Hygiene

    2130—Lights Out (Set the Fire Watch)

Tuesday

    0530—Reveille

    0600—Physical Training

    0700—Hygiene

    0730—Breakfast

    0800—Room/Rack Inspection

    1000—Drill

    1200—Lunch

    1300—Classroom GMT

    1500—Drill

    1700—Dinner

    1800—Leadership Discussion

    1900—Platoon Time/Uniform Inspection Preparations

    2100—Hygiene

    2130—Lights Out (Set the Fire Watch)

Wednesday

    0530—Reveille

    0600—Physical Training

    0700—Hygiene

    0730—Breakfast

    0800—Room/Rack Inspection

1000—Drill/Uniform Inspection

1200—Lunch

1300—Classroom GMT

1500—Drill

1700—Dinner

1800—Leadership Discussion

1900—Platoon Time

2100—Hygiene

2130—Lights Out (Set the Fire Watch)

Thursday

0530—Reveille

0600—Physical Training

0700—Hygiene

0730—Breakfast

0800—Room/Rack Inspection

1000—Drill

1200—Lunch

1300—Classroom GMT

1500—Drill Inspection

1700—Dinner

1800—Leadership Discussion

1900—Platoon Time

2100—Hygiene

2130—Lights Out (Set the Fire Watch)

Friday

0530—Reveille

0600—Physical Training

0700—Hygiene

0730—Breakfast

0800—Final Room/Rack Inspection

1000—Final Drill Inspection

1100—Concluding Discussion w/ CO

1200—Battalion BBQ

1400—NSI Ends—MIDNs Return to the Institution for Dormitory "Move In"

Practical Advice for MIDNs Attending New Student Indoctrination

Many freshmen NROTC midshipman are nervous about New Student Indoctrination. The Welcome Aboard packet you received from your host NROTC unit may well have presented NSI (and justly) as a foundational event of your time in the NROTC program. If college represents your first significant time away from your family and support system, it is perfectly natural to be feeling some nervousness. Take heart from the fact that NSI represents an incredible opportunity to bond with a group of similarly successful and patriotic young men and women, some of whom will be your shipmates throughout your time in NROTC. Before concluding this chapter, we recommend the following basic advice to help you succeed during your NSI and lay the foundation for an outstanding first semester in NROTC.

1. *Keep a positive attitude!* Nothing is more important during NSI than keeping and maintaining a positive attitude. Although NSI is *not* boot camp, there will almost certainly be a level of volume and accompanying stress not typical

A Marine lance corporal teaches midshipmen how to utilize an M9 during the Career Orientation and Training for Midshipmen's (CORTRAMID) "Marine Week" at Marine Corps Base Camp Pendleton, California. *U.S. Marine Corps photo by Tayler P. Schwamb*

of normal interactions between peers. The stress is a deliberate part of the program—it is there to train you to focus on what is important and to be able to respond even when your sensors are overloaded. If you make a mistake or feel that you are being "trained" more than other midshipmen, just take a deep breath, recommit to performing at standards, and keep a cheerful disposition. Some of your classmates may struggle with this initial foray into NROTC, and your positivity may help improve their perspective and ability to cope. You are in the position you are, as an NROTC midshipman, thanks to the strength of your character and academic record. Be confident that you deserve to be where you are—even if the gunnery sergeant seems to be giving you reason to think otherwise!

2. *Don't take corrections personally.* Depending on your upbringing, NSI may represent the first time you have been yelled at for seemingly minor faults. After all, who should care so much if your thumb isn't tucked "just so" while saluting? After all, it looks pretty much the same as everyone else's! However, such details *do* matter in a military organization predicated on integrity and shared commitment to upholding standards. Take absolutely nothing personally when training-staff members correct your faults in bearing, drill, uniform, etc. The training staff is there to ensure that you and the other new midshipmen can quickly fit into an NROTC battalion. What may seem like harassment over trivia is in reality training on the critical importance of attention to detail in military affairs—an attention to detail that your future Sailors and Marines will expect of you, and you of them.

3. *Sound Off!!!* Nothing is likely to infuriate your training staff more than not responding *loudly* and directly to their questions. If in doubt, yell louder than you think you should. In the unlikely event that you are actually too loud, training staff will likely applaud your motivation and tell you to tone it down a bit. In the naval services we respond with "Aye, Aye, Sir/Ma'am!" to directions and "Yes, Sir/Ma'am!" to questions. We are not encouraging you to yell "Aye, Aye, Sir!" at everything you hear, but a soft-spoken response to a direction or question will almost certainly result in your providing the appropriate response many more times than you would have cared to. If you think you are loud enough but the midshipman platoon sergeant won't "get off your case," be even louder. It is not at all uncommon for the majority of an NSI cohort to be voiceless a couple of days in. Do not worry: we promise you that

your voice will promptly return after NSI and that your memory of croaking through NSI will be just like those of your shipmates.

4. *Stand up if you are tired.* As shown in the schedule above, there is typically an eight-hour rest period between lights out and reveille. However, because of standing fire watch, inability to sleep from excitement/nervousness, or other factors, you may not actually get enough sleep each night. It is natural to feel tired over the course of NSI—particularly during classroom instruction. However, falling asleep on watch is one of the cardinal sins of naval life. While falling asleep during GMT is not nearly as heinous, during NSI it will be treated as if it were. If you feel yourself nodding off, do the responsible thing: simply stand up in the back of the room until the period of instruction is over. It is *much* harder to fall asleep standing up—your staff members will appreciate your self-discipline in recognizing and dealing with your tiredness. You will also set a proper example for any similarly sleepy peers.

5. *Have fun!* As stated before, NSI is a challenging, unifying, and memorable part of each NROTC midshipman's time in the program. Take advantage of any opportunity to display your sense of humor. Training staff will almost certainly insert some manner of ridiculousness into the training regimen, to break up the monotony—use these occasions to demonstrate your personality and create memories with your new shipmates.

Conclusion

Indoctrination to NROTC is a powerful shared experience for you and your shipmates. Perhaps more than any other event during your time in NROTC, New Student Indoctrination coalesces your class and cohort as distinct groups. It is likely that you will form lasting friendships and memories far beyond those resulting from your university's orientation. While you may be nervous or be stressed anticipating the event, embrace the opportunity as a rite of passage initiating you into your new NROTC family. You are sure to collect some of your first "sea stories" to share!

"At the time of my NSO, the NROTC unit commanding officer was CAPT Trost. During periods of rehydration, midshipmen would be encouraged to offer a toast to our beloved leader, CAPT Trost. Our NSO training staff was an unusually poetic lot and desired that all toasts rhyme—the challenge became to offer the longest, most poetic toast.
An example:
I here offer a toast!
To Captain Trost!
Whom we admire the most!
Who is humble and does not boast!
Who has sailed from coast to coast!
It has been over 12 years since my NSO but I can still vividly recall me and my shipmates holding our canteens high and shouting our toast to the honor of CAPT Trost!"

—LIEUTENANT CORDIAL

8 NROTC Program Requirements

WITH THE FIRST LITTLE BIT of salt on your collar, having completed New Student Indoctrination, you are now ready to deeply delve into all of the programmatic requirements for an NROTC midshipman. As you begin to get the hang of college and NROTC, you will need to plan for specific program requirements that you will be held to during your time in the NROTC program. We will discuss that now in detail: the program's academic requirements, then the physical fitness requirements, and in closing the command and leadership requirements. Critically, NROTC midshipmen must demonstrate proficiency in all required "Professional Core Competencies" (PCCs) prior to commissioning as naval officers. You will find a full listing of PCCs in appendix III.

Make no mistake about it, these requirements are exactly that—standards that must be met in order to be eligible for a commission as a naval officer after earning your undergraduate degree. If you have any questions concerning program requirements, be sure to discuss the matter with your class advisor to ensure you are not caught flat-footed with a critical deadline looming.

Academic Requirements

If you completed courses for college credit (Advanced Placement, International Baccalaureate, community college, etc.) prior to joining the NROTC program, you may count these credits toward program requirements as long as your academic institution accepts them as counting toward the completion of a baccalaureate degree. The only exception to this policy is that you must take at least one semester/quarter each of calculus and physics in a university classroom environment. Thus, even if you "aced" the AP Calculus BC exam and your university

RADM Mike Bernacchi, commander of Naval Service Training Command (NSTC), and MCPO Jimmy Hailey III, NSTC command master chief, speak to Texas A&M NROTC midshipmen during an admiral's call. *U.S. Navy photo by Frederick Martin*

is willing to check off both Calculus I and II toward your degree, you are still required to take a university calculus course; in this case the logical course would be Calculus III.

Students participating in the NROTC program must complete a three-pronged academic program: (1) the academic institution's baccalaureate degree program with an NROTC-approved major (for details, please refer to chapter 5); (2) NROTC-specified courses offered by the academic institution, and (3) specified naval science courses taught by the NROTC unit.

Working with your institution's academic advisor, develop a degree plan, detailed by semester, that ensures that you will complete all required coursework within the four years your NROTC scholarship agreement allows to graduate with the appropriate degree. An approved degree plan is a required component of your student file and will be a topic of conversation during counseling sessions with your NROTC class advisor.

In developing your degree plan, keep in mind that you must maintain status as a full-time student to remain in good standing with the NROTC program. Standard course loading for an NROTC student is usually between fifteen and eighteen credit hours per semester; each student's individual academic program will depend on the degree sought and university policies. Under no circumstances can an NROTC student fall below the minimum credit hours the school requires per semester of full-time students, regardless of progress toward the degree. Even in your senior year, when many of your peers will be cruising through nine credit hours of ceramics and basket weaving, you must maintain a full course load.

Subject areas mandated by NROTC but not included in the unit's naval science curriculum include not only calculus and physics but also foreign affairs, American history, military history,

> "I struggled significantly with my academics in my first semester of college, but once I learned how to manage my time and realized how important it was to study constantly towards my classes, I got the hang of things. This relates to NROTC because your GPA will ultimately affect your service selection, so you want to be on the ball with your grades from the start."
>
> —MIDSHIPMAN 2ND CLASS OTT, University of Virginia NROTC

and foreign languages, all of which broaden your education. Engineers and technical majors in particular may have to work hard to fit mandated liberal arts courses into their degree plans. The NROTC unit staff will maintain a listing of approved courses to meet non–naval science requirements. In addition, the unit's academic officer can approve courses not listed, if they meet the criteria established in NROTC directives. If you desire to take such a course, perhaps a newly established one, discuss the matter with your class advisor. In most cases all it takes is a copy of the course syllabus to demonstrate that it meets the standards.

The final set of NROTC program academic requirements comprise the Naval Science courses taught by NROTC unit staff. The sequencing of these courses and when they are offered differ from school to school, based on the Professor of Naval Science's preference, but Introduction to Naval Science will be the first course offered, in the first semester, and Leadership and Ethics the final one, during your senior spring semester. As mentioned in chapter 2, the PNS will teach Leadership and Ethics, and the executive officer will teach the Leadership and Management course. Other courses will be divvied up among the NROTC unit staff officers.

Last, Naval Science requirements are different for the different NROTC options. We will cover Navy-Option naval science courses, then Marine-Option courses. Also, as naval warfare evolves and adapts to ever more complex environments, the professional and educational needs of its officer corps must likewise change. Naval science courses may from time to time be supplemented, adjusted, or eliminated altogether to allow curriculum space for more pressing material.

NAVY-OPTION NAVAL SCIENCE

The descriptions of naval science courses below are provided as guides to the scope and types of material covered in each. Your academic institution's description may differ slightly. If such is the case, the school's description is likely to be more accurate. Regardless, instructors are given some academic freedom in developing their curricula, so focal points may differ from unit to unit and course to course.

Introduction to Naval Science. Taught during the fall semester, Introduction to Naval Science is the first course taught to newly arrived midshipmen and serves as a continuation of introduction to the naval services they received at New Student Indoctrination. If you join the NROTC program as a College Programmer (that is, not a computer-programming major but a midshipman in the NROTC College Program, discussed in chapter 9), work with your class advisor to fit this course into your overall curriculum. It is a general introduction to the U.S. Navy (USN) and U.S. Marine Corps (USMC) that emphasizes their organizational structures, warfare components, and assigned roles and missions. It covers all aspects of the naval service, from its relative position within the Department of Defense to "specific warfare communities" and career paths. It also includes basic elements of leadership and of USN's and USMC's core values. The course is an initial exposure to many elements of naval culture and provides students a conceptual framework and working vocabulary for use on summer cruise.

If your unit assigns a class advisor especially for freshmen midshipmen, then that advisor is the natural choice to teach this course, as it allows frequent interaction with their midshipmen. The course is fairly straightforward, and tests will likely ask you to define terms, recognize naval "assets," and explain the scope and purpose of the U.S. Navy as a part of the Defense Department.

Sea Power and Maritime Affairs. This course is a study of the U.S. Navy and the influence of seapower on history from both a historical and political-science viewpoint. It explores the major events, attitudes, personalities, and circumstances that have given the U.S. Navy its proud history and rich tradition. It deals with issues of national imperatives in peacetime as well as war, various maritime philosophies that have been interpreted into naval strategies and doctrines, budgetary realities that shaped the forces of an era, and the pursuit of American diplomatic objectives. It concludes with a discussion of the Navy's strategic and structural changes at the end of the Cold War and its new focus, mission, and strategy in the post–September 11, 2001, world.

For liberal arts majors, this course will be very similar to other history/political science courses, in that it is a broad overview of important events, themes, and principal actors. Your instructor will likely use the course as a means to develop your personal speaking and briefing skills and have you write a series of analytical papers on given subjects.

Leadership and Management. This course introduces the fundamental concepts of leading Sailors and Marines that will be expanded on throughout your NROTC years, in a "continuum of leadership development." It identifies the elements of leadership vital to the effectiveness of Navy and Marine Corps officers by reviewing the theories and parameters of leadership and management both within the naval service and outside it, progressing through values development, interpersonal skills, management skills, and application theory. Practical applications are explored in experiential exercises, readings, case studies, and laboratory discussions.

This course is typically taught by your NROTC unit executive officer. The XO's practical leadership experience, personal anecdotes, and professional knowledge will all enhance the course. Similar courses are taught in undergraduate business and management schools, but this one is particularly focused on the challenges of and skills necessary for military leadership. It typically involves a substantial amount of reading, case-study analysis, seminar discussion, and public speaking.

Navigation. This course is an in-depth study of the theory, principles, and procedures of plotting, piloting, and electronic navigation, their applications, and an introduction to the use of "maneuvering boards" (a way of quickly solving relative-motion problems that you'll be using in simulators and at sea). Students learn piloting techniques, the use of charts, the use of visual and electronic aids, and the theory of operation of both magnetic and gyrocompasses. Students develop practical skills in plotting and electronic navigation. Other topics include tides, currents, effects of wind and weather, voyage planning, and the international and inland rules of navigation (the "Rules of the Nautical Road"). The course is supplemented with case studies involving moral, ethical, and leadership issues that can arise in this connection. Celestial navigation—using the sun, moon, and stars as "lighthouses of the sky"—will also be introduced.

For the professional naval officer, regardless of designator, basic skills in navigation are essential. This course is most applicable to future Surface Warfare Officers, who during the first sea tours will serve as deck watchstanders, but the principles taught will serve submarine, aviation, and Special Warfare Officers as well. This course aims to increase the professional knowledge and practical skills of midshipmen and enhance the benefit of the training they will receive during summer cruises. This course is one of the more challenging naval science courses, as it calls on you to demonstrate mastery of a number of skills, but may also be the most rewarding to midshipmen who take their profession seriously.

Naval Ship Systems I (Engineering). In this course, students learn ship design, hydrodynamic forces, stability, propulsion, electrical theory and distribution, hydraulic theory and ship control, and damage control. The course introduces the basic concepts of theory and design of steam, gas turbine, diesel, and nuclear propulsion plants. Case studies on leadership and ethical issues in the engineering arena are also covered.

This course is the first in a two-course sequence that introduces in technical detail the system and "systems of systems" that constitute naval vessels, sensors, and weapons. The structure and content of this course will be most familiar to engineering and other technical majors but approachable to liberal arts majors with the NROTC-required calculus and physics background. This course is typically taught by your unit's nuclear power officer (NPO). Tests in this course will include solving engineering equations and problems encountered by young naval officers.

Naval Ship Systems II (Weapons). This course outlines the theory and employment of weapons systems. Students explore the processes of detection, evaluation, threat analysis, weapon selection, delivery, guidance, and explosives. Fire-control systems and major weapons types are discussed, in terms of their capabilities and limitations. The physical aspects of radar and underwater sound are described. The concept of "command, control, communications, computers, and intelligence" is explored as a framework for weapons system integration, as are the tactical and strategic significance of "command and control warfare" and "information warfare." Supplementing these topics are case studies involving the moral and ethical responsibilities of leaders in the employment of weapons.

The second of two naval ship systems courses, this course focuses on the fighting components of naval vessels more than on their engineering support aspects. Tests in this course will be similar to those in the engineering course and will assess midshipmen's understanding of the basics of how weapon and sensor systems on the Navy's warships work.

Naval Operations and Seamanship. This course is a continued study of relative motion, formation tactics, and ship employment. It includes introductions to naval operations and operations analysis, ship behavior and characteristics in maneuvering, the practice of shiphandling, afloat communications, naval command and control, naval warfare areas, and joint warfare (i.e., services working together). Again, there are case studies on relevant moral, ethical, and leadership issues.

This course is typically taught to fall-semester senior midshipmen, building upon their summer cruise experiences and formally instructing them in watchstanding, naval operations to be expected on deployment, and naval operations. This course will take advantage of wargaming techniques and any ship-simulator resources available to the unit, stressing both practical seamanship skills and basic "operational-level" thinking.

Leadership and Ethics. This course completes the final preparations of soon-to-be ensigns and second lieutenants for service in the Navy and Marine Corps. The course integrates an intellectual exploration of Western moral traditions and ethical philosophies with such topics as military leadership, core values, professional ethics, the Uniform Code of Military Justice, Navy Regulations, the roles of enlisted members, junior and senior officers, command relationships, and the conduct of warfare. The course aims to combine a foundation of moral traditions with actual current and historical events in the Navy and USMC, to prepare midshipmen for the roles and responsibilities of leadership in the naval service of the twenty-first century.

Above all else, the military services require officers whose character and integrity can serve as the foundation of effective operations in peace and war. This course is similar to Leadership and Management but distinct in its focus on the underlying philosophy of leadership and morality. It will employ extensive reading, case-study analysis, seminar discussion, and public speaking. Many midshipmen find this course the most satisfying in the NROTC program: it affords them extensive time with the most senior naval officer in the unit, and it serves as a purposeful pause, a step back from the "nuts-and-bolts" subjects of other naval science courses.

Naval Science Laboratory. In addition to the naval science courses listed above, each NROTC unit will schedule a weekly two-hour Naval Science Laboratory course for the entire midshipmen battalion. The Naval Science Laboratory is a flexible opportunity for the PNS to direct such professional development training as close-order drill, personnel uniform inspections, and GMT. Guest speakers often attend laboratory sessions to brief the battalion on their areas of expertise. Senior officers from the Navy's unrestricted line communities visit periodically to discuss the advantages and experiences of a career in their community. All midshipmen attend the weekly Naval Science Laboratory throughout their time in the NROTC program. This course's two-hour meeting can make scheduling a challenge. If you have conflicting course obligations, your class advisor will work with you on an individual solution.

MARINE-OPTION NAVAL SCIENCE COURSES

Marine-Option midshipmen complete a distinct naval science curriculum. Total naval science course requirements are reduced from eight to six. All NROTC midshipmen, regardless of option, take Introduction to Naval Science, Leadership and Management, and Leadership and Ethics. Marine-Option midshipmen are not obliged to take Naval Engineering, Naval Weapon Systems, Navigation, or Seamanship and Operations, although if their degree plans allow and they are interested, they may choose to take them as electives. Marine-Option naval science courses are taught by the NROTC unit's Marine Officer Instructor. The MOI may be assisted as necessary by other staff members, particularly in areas directly relatable to Navy roles, such as amphibious shipping and naval surface fire support. There are two naval science courses specifically for Marine-Option midshipmen.

Evolution of Warfare. In this course, students trace the development of warfare to the present day. It is designed to uncover the causes of continuity and change in the means and methods of warfare. It addresses the influence of political, economic, and societal factors on the conduct of war, paying considerable attention to the role of technological innovation in changing the battlefield. Students will explore the contributions of preeminent military theorists and battlefield commanders to our modern understanding of the art and science of war.

Fundamentals of Maneuver Warfare. In this course, students study broad aspects of warfare and their interactions with the "doctrine" of "maneuver warfare"—that is, the Marine Corps' officially adopted and formally elaborated approach to combat. It focuses on the USMC as the premier maneuver-warfare institution. In part through case studies, it addresses historical influences on current tactical, operational, and strategic aspects of maneuver warfare. It focuses on the evolution of the Marine Corps as a maneuver-warfare organization, with particular attention to its present-day structure and capabilities as a forward-deployed, rapid-deployment force, as well as to the development of "expeditionary-" and maneuver-warfare concepts. Enrollment preference is given to NROTC students.

Physical Fitness Requirements

Physically, the military profession is inherently arduous. To succeed in battle requires the fitness, strength, and toughness to take a hit and continue fighting. To ensure that its members have those qualities, the Navy and Marine Corps mandate regular physical fitness assessments. Once again, do not forget that your scholarship cannot be activated until you prove that you can meet either the Navy or Marine Corps physical requirements during New Student Indoctrination. Throughout your time in the NROTC program as you prepare to become a naval officer, you must maintain physical readiness. Each semester you will run both an "inventory" physical readiness assessment to help gauge your status, as well as an official physical readiness assessment each semester that will serve as a measure of your current condition. Service requirements differ so we will treat first the Navy and then the Marine Corps.

NAVY PHYSICAL FITNESS ASSESSMENT

The Navy Physical Fitness Assessment (PFA) is the Navy's means of testing the physical readiness of its members. The PFA is composed of a Body Composition

Assessment (BCA) and Physical Readiness Test (PRT). Midshipmen must meet the standards of both.

The BCA measures a member's height and weight and compares them to the standards. Exceeding the allowable weight for a given height will require an assessment of "body composition," to ensure that the body fat percentage is within standards. Appendix V lists height/weight tables and measurement standards for body composition.

NAVY PFA EVENTS

Body composition within Navy standards
Max curl-ups in 2 minutes
Max push-ups in 2 minutes
1.5-mile run

The PRT consists of timed push-ups, curl-ups, and a 1.5-mile run. Repetitions are counted and scored relative to the standards, based on gender and age. As we've discussed, success on the PRT is largely a function of consistent, safe, and challenging physical training, along with proper nutrition and rest habits. It is important to note that meeting PRT standards does *not* mean a midshipman doesn't have to meet BCA standards also. Extraordinary circumstances, such as a varsity football lineman unable to meet BCA standards but otherwise in excellent shape, are handled on a case-by-case basis.

The Navy grading scale is broken into distinct tiers that correlate to certain levels of performance. NROTC midshipmen must complete all events of the PFA with at least a "Good Low" score. For example, the minimum number of satisfactory push-ups for a nineteen-year-old male NROTC midshipmen is fifty-one; the maximum score is ninety-two. Failing any event of the PFA results in the failure of the entire test—you cannot compensate for a failing run time by maximizing your score on both push-ups and curl-ups.

Although Navy-Option midshipmen are required to be within standards throughout their time in the NROTC program, failure on a single PFA will not necessarily end their prospects for commissioning—*except in their senior year.* Midshipmen will be ineligible for commissioning without a successful PFA that year.

MARINE-OPTION PHYSICAL FITNESS PROGRAM
Marine-Option midshipmen are held to the standards of the Marine Physical Fitness Program. Marine-Option midshipmen must complete, within standards, the Marine Physical Fitness Test (PFT), the Combat Fitness Test (CFT), and the Body Composition Program (BCP). The PFT is a three-event test comprising pull-ups, crunches, and a three-mile timed run. The CFT, a more functional test of your

MARINE PHYSICAL FITNESS PROGRAM

USMC Physical Fitness Test (PFT)
Maximum pull-ups
Maximum abdominal crunches in 2 minutes
3-mile run

Marine Combat Fitness Test (CFT)
800-meter sprint
Ammunition can overhead lift
Mini–obstacle course (low crawl, agility drills,
dummy grenade throw, buddy drag and carry)

physical capabilities, is also made up of three events. The first, "movement to contact," is an eight-hundred-meter sprint. Second, the "ammunition lift," is a timed test of overhead presses of a thirty-pound ammunition can. The final event is a mini–obstacle course that includes a low crawl, agility drills, a simulated grenade throw, and "buddy drag and carry." The BCP measures height and weight and, if weight exceeds allowable limits, body-fat percentage is determined. Outstanding performers on the PFT/CFT are exempt from body fat percentage requirements but must still be measured and their results recorded.

Purdue University NROTC midshipmen participate in an endurance race on The Ohio State University campus. *U.S. Navy photo by Eva Pahl*

Standards are especially rigorous for Marine-Option midshipmen preparing for Officer Candidate School (OCS). We have included Marine standards in the chart and in appendix V for various ages of NROTC midshipmen. The minimum passing score for both the PFT and CFT is 235 out of 300. In a midshipman's first year in the NROTC program, a 200 PFT is acceptable for the Marine Option, but 235 prevails after that. However, in order to increase their probability of success at OCS, midshipmen are trained to score above 265. As on the Navy PFA, failure on any one event in a test means a complete test failure. As you would expect, poor physical performance will ruin your prospects of success as a Marine-Option midshipman.

For most young people, meeting the physical standards of the NROTC program requires nothing more than full participation in the unit's physical readiness events, which will almost certainly be held more than once per week. For midshipmen who are struggling, units run Fitness Enhancement Programs (FEPs), additional (mandatory) training sessions, to help bring them up to standards. In NROTC, physical fitness is as important as academic excellence—failing your PFA will lose you your scholarship about as quickly as will failing your classes.

Command and Leadership Training

The final component of NROTC requirements is the set of military and professional exercises and events broadly classified as "Command and Leadership Training." Being effective and successful as an officer requires such practical leadership skills as prioritization, problem solving, delegation, public speaking, decision making, and risk assessment and mitigation. To exercise and develop these skills, all midshipmen are afforded such opportunities as these:

- Close-order drill team
- Competitive military/physical fitness exercises
- Battalion management and administration
- Planning and coordination of major battalion functions
- Intramural and athletic competitions.

These activities provide invaluable opportunities for personal growth and leadership development in NROTC. They are typically organized on a volunteer basis and constitute subsets of the overall battalion. They are great ways to

University of Missouri NROTC drill platoon performs close-order drill.
U.S. Navy photo by Eva Pahl

meet and develop relationships with midshipmen with similar passions for drill, physical fitness, or athletics. Relatively junior midshipmen are often appointed as team or assistant team leaders, positions of leadership that might not otherwise be available to them. Specific opportunities available differ from school to school, but each NROTC unit offers ways to get involved with teams designed to help increase your military and professional expertise.

Extracurriculars and NROTC

Before concluding the chapter, we would like to discuss briefly what effect NROTC program requirements may have on other extracurricular activities within your institution. A prime advantage, of course, of the NROTC program as compared to other commissioning programs is that it offers a largely "normal" college experience while providing a full-tuition scholarship. For many students, the college experience is enriched by participating in varsity athletics, intramural sports, Greek organizations, student clubs, professional societies, academic clubs, volunteer service, and so on. NROTC leaders are fully aware and appreciate the value

"NROTC regularly challenges me both physically and mentally, but it is most valuable when it challenges my leadership skills, allowing me an environment where I can freely make mistakes and learn from them. I believe my confidence and skill as a leader and manager have all benefited, and I am very grateful for that."

—MIDSHIPMAN 3RD CLASS ALEXANDER, University of Minnesota NROTC

"One of the best parts about going to a civilian institution and belonging to an NROTC unit is the ability to experience the best of both worlds—the camaraderie of the unit plus the variety and freedom of the normal college experience. I thoroughly enjoyed my NROTC experience; some of my best friends to this day were part of that tight-knit group. However, what I liked even more about college was the opportunity to branch out, try new things, and pursue other interest areas outside of the military. On top of playing several different intramural sports, I participated in a lot of groups dedicated to improving the student experience, and was elected to several positions to represent my class, dormitory, and ultimately becoming the Student Body President. The opportunities that went along with these responsibilities were easily the most impactful and memorable during my days at Notre Dame— and they definitely didn't hurt on internship, job, and graduate school applications, either."

—COMMANDER MURPHY

of these activities in developing outstanding naval officers. To make this clear, up front: if your activity has value in your personal and professional development, your NROTC unit staff will work with you.

Take as an example varsity athletics. Participation in collegiate varsity athletics is, in and of itself, an incredible opportunity for personal growth, physical fitness, and leadership development. It's a "huge deal," requiring an extraordinary amount of your time, but rest assured that being a varsity athlete, even at the Division I level, is perfectly compatible with participation in the NROTC program. However, the unique stressors and time commitments levied on varsity athletes may require action on your part to ensure you meet commissioning requirements. In all cases, keep your class advisor informed as to your team's practice routine, workouts, meetings, and game schedule. The PNS would have to excuse you formally from routine NROTC events, such as battalion physical training exercises, that conflict with your team's scheduled workouts. Update your class advisor as your team commitments change, so additional adjustments can be made.

Similar communication should be going on with your coaching staff, so that they understand and are on board. The only hard-and-fast requirements to receive your commission are satisfactorily completing the academic program, meeting physical and medical standards, completing New Student

Indoctrination, Sea Trials (for Navy Option) or Officer Candidate School (Marine Option), and a first-class midshipmen cruise.

Conflicts between desired extracurriculars and mandatory NROTC events will be handled on a case-by-case basis between you, battalion leadership, and the unit staff. As a rule, since either NROTC is paying you a scholarship or you are seeking to earn one, mandatory NROTC events (naval science courses, Naval Science Laboratory, physical training exercises, etc.) will have priority over optional extracurriculars. With that being said, do communicate with your chain of command your desire to attend a scheduled extracurricular well in advance if it would mean permission to miss an NROTC event. Be prepared to "make up" any lost training at a later date to ensure you do not fall behind your peers. While this policy may seem harsh, you will likely find your unit staff helpful and accommodating; they understand that developing your personal interests is a vital aspect of the college experience. If you are proactive in notifying your chain of command and creative in proposing a responsible work-around, your unit staff will probably accommodate you.

In fact, it is a common occurrence for midshipmen to request to miss mandatory events. There will be some formal administrative process in place. Abide by its steps and follow up with your leadership to ensure that your request is acted upon in a reasonable time.

As an example of the proper way to go about seeking permission to miss a mandatory event, consider "Midshipman Squared Away," a member of the university chess team, who is hoping to attend an intramural chess meet against a cross-town school. The chess match is scheduled at the same day and time that Midshipman Away normally participates in his platoon's physical training session. Knowing that his battalion runs platoon-level physical training sessions throughout the week, Midshipman Away looks at the schedule and discovers he can attend a different platoon's session the following day. Midshipman Away submits his request in writing a few weeks before the match and outlines his intention to make up the missed physical training session. His chain of command accepts his plan and approves his request.

Contrast Midshipman Away's proactive and responsible actions with what Midshipman Johnny Late does. Midshipman Late, a member of the school's club debate team, would like to miss Naval Science Laboratory in order to attend a club-sponsored VIP guest speaker event on a Wednesday. The club scheduled the lecture months ahead of time and plastered flyers throughout the campus to generate awareness. Midshipman Late waits until the week of the event to request permission to miss Naval Science Lab (also held on Wednesday) and develops no plan to make up the training. Midshipman Late submits a hastily written request to his leadership immediately after battalion physical training on Monday morning, despite the requirement of the unit's request procedures for, special circumstances aside, two weeks' advance notice. Midshipman Late's chain of command recommends disapproval; the PNS agrees and denies the request. Midshipman Late is discontented, both at himself for procrastinating and at the chain of command for denying his request. What would otherwise have been a "no-brainer" is now an unpleasant experience and missed rare opportunity to hear a distinguished speaker in person.

Again, however, your obligations to the NROTC program are, ultimately, just that, obligations, and you will have to subordinate extracurriculars and in cases of conflict set them aside, unless you have explicit permission from your leadership.

Conclusion

We have discussed in detail the various academic, physical fitness, and professional requirements for midshipmen within the NROTC program. It is your responsibility as a young professional to understand fully your obligations to complete both your degree and professional requirements successfully and on time in order to be commissioned in your projected year. Your class advisor and other unit staff will work with you as a team to help steer you toward success and your commission. If at any time you do not completely understand the requirements and your path to graduation and a commission, you should schedule an appointment with your class advisor. As the baseball great Yogi Berra quipped, "If you don't know where you're going, you'll end up someplace else." Make sure you know where you're going!

9 The College Program

WE HAVE MENTIONED the College Program previously in this book but feel that the subject deserves a chapter dedicated to it. The College Program is a "walk-on" method designed to encourage and allow motivated, capable college students to enter the NROTC program in order to earn commissions in the unrestricted line of the Navy or Marine Corps or the Navy Nurse Corps. For many reasons, college students may have not been aware of the NROTC program in high school or been motivated to enter directly out of high school. Some high school counselors are unaware of this option. Some students as well, lacking the benefit of a friend or relative in the military, may have been unaware that programs like NROTC even exist. For these students, sitting in their freshman classes with peers dressed in uniform, seeing midshipmen around campus, or having NROTC midshipmen assigned as roommates may have been their first glimpse of the possibility of a career as an officer in the naval services. Others did know about it and made the attempt but weren't competitive for the National Scholarship because of academic struggles or marginal performance on standardized tests during their high school careers; now they're excelling at the undergraduate level and remain interested in earning scholarships.

For these students, once they have more than thirty credit hours on their transcripts, the NROTC College Program can be an outstanding opportunity to earn first a full-tuition scholarship and then a commission as a Navy or Marine Corps officer. In this chapter, we will cover in detail the NROTC College Program, including requirements for applicants, applications procedures, scholarship award timelines, and service obligations.

Why did you join the College Program?

I joined the College Program during the summer before my freshman year of college. While I did not apply for the scholarship while in high school, I knew I wanted to pursue a career serving my country. By joining the College Program, I was able to put myself on the path to join the Navy.

What was the application process like for the College Program?

The application process for the College Program was simple and straightforward. Once you make contact with your respective NROTC unit, they will send you a packet of documents to fill out. These are self-explanatory and simple forms—if you complete these forms in a timely manner, you will start NROTC on the exact same footing as scholarship MIDNs. If you are applying for the scholarship as a College Program MIDN, you have significant advantages that you should use in order to secure a scholarship. Seek guidance from MIDNs and officers at your unit before applying. Ask your NROTC unit for a letter of recommendation for the scholarship. The specific application process is not difficult, but you need to make sure you put your best foot forward. Spend time editing and reviewing your essays, have a friend review your application, and make sure you are in contact with your NROTC advisor when preparing the application.

Were you treated differently as a College Program MIDN vs. scholarship MIDN? If so, how?

I was *never* treated in a derogatory fashion because of my status as a College Program MIDN. I had several influential mentors (both midshipmen and officers) who, once informed of my College Program status, pushed me to excel academically and in ROTC in order to assist my chances of receiving a scholarship. I credit their guidance and a letter of recommendation from my NROTC unit for my earning a scholarship in the spring of my freshman year. College Program MIDNs are often held to a higher standard in order to assist them in earning a scholarship. While this may put extra burdens on a College Program MIDN, it will greatly help in the application process for a scholarship.

Any recommendations for students interested in NROTC but who didn't pick up a scholarship in high school? What do you wish you had done differently?

If you are still interested in the scholarship, join the College Program and do your absolute best your first semester of college. Work hard to get stellar grades, develop a good PT plan, and dedicate yourself to being the best MIDN possible. Your command will recognize your dedication and will assist you in earning the scholarship.

—ENS J. Olsen, USN, The George Washington University NROTC Class of 2019

Overview

In simplest terms, the College Program is a way for students already in college to earn a commission through the NROTC program. As mentioned in chapter 3, the number of National Scholarships awarded each year is determined by the expected "officer accession demand"—that is, estimates by "warfighting community" (air, surface, submarines, etc.) managers who regularly estimate the number of new, "entry-level" officers required. From these estimates are derived the aggregate number of scholarships awarded—the need for one thousand ensigns four years from now means that a thousand scholarships will be awarded to high school seniors this year. However, due to natural "attrition"—incompatibility with naval service, medical disenrollments, and myriad other factors—some fraction of students initially awarded scholarships will not complete the NROTC program and so will not be among those thousand officer "accessions" required. For that reason, motivated and high-performing students are awarded College Program scholarships each semester.

To be clear, to be in the College Program is not to be seen as a "second-best" midshipman. To outside observers, it is impossible to distinguish a College Program NROTC midshipman from one with a National Scholarship. All midshipmen perform the same professional training, are held to the same academic and physical standards, and wear the same uniform. A vibrant College Program makes for healthy NROTC units and furthers the best interests of the naval service. Just as motivated, competitive walk-on players on an athletic team improve its overall performance by replacing substandard scholarship players, a strong College Program ensures that the Navy commissions the best possible class of midshipmen each year by filling the gaps left by dropped scholarship students.

COLLEGE PROGRAM ELIGIBILITY REQUIREMENTS

In order to apply to be an NROTC midshipman you must first meet the following basic requirements (essentially the same as for the National Scholarship listed in chapter 3):

1. Be an American citizen, naturalized citizen, or have submitted naturalization papers.
   a. Scholarship selectees must be American citizens in order to activate the scholarship.

b. Scholarship selectees must obtain their citizenships and activate their scholarships within the first academic year after the stated scholarship offer "begin" date listed in their scholarship notification letter or their scholarship offers will be rescinded.

c. Retroactive benefits will not be approved for selectees who delayed activating their scholarship due to not obtaining their U.S. citizenship.

d. Applicants with dual citizenship may apply and, if selected, activate their scholarships but must renounce their citizenship to the other countries and surrender their passports for them in order to continue in the NROTC program.

2. Have no moral obligations or personal convictions that will prevent bearing of arms and supporting and defending the Constitution of the United States against all enemies, foreign and domestic, or to taking an oath to perform such acts.

3. Be at least seventeen years of age on or before 1 September of the year of enrollment and less than twenty-seven years of age on 31 December of the year an applicant expects to graduate, complete all NROTC training requirements, and be commissioned. Those with prior or current active duty in the armed forces may be granted age waivers equal to the number of months served. Those granted the maximum age waiver must not have reached their thirtieth birthday by 31 December of the year in which graduation and commissioning are anticipated.

4. Meet physical requirements for the NROTC program.

5. Possess a high school diploma or equivalent certificate.

6. Be accepted for admission as a full-time student at a participating NROTC college or university.

THE COLLEGE PROGRAM BASIC COURSE

The College Program Basic Course is offered to college students who have not been awarded any form of NROTC scholarship but are interested in service as commissioned officers in the Navy or Marine Corps. To be considered a College Program midshipman, you must have applied for enrollment at a school with an NROTC unit and have signed a contract agreeing to complete designated naval science courses and to complete a summer training period if selected for Advanced Standing. College Program Basic Course students must have at least two years of

University of Wisconsin, Madison NROTC midshipmen perform buddy carries running down Bascom Hill on campus. *U.S. Navy photo by Scott A. Thornbloom*

undergraduate coursework remaining. Basic Course midshipmen are civilians but must meet the same academic and physical requirements as scholarship midshipmen.

The first step in the process of application to the Basic Course is to contact the recruitment officer on the local NROTC unit staff. If your academic institution is a cross-town affiliate of a host NROTC unit, staff members will very likely be physically located on the host school's campus. For example, prospective College Program students at Drexel University would need to contact the NROTC staff residing at its host unit, the unit at the University of Pennsylvania. Check your institution's or NROTC's website for information for cross-town affiliates.

The recruitment officer, one of the NROTC unit active-duty staff members, will explain the application process and detail the forms to be completed. The NROTC College Program Application (NSTC Form 1533/133) requires basic background and educational information: extracurricular activities, athletic activities, employment, academic performance, drug use, and whether or not you would have any reservations about bearing arms in support of your nation. The Professor of Naval Science may also mandate that you complete a physical fitness assessment or test to ensure you are likely to meet physical qualification standards before accepting you as a member of the Basic Course.

Overall, earning acceptance into the Basic Course is not difficult; if you meet the basic requirements and are motivated to serve, you should have no trouble joining the NROTC program. Throughout your application process, stay engaged with the staff and responsive to it should any issues arise. By the start of their junior academic year, NROTC midshipmen in the Basic Course will have been either offered a scholarship or Advanced Standing or disenrolled.

ADVANCED COURSE

The Advanced Course, also known as Advanced Standing, is a pathway to a commission in the Navy or Marine Corps offered in lieu of a two-year scholarship to qualified midshipmen. We discussed these scholarships in chapter 3. All students with only two years remaining until graduation who are not offered a sideload scholarship (chapter 3) are automatically considered for the Advanced Course. Selection boards for the Advanced Course convene at NSTC and Marine Corps Recruiting Command (MCRC) during the summer and consider students between their sophomore and junior academic years. The applicants selected will be notified via their NROTC units. At that point they must be accepted into the Advanced Course by their NROTC unit's commanding officer and pass a Department of Defense Medical Review Board physical examination in order to be eligible to enlist, as required, in the Navy Reserve or Marine Corps Reserve. Finally, a new Advanced Standing midshipman also must agree to complete Sea Trials and a first-class cruise (see chapters 13 and 14), as required to satisfy statutory requirements for commissioning.

In return for enlistment, the Advanced Standing midshipmen will receive necessary uniforms, naval science textbooks, and a small monthly subsistence allowance (for a period of no more than twenty months prior to commissioning). You need not have participated in the NROTC unit with the College Program Basic Course to be eligible for the Advanced Course. However, it may be to your benefit to join it as soon as you are able. Because students with less than two years remaining to graduate are ineligible for the Advanced Course, if you do not join the Basic Course you will effectively only have one opportunity to select for a sideload scholarship or secure Advanced Standing.

Advanced Standing may seem like a "raw deal" as compared to securing a scholarship, but successful completion of the NROTC College Program Advanced Course guarantees you the same commission in the U.S. Navy or Marine Corps that scholarship midshipmen will receive. The monthly subsistence payment is equal to that of second- and first-class scholarship midshipmen, as are the opportunities for your first-class summer cruise. Advanced Standing midshipmen are eligible for all service-assignment designators and wear exactly the same uniform and insignia as other midshipmen within the unit.

Some students offered Advanced Standing consider disenrolling from the NROTC program and seeking a commission directly through Officer Candidate School after graduation. After all, if you know you are never going to be on scholarship, why continue to wake up early, attend the additional naval science courses, and deal with the other NROTC commitments? Why not just enjoy the rest of your college years as a "normal" student and simply apply to OCS afterward? While this may be a natural response to the disappointment of not being offered Advanced Standing, remember that scholarship availability is limited and the competition is very strong: Many outstanding applicants each year are offered neither a scholarship nor Advanced Standing. Before making a hasty decision, we recommend you consider the potential advantages and disadvantages.

First, there is no guarantee that two years from now your application to OCS would be accepted. The Navy and Marine Corps accession needs change without advance notice based on world events, political elections, and various other factors that affect fleet manning forecasting models. You should weigh carefully the value of the professional development and training available through continued involvement with the NROTC program as against the relatively minor time commitment required. Again, once accepted into the Advanced Course you have only to complete the requirements to be guaranteed a commission and, potentially, a rewarding career.

Second, Officer Candidate School itself is demanding and stressful. OCS is designed to transform civilians rapidly into officers; it is much more akin to a traditional "boot camp" military indoctrination environment than you are likely to encounter at an NROTC unit. There is certainly value to this type of training—OCS has a long history and tradition of successfully morphing civilians into members of the finest military in the world—but the reality is that not everyone completes OCS. That is, even if you are accepted as an Officer Candidate, you may not complete the course. Accepting Advanced Standing requires only that you continue to excel within the NROTC environment with which you are already familiar.

Last, deeply consider your motivations for service. Officers in the U.S. Navy and Marine Corps are entrusted with leading young men and women who volunteer to defend our country, potentially at the sacrifice of their lives. Any offer of a guaranteed commission in the naval services is a profound statement of belief in your potential to grow into such a trust. If you feel "rejected" in not having been offered a scholarship, we recommend that you take some time to count your blessings and remember that you are being offered an opportunity to perform both an invaluable service to your country and to help lead some of our country's finest sons and daughters.

Practical Advice for College Programmers

For students who are in the running for a scholarship, the process can be physically and emotionally draining. While to all appearances you are exactly the same as scholarship midshipmen, until you are offered a scholarship or an appointment to Advanced Standing you will not have the security of knowing that an honorable and worthwhile career awaits you upon graduation. Competition is fierce, and only a small percentage of College Program students will be offered scholarships. Further, the criteria the scholarship board applies can seem opaque. However, successful applicants tend to have certain characteristics.

First, they have the strong endorsement of their class advisor and PNS. All the applications the selection board will be sifting through are highly qualified, and most of the competitive packages have similar GPAs and physical fitness scores. The deciding factor can easily be the strength of the endorsement from the NROTC unit commanding officer. The commanding officer is a seasoned naval officer who is keenly interested in developing the highest-quality young men and women into naval officers. Your direct interaction with the commanding officer may be limited, but he or she will take seriously the reports and counsel of your class advisor and the executive officer. In addition to performing at a high level on your academics and physical fitness requirements, displaying a cheerful, professional demeanor can go a long way. Consistently do the little things right—show up on time, be in a smart, properly fitting uniform, always try your best, help your struggling shipmates, respond to e-mails and "taskers" promptly, and actively participate in your naval science classes. Even if your GPA and PRT scores are very good, if you are not perceived as fully engaged, that is what the unit's commanding officer will hear, and the highest endorsement may go to a slightly lower-scoring midshipman who is obviously hungry for a commission. Don't handicap your own chances at a scholarship.

Second, recall that although no directive may explicitly say so, students performing well in Tier 1 or Tier 2 majors will be advantaged over similarly performing students in Tier 3 majors. The Navy seeks to commission some 85 percent of each NROTC class with degrees in engineering or the hard sciences, so the sideload and Advanced Standing boards will take your expected degree into account. If you are truly committed to earning a scholarship or commission through the NROTC program, it may be to your benefit to pursue a Tier 1 or Tier 2 major. But as discussed earlier, switching majors to a difficult engineering program for which you are ill suited will not get you anywhere. It may be prudent to have a frank conversation with your institution's academic advisor about your ability to excel in a different degree program in hopes of enhancing your record in the Navy's eyes. You must also keep in mind that you need to be able to complete your degree within four years, the four years starting when you began college, not when you joined the NROTC program.

Next, you obviously need to excel in your academics and on the PRT course. Understanding that the competition for limited nationwide scholarship spots is severe, you can see that you will have very little likelihood of securing a scholarship award if your grades are only just above NROTC standards.

Also, you need to stay out of trouble, particularly concerning violations of character such as lying, cheating, or stealing. Fair or not, whereas scholarship students involved in aptitude violations may be placed on probation but not lose their scholarships, a College Programmer trying to break away from the pack and earn a sideload scholarship may be marked as a troublemaker. A stronger endorsement is likely to go to another who has stayed out of trouble. Keep your nose clean.

Also, it is critical that you be honest with yourself in assessing your performance and your prospects of earning a scholarship or being offered Advanced Standing. If you are struggling to balance academic, physical, and NROTC obligations well enough to make yourself competitive, you may be better advised to focus solely on your academics and apply for a commission through the Navy's or Marine Corps' Officer Candidate School after graduation. An OCS application with a higher GPA will be likely be viewed more favorably than one with a lower

GPA. Once you arrive in the fleet, no one will care whether you earned your commission through NROTC, USNA, or OCS—or what your GPA or major was, for that matter. Your primary goal, if this is your situation, should be the commission and the opportunity to lead Sailors or Marines, not a scholarship.

Finally, it is important to not concern yourself with your performance relative to your peers. The scholarship and Advanced Standing boards will review your package on its own merits. Doing well within the NROTC program is in many ways similar to golf—you ought to play the course, not the other golfers. Successful golfers focus on what they can influence, on how good a shot they can make on each stroke. Where competing golfers' balls land has nothing to do with the quality of their next shots. It can be easy to be disheartened, particularly when you see students awarded National Scholarships out of high school just skating by with performances just above the minimums. You will not enhance your own performance, though, and you may degrade it, by judging others or bemoaning the seeming inequity. Keep your head up and your attitude positive, and you will give yourself the best chance of succeeding in the College Program to secure either a sideload scholarship or Advanced Standing.

Conclusion

The College Program is in many ways the secret weapon of the NROTC program. Each year, outstanding college students earn full-tuition scholarships and benefit themselves, their commissioning classes, and the future naval officers corps. Are you still on the fence as to whether or not to give the Basic Course a try? We strongly encourage you to give it a go. As a Basic Course College Programmer, you are under absolutely no obligation to the U.S. government. While you will be expected to perform up to standards as long as you participate in the NROTC program, it is completely up to you how long you do so. You may find yourself enjoying the challenge of the physical training, the warmth of the camaraderie, and the intellectual rigor of naval science courses. If nothing else, it may offer a brief glimpse into the training, commitment, and enthusiasm of your fellow citizens of the United States who will one day serve in uniform. We wish you the best of luck!

10 Life as an NROTC Midshipman

WITH A BETTER UNDERSTANDING of the NROTC program, how to apply for a scholarship, and the academic and physical requirements, you may be asking yourself, "So what does an average day for an NROTC midshipman actually look like?" Young people look forward to their college years as some of the best of their lives—will you still be able to have a good time as a midshipman?

In this chapter, we will discuss what would be considered the "normal" day in the life of a midshipman. Variety is the spice of life within the NROTC program, so keep in mind that the individual NROTC unit and institutional cultures will play a big part in your day-to-day experience. Studying at a cross-town affiliate will have an effect, as will studying at a military institution, such as the Virginia Military Institute or The Citadel. Studying at an idyllic land-grant college like the University of Idaho will be different from studying at an urban institution fully integrated into its city, such as Boston University. For the purposes of this chapter, we assume a student studying at a civilian college or university that is a host institution and whose setting is in neither of those extremes. When considering potential schools to attend and at which to join NROTC, we strongly encourage you to schedule a visit with the local NROTC unit to see in person and to get a taste of what a day in the life of a midshipman is like.

Uniform Wear and Haircuts

The most conspicuous aspect of being an NROTC midshipman is that you will be required to wear your uniform at least once a week while on campus. Male midshipmen will be obliged to cut their hair to naval standards. Female midshipmen must also, but naval standards generally require only putting up longer hair in a bun; it can be down again when out of uniform. The NROTC unit commanding officer will promulgate local policy, but "uniform day" typically coincides with one of the days of your naval science class and the weekly Leadership Lab. On those days, uniforms are to be worn while attending your university classes and transiting about campus. Exercise or extracurricular activity that requires different outfits are usually allowable exceptions. Be sure to ask your class advisor for details if you have any questions.

The standard NROTC uniform is Service Khaki. Service Khaki is a standard U.S. Navy uniform consisting of a khaki buttoned, collared shirt and creased khaki trousers. Standard-issue name tags and midshipman insignia are also worn. The appropriate cover (in the service, the hat on your head is a "cover") associated with each type of uniform, with its appropriate insignia, is worn when out of doors. Black leather shoes with black socks are the standard footwear. Marine-Option midshipmen wear the same uniforms as Navy-Options but are distinguished by special collar devices and name tags. For female midshipmen, pumps and khaki skirts are optional.

At some NROTC units, midshipmen wear not khakis but camouflage "utility" uniforms, like the working uniform worn in the fleet. You may be familiar with such uniforms from movies or television: a "blouse" (as certain shirts or jackets are

NROTC midshipmen candidates participate in a uniform inspection at Recruit Training Command (RTC). *U.S. Navy photo by Amanda S. Kitchner*

known even for males, though these are "unisex"), pants, high lace-up boots, and cover. Again, midshipmen will wear appropriate NROTC rank insignia. In these uniforms, identification name tapes are sewn directly into the blouse and pants, along with service, either U.S. Navy or Marine Corps. Camouflage uniforms are usually worn to engage in "dirty" work, such as off-campus field exercises or for certain Marine Corps–style obstacle course or physical training exercises.

For special events, you will also be issued "dress" uniforms. Based on your geographic location and season of the year, these are Service Dress Blue (SDB), Summer Whites, or Dress Whites. Service Dress Blues are coat and tie, with insignia sewn into the coat's cuffs; Summer Whites are essentially a white version of Service Khaki worn during warm weather months; and Dress Whites—also called "choker whites"—are the classic naval uniform with the raised collar and shoulder boards. No matter the uniform, you are sure to turn heads about campus.

While your NROTC uniforms may not be as comfortable as the sweatpants, slippers, and tank tops your peers are wearing to class, we are confident that you, as a more professionally minded student, wouldn't be wearing that to class anyway. Well-fitting uniforms are comfortable enough, pleasant in appearance, and give

Northwestern University NROTC midshipmen low crawl through a volleyball court during an endurance race. *U.S. Navy photo by Scott A. Thornbloom*

Chief of Naval Operations ADM John M. Richardson speaks to NROTC midshipmen during a dinner in the Purcell Pavilion Monogram Room on the University of Notre Dame campus. *U.S. Navy photo by Andrew Slattery*

Midshipmen from the Boston Consortium take the oath of office on board USS *Constitution. U.S. Navy photo by Scott A. Thornbloom*

their wearer a sense of confidence and smartness that less professional clothing does not. You will likely find yourself sitting up a little straighter on the days you are wearing your uniform (a practice that should carry over to your nonuniform days, by the way). Besides, on uniform days you won't have to decide what to wear!

Your uniforms should always be clean, ironed, and starched. Your shirt should be tightly tucked in. A standard white tee-shirt (sleeveless, vee neck, or crew neck) is required to be worn beneath for males (optional for females). Shoes should be clean, shined, and free of scuff marks. Your "gig line," an imaginary line drawn from your shirt's overlapping sides near the buttons down to your belt buckle should be straight. Any and all ribbons or other devices you are authorized to wear should be clean, shiny, and appropriately placed above front pockets or on collar tabs (and on the correct side!).

NROTC midshipman follow the standard U.S. Navy uniform regulations, which you can explore online at http://www.public.navy.mil/bupers-npc/support /uniforms/uniformregulations/Pages/default.aspx. The website may seem intimidating, but it is the sole authoritative source for proper uniform wear. Do yourself a favor and look up the standard in the regulations instead of wearing your uniform the way your buddy told you. Marine-Option midshipmen who wear Marine uniforms can find the equivalent online at the Marine Corps Public Electronic Library website, searching for "Uniform Regulations" at https://www.marines.mil/News /Publications/MCPEL/. In either case, rest assured that your New Student Indoctrination will cover uniform wear extensively and answer many of your questions. If you are ever in doubt, be sure to consult the regulations and confirm your interpretation with a senior midshipman—who will be impressed by your foresight and professionalism.

Much of the anxiety surrounding uniform wear on campus comes from apprehension over peer perception. It is common to not want to "stick out" and seem different from other, "normal" college students. But consider: as a naval officer, one of your primary duties as a leader will be to demonstrate moral and physical courage. Wearing the conspicuous cloth of the nation may make you uneasy, but it is in itself a trivial act of wearing a certain type of clothing. You may be called on later to dare more than that; for now, you should feel proud and honored to wear your uniform.

Some of your classmates, who have never seen someone in military uniform, may ask why you are wearing the uniform that you are. Proudly and simply respond that you are a member of the school's NROTC unit and explain that you are wearing the uniform of a midshipman, a student training to be an officer in the U.S. Navy or Marine Corps. Many students either have a relative or know of someone who is or has been in the service and can appreciate your willingness to serve. In reality, most NROTC units are on campuses that also host Army and Air Force ROTC units, so cadets and midshipmen in uniform are not uncommon sights. Take pride in your uniform and the service that it represents!

When not required to be in uniform, you are largely free to wear whatever clothing you prefer. Many NROTC units, however, establish basic guidelines for personal clothing, along lines that would be typical for active-duty officers. Discouraged would be provocative clothing, excessively worn and tattered clothing, and clothing bearing offensive statements. On days you attend naval science events out of uniform, you may be required to wear slacks or a skirt along with a smart, tucked-in shirt or blouse.

Customs and Courtesies

Besides uniform wear, the other practical matter to keep in mind when walking about campus is the observance of proper military customs and courtesies with other midshipmen, cadets, commissioned officers, and active-duty personnel. When meeting another member of the uniformed service, tradition and regulations dictate an appropriate greeting and salute by the junior to senior and a proper acknowledgment in return.

As a hierarchical organization, the U.S. military has a rigid structure of subordination, from the lowliest new recruit up to the commander in chief, the president of the United States. How to salute properly will be covered extensively during your New Student Indoctrination, but a brief explanation is called for here as well.

In the naval services, we salute only when in uniform, out of doors, and covered. Juniors, upon noticing that a senior officer is approaching, will raise their right hands smartly with hands stiffly outstretched and point of the middle fingers resting on the tip of the cover. The senior will acknowledge their salute by "returning" it. The junior's salute should be accompanied by the greeting appropriate to the time of day—for example, "Good Morning, Sir/Ma'am." The senior will respond accordingly, then drop his or her salute; the juniors then "cut" their salutes as well, returning their arms smartly to their sides, and carry on. This may happen while walking or standing; in either case, continue about your business unless the senior desires to speak to you. If the senior fails to recognize your salute, do not make a scene but give them the benefit of the doubt—simply hold your salute until they have passed. With practice, this seemingly arcane ritual will become second nature, an opportunity to present yourself with pride and professionalism.

A Normal Day in the Life of an NROTC Midshipman

For most, college represents their first extended period being largely in control of their own time. Your mother will not wake you up in the morning or remind you to do your laundry. You will have to do coursework on time, as you did in high school, but in college how you manage that will be largely your own problem. Social and extracurricular activities in the exciting college environment will compete for your time and attention. On top of it all, as we've noted before, you as an NROTC midshipman will have obligations that most of your classmates do not.

Perhaps the biggest difference in the daily schedules of ROTC (of whatever service) students and the others has to do with the early mornings. As we saw in an earlier chapter, and for better or worse, military organizations tend to schedule events early in the morning. In any case, NROTC units, seeking to schedule battalion-wide events around the schedules of hundreds of midshipmen, frankly find it easiest to hold them before university classes begin.

To give a brief example, consider the following "notional" schedule—what a normal day might look like:

M/W/F (Freshman w/ 18 hours)
 0545: Wake-up alarm
 0630: Battalion physical training exercise at intramural sports fields
 0715: PT ends
 0715–0755: Shower, change, breakfast
 0800: Introduction to Naval Science
 0905: Calculus I
 1010: Freshman class A
 1100–1310: Lunch/break/office hours
 1310: Freshman class B
 1400–1600: Study in library w/ friends
 1600: Workout at student gym
 1700: Dinner in dining hall w/ friends

1730: Naval Science Laboratory (Wednesday)
1800: Calculus tutor session (Monday and Friday)
1900–2100: Homework in library
2230: Return to dorm

T/Th (Freshman w/ 18 hours)
0715: Wake-up alarm
0715–0755: Shower, change, breakfast
0800: Freshman class C
0945: Freshman class D
1100–1300: Lunch/break/office hours
1300: Volunteer at food shelter
1400–1600: Study in library w/ friends
1600: Workout at student gym
1700: Dinner in dining hall w/ friends
1900–2100: Homework in library
2230: Return to form

Saturday (Freshman w/ 18 hours)
1000: Wake up
1030–1130: Brunch w/ friends
1200–1500: Study in library
1700: Tailgating
1900: Kickoff!

Sunday (Freshman w/ 18 hours)
Relaxed day, religious services, study time, *call your family,* etc.

We invited current NROTC midshipmen to share their experience managing their time commitments.

> "Time management is going to be your biggest challenge. Be ready for it instead of being intimidated by it."
>
> —MIDSHIPMAN 4TH CLASS LENNON,
> University of San Diego NROTC

NROTC Extracurricular Opportunities

Participating in the NROTC program affords you opportunities to engage in military- and naval-related events. These will vary from unit to unit, but most will have organized ways to "give back" to the campus and community, perhaps as color guards or various warfare-community clubs. Most units also have competition drill teams and many field physical training teams that compete at the many NROTC meets held across the country.

As mentioned in chapter 8, participation in the full spectrum of extracurriculars available to an undergraduate student is both compatible with demands of NROTC and encouraged of midshipmen. Just be sure to communicate your plans with your battalion and staff leadership to reconcile any conflicts.

> "Managing commitments between varsity athletics, college academics, and NROTC is difficult, but rewarding. I run twice a day due to my cross-country and track commitments, and still make time for PT and NROTC classes and labs. It's much harder to find classes to fit that kind of schedule than just doing one or the other."
>
> —MIDSHIPMAN 4TH CLASS SVENDSEN,
> University of Rochester NROTC

Conclusion

As we hope you can tell, being both a fully engaged undergraduate student and an NROTC midshipman is perfectly feasible. You may have some earlier mornings than your civilian peers, but the discipline you develop to report on time for mandatory events will serve you well both in and out of the military. While much of the midshipman experience is similar from school to school—the notional schedules and experiences shared in this chapter ought to help—the best way to get a sense of the particular circumstances typical of midshipmen at your desired school is to visit in person. We look now in more detail at some of the outstanding NROTC units across the nation.

11 NROTC Unit Highlights

AS A FINAL INTRODUCTION to the Naval Reserve Officers Training Corps, we would like to showcase a few of the remarkable NROTC units around the country. Each and every school affiliated with the NROTC program has a distinct history, culture, and tradition that adds to the experiential, cultural, and academic diversity of the naval officer corps. This diversity in turn strengthens the overall effectiveness of the naval officer corps and helps individuals to complement each other with their differing perspectives and experiences. Compared to the more rigid commissioning path of the U.S. Naval Academy, NROTC offers considerable diversity of experience while still offering excellent professional training and the path to a commission in the U.S. Navy or Marine Corps.

The schools and NROTC units highlighted here were chosen to give a meaningful snapshot of the different types of schools affiliated with the NROTC program. From a large, public, land-grant school to a historically black college to the Ivy League, schools that may be great fits for all different types of students are affiliated with the NROTC program and offer the benefits of a world-class civilian education and the professional training and path to a commission in the naval services.

University of Washington–Seattle, Washington

The University of Washington (UW) is a public research university on campuses in the vibrant Seattle/Tacoma area of Washington State. UW's total student body is approximately 54,000, with approximately 12,000 completing their degrees annually. UW offers over 1,800 undergraduate courses each year and undergraduate degree paths in more than a hundred majors. The University of Washington consistently ranks high in national and international rankings of public universities and maintains a most prestigious alumni group, with Nobel Prize laureates, Pulitzer Prize winners, Fulbright Scholars, Rhodes Scholars, and Marshall Scholars. The University of Washington Huskies are justifiably proud and loyal to their alma mater.

The University of Washington's NROTC unit is one of the six original units established by Congress in 1926 and has built upon this proud legacy by commissioning outstanding junior naval officers into the U.S. Navy and Marine Corps ever since. When asked what makes the University of Washington NROTC so special, a senior Husky midshipman enthusiastically responded as we've recorded (Midshipman 1st Class Warnick).

A premier event each year for the Husky Battalion is "Northwest Navy," an annual competition between the University of Washington, Oregon State University, Washington State University/University of Idaho, and the University of Utah NROTC units in drill, athletics, and academics. Midshipmen from each unit travel to that year's host school to compete against their fellow midshipmen in a series of events for the coveted Northwest Navy Trophy. The event is a terrific opportunity not only to compete but also to meet and bond with midshipmen from different units and soon-to-be peers as junior officers.

Midshipmen have many different reasons for joining the NROTC program and seeking a commission in the U.S. Navy or

"UW is home to one of the original six NROTC units, and during my time as a midshipman I've only heard the best about the people we've put out from the program here. It really seems like the officers that graduate from UW are a cut above. Plus, we're the only commissioning source outside of the Academy that has a sailing program! Go Dawgs!"

—MIDSHIPMAN 1ST CLASS WARNICK, University of Washington NROTC

"Every year, our unit gets together with the other NROTC units in the Pacific Northwest to compete in Northwest Navy, a day event composed of competitions in activities like drill, swimming, tug-of-war, and various physical challenges. Every four years we get a chance to host the event at our campus and the other years we travel out to the designated hosting school's area, ranging from Oregon all the way to Utah. This event brings our own unit closer together while allowing us to meet other midshipmen we may one day serve alongside."

—MIDSHIPMAN 2ND CLASS SELTMANN, University of Washington NROTC

"I chose to be a part of the NROTC program because I wanted to be a part of something bigger than myself. I felt that serving my country and being a part of the Navy would allow me to develop further as a leader."

—MIDSHIPMAN 4TH CLASS WEISS, University of Washington NROTC

Cherry blossoms in bloom on the campus of the University of Washington.
U.S. Navy photo by Eva Pahl

University of Washington NROTC midshipmen compete in a tug-of-war.
U.S. Navy photo by Eva Pahl

Marine Corps. The long tradition of excellence maintained by the University of Washington NROTC unit is a testament to the quality and patriotism of the young men and women who have earned their commissions through the Husky Battalion. When we asked the UW midshipmen about their motivations for joining the NROTC program, a freshman midshipman reflected the responses of many (Midshipman 4th Class Weiss).

The University of Washington NROTC unit may be an excellent option for students seeking an active college community near the heart of a large, diverse

---

"After high school I attended a local community college for two years. It was during my second year at the community college, as I was applying to transfer to a university, that I found out about the NROTC program. I applied for a two-year scholarship at the NROTC University of Washington (UW) Unit (aka, the 'Husky Battalion').

"Because I would be entering the unit as a college junior (2nd class Midshipman), I would be starting out behind my peers in terms of the naval and military knowledge typically learned during freshman and sophomore years (as a 4th class and 3rd class Midshipman). In order to 'catch up,' all 2-year-scholarship students attended the seven-week Naval Science Institute (NSI) at Naval Station Newport, R.I., the summer before joining our respective NROTC units. NSI was essentially a crash course in naval indoctrination. In addition to being taught by Marine Corps drill instructors how to wear a uniform, stand in formation, and march, we also received classes in naval history, naval engineering, and naval weapons systems. We also did a lot of PT.

"That fall I arrived on campus at UW and quickly fell into the university and NROTC routine. Once a week (typically Tuesdays) we would wear our uniforms and the entire battalion would muster early in the morning before classes, usually for battalion-wide instruction or training on some topic relevant to naval service. Another day each week (typically Thursdays), we would muster early in the morning for battalion-wide PT. Each quarter (UW continues to divide the school year into quarters, vice semesters), each midshipman would also enroll in a naval science class—navigation during my 2nd class (junior) year, and leadership and ethics during my 1st class (senior) year. At a school with over 30,000 undergrad students, the Husky Battalion midshipmen quickly became each other's core group of friends and support network.

"For my 1st class cruise the summer between my junior and senior years, I was assigned to USS *Denver* (LPD 9). I flew to Hawaii to meet the ship in Pearl Harbor along with another of my fellow Husky Battalion midshipmen. We rode the ship across the Pacific on her way to an Arabian Gulf deployment and debarked from her during a port visit in Singapore. We got to spend three days in Singapore before flying home. As a college kid who had only ever been outside of North America one other time, the experience of sailing across the Western Pacific and a port visit in Singapore was amazing.

"After the cruise I returned to UW for my second year at the NROTC unit, and the following spring, I graduated with a BA in Political Science and was commissioned as an ensign in the Navy. A month later I reported to my first ship, USS *Mason* (DDG 87)."

—LCDR C. Roberts, USN, University of Washington NROTC Class of 2003 metropolitan area and at the same time offers an outstanding education and professional development.

Additional information on the University of Washington NROTC unit can be found at its website, http://nrotc.washington.edu/.

University of Notre Dame–South Bend, Indiana

The University of Notre Dame is located in South Bend, Indiana, a medium-sized city two hours east of Chicago, Illinois. Notre Dame is a private, Catholic research university and is home to some eight thousand undergraduate and four thousand graduate students. Notre Dame consistently ranks in the top twenty in national rankings for institutions of higher learning and boasts a very proud tradition of excellence—in the classroom, on the athletic field, and in the development of military leaders of character. The university maintains large ROTC programs associated with all the U.S. military services but has a particularly strong attachment with the U.S. Navy. During World War II, the then–all male Notre Dame was at one point threatened with insolvency because so large a part of its student body left school to serve in the military. Fortunately, the Navy decided to make Notre Dame one of four host schools for its wartime V-7 program, stabilizing the school's revenues. As a sign of their mutual appreciation, Notre Dame and the U.S. Naval Academy have played each other in football every year since. Another indication of strong institutional ties is the annual motivational run around campus with the university's president—since 2005, Father John Jenkins; at the end, the run passes through the home team's entrance tunnel into historic Notre Dame Stadium.

School and team spirit are huge aspects of life at Notre Dame. Notre Dame's Fighting Irish teams are cheered on by its devoted student body, extensive alumni network, and national fan base. Students live throughout their time on campus in single-sex dorms to which they are assigned, each with a resident rector. There they can study, compete for their dormitory team in a wide range of intramural sports leagues, and find opportunities to grow spiritually.

Fighting Irish midshipmen responded to our questions about their school and unit with many outstanding qualities, but one junior midshipman best expressed a sentiment that is particularly widely held and which we reprint (Midshipman 2nd Class Mortemor).

Another junior midshipman enjoys the variety of opportunities that pursuing a degree at a high-quality civilian institution offers while also participating in the NROTC program and pursuing a commission in the naval services (Midshipman 2nd Class Dosch).

Notre Dame cadets and midshipmen run through the home-team entrance tunnel to Notre Dame Stadium to finish a PT run. *U.S. Navy photo by Scott A. Thornbloom*

A major event for Notre Dame NROTC is its annual Naval Leadership Weekend, which consistently attracts senior civilian and military leaders from across the nation. Each February, over 250 midshipmen from NROTC units across the country brave the bitter winter weather of northwestern Indiana to participate in a series of lectures, workshops, leadership scenarios, and other events to help expand their leadership toolkit and prepare for their coming roles as commissioned naval officers. Past speakers have included a Chief of Naval Operations, ADM John Richardson; a Commandant of the Marine Corps, Gen Robert Neller; and a commander of U.S. Fleet Forces Command (and Notre Dame alumnus), ADM Christopher Grady.

"My favorite thing about NROTC at Notre Dame is the comradeship that is held throughout the battalion. We are all friends and it is great to be a part of an organization where everyone supports each other in pursuing a common goal."

—MIDSHIPMAN 2ND CLASS MORTEMOR,
University of Notre Dame NROTC

"Opportunities for experience and service are readily available to me. We have trips for community service, the gun range, and leadership conferences, etc."

—MIDSHIPMAN 2ND CLASS DOSCH,
University of Notre Dame NROTC

ADM Christopher Grady, Commander, U.S. Fleet Forces Command, addresses midshipmen at Notre Dame's annual Naval Leadership Weekend. *U.S. Navy photo by Scott A. Thornbloom*

As in all the schools that make up the NROTC family, Notre Dame midshipmen seek commissions in the naval services for many worthwhile reasons, and a junior midshipman expressed a characteristic feeling of the Fighting Irish Battalion (Midshipman 2nd Class Slattery).

Notre Dame may be an excellent choice for students seeking a school with a proud heritage of academic excellence, religious faith, and military service. Etched above the eastern entrance to the university's main church, the Basilica of the Sacred Heart, are words that reflect the devotion of many Fighting Irish, "God, Country, Notre Dame."

Additional information on Notre Dame NROTC can be found at its website, http://nrotc.nd.edu/.

> "I wanted to serve my country and be a part of something bigger than myself. There is a lot of tradition in the Naval service, and I wanted to be a part of that. Also, I had good mentors and people to look up to in high school who had served or were serving in the Navy."
>
> —MIDSHIPMAN 2ND CLASS SLATTERY, University of Notre Dame NROTC

"I am the oldest of four children to Nigerian immigrants. I had no military service in my family and did not ever dream of serving in the military. The summer before my high school senior year, I visited the University of Notre Dame because my family was moving from Tennessee to Ohio and I was looking for great schools in the Midwest. My family and I fell in love with Notre Dame from the moment we stepped on campus! I knew this was where I wanted to spend my formative years of higher education. But then we were smacked in the face with the 'sticker shock.' How would my parents be able to afford this tuition with three other children still in the home? One week into my senior year, my Mom and I attended a college fair, and as luck would have it, I saw a man in a white uniform standing at a booth. He asked us if we had ever heard of the Navy ROTC Scholarship. We said no. After he described the details of the scholarship, my only question was, 'Will you pay for me to go to Notre Dame?' 'Son, if you qualify for the scholarship and get accepted to Notre Dame, then you'll be saying "Go Irish!" the rest of your life!'

"I can honestly say that receiving this scholarship and serving in our Nation's Navy have been the most impactful experiences in my life. I was commissioned as an officer in 2002 and since then, I have had the honor and privilege to travel to over 30 countries, represent the Navy on Capitol Hill, earn a Master's from the Naval War College, work as a Staff Officer in the Pentagon, and lead and serve with some of the most amazing and hardworking people that our country has to offer. As I prepare to return to sea duty as the Executive Officer (and hopefully Commanding Officer one day) of a destroyer based in historic Pearl Harbor, Hawaii, I can't help but look back on my life and how this kid with an African name who grew up in Tennessee ended up graduating from Notre Dame and serving in the World's Greatest Navy. Thank God for Navy ROTC . . . and Go Irish!"

—CDR K. R. Ndukwe, University of Notre Dame NROTC Class of 2002,
Prospective Executive Officer, USS *Halsey* (DDG 97)

Virginia Polytechnic Institute and State University–Blacksburg, Virginia

Virginia Polytechnic Institute and State University, more popularly known as Virginia Tech (VT), is a midsized public, land-grant, research university with its main campus in central Virginia. Virginia Tech is consistently ranked in national publications as one of the best public universities and is particularly recognized for its outstanding College of Engineering. The mascot of Virginia Tech is the Hokie, a term created in the late nineteenth-century university when a contest was held seeking a new cheer for Virginia Tech's successful athletics teams. "Hokie Nation" is one of the most proud and loyal such "communities" in the country, as Virginia Tech students excel both in the classroom and on athletic fields.

Burress Hall on the campus of Virginia Polytechnic University. *U.S. Navy photo by Scott A. Thornbloom*

Virginia Tech midshipmen perform firefighting hose-handling drills during professional training on campus. *U.S. Navy photo by Scott A. Thornbloom*

Notably among NROTC-affiliated schools, Virginia Tech maintains a Corps of Cadets, which imposes the rigor and discipline inherent of a military school while offering a civilian education. Similar curricula are offered at other NROTC-affiliated military schools, such as The Citadel, Norwich University, the Virginia Military Institute, and Texas A&M University. Even more than traditional institutions with NROTC units, a school like Virginia Tech offers both a full-time military cadet experience and an outstanding civilian education curriculum. All NROTC midshipmen seeking to study at Virginia Tech must also become members of the Corps of Cadets. However, not all Corps of Cadets students will be seeking commissions in the naval services; both the Army and Air Force maintain ROTC programs at Virginia Tech as well. In addition, many Corps of Cadets students are there not to prepare for careers in the military but to develop their discipline and leadership abilities prior to beginning civilian careers. A Virginia Tech senior midshipman describes his unit as we have reprinted here (Midshipman 1st Class Liddon).

Virginia Tech Corps of Cadets in formation. *U.S. Navy photo by Scott A. Thornbloom*

In addition to the added structure and discipline inherent in a corps of cadets, the presence of a large body of military-focused students fosters camaraderie and competition, helpful for a future in physically demanding, team-based specialties of the naval services. For example, Raider Company is Virginia Tech NROTC's Marine Corps–focused training team; it takes advantage of the large number of Marine-Option midshipmen to train in small-unit leadership, physical fitness, and discipline. A junior Virginia Tech NROTC midshipman highlights the benefits of this large military-focused student body (Midshipman 2nd Class Marin).

Midshipmen interested in possible careers in Naval Special Warfare or Explosive Ordnance Disposal find assistance in their development in Virginia Tech's Naval Special Preparatory Team. Virginia Tech NROTC is consistently one of the top-producing schools for Naval Special Warfare candidates who go on to attend the rigorous

> "The Virginia Tech NROTC program is unique in the fact that VT is a Senior Military College. This means that everyday we live a regimented military life instead of only wearing a uniform once a week. We live in barracks, we wear a uniform every day, and we hold ourselves to higher guidelines every day. When you sign up for ROTC at Virginia Tech, you're not signing up for PT, ProLab, and wearing a uniform once a week. You're signing up for a military atmosphere 24/7."
>
> —MIDSHIPMAN 1ST CLASS LIDDON, Virginia Tech NROTC

A Virginia Tech midshipman performs physical training.
U.S. Navy photo by Scott A. Thornbloom

Basic Underwater Demolition/SEAL (BUD/S) school in Coronado, California. Most NROTC units have at least a couple of interested candidates for such programs, but senior military colleges like Virginia Tech tend to attract a much larger proportion and have proven track records of preparing midshipmen for success in these more physically and mentally demanding military specialties.

It must be stressed that although the Corps of Cadets is a defining characteristic of NROTC at Virginia Tech, the school remains a large, public, and "normal" college in terms of atmosphere and opportunities. This "hybrid" quality may be attractive to students who would benefit from the added structure and discipline of a corps-of-cadets curriculum but do not want to forgo entirely the advantages of a larger civilian institution. A junior Hokie raised for us this point as particularly beneficial (Midshipman 2nd Class Kassman).

More information concerning Virginia Tech NROTC can be found at its website, https://liberalarts.vt.edu/rotc/navy.html.

Cornell University–Ithaca, New York

Cornell University is a private, research university in the scenic Finger Lakes region of New York State. Cornell, one of the eight Ivy League schools, is consistently ranked as one of the very best schools in the United States. Cornell comprises seven undergraduate colleges and seven graduate divisions on its main campus; its

"Virginia Tech NROTC goes hand-in-hand with the Virginia Tech Corps of Cadets when it comes to leadership development. Every midshipman going through the program must be a member of the Corps of Cadets. This gives each midshipman more followership and leadership opportunities for them to grow as leaders. The sense of family and pride cultivated in both organizations further influence midshipmen to give it their all and strive for the best."

—MIDSHIPMAN 2ND CLASS MARIN,
Virginia Tech NROTC

"Our program is unique because it is a part of a larger school population, allowing our midshipmen to develop themselves in a military environment but also working with civilians and staying active holding leadership roles in other organizations. Additionally, the NROTC unit is very active around campus helping with parking during football games, community service involving the Toughest Hokie and many other events around campus."

—MIDSHIPMAN 2ND CLASS KASSMAN,
Virginia Tech NROTC

overall student body numbers approximately 15,000 undergraduate and 8,500 graduate students. As one of only three private land-grant academic institutions in the United States, Cornell has since its founding in 1862 made available military training to its students. The Navy formally affiliated with Cornell University during World War II, in connection with the V-12 program, which produced thousands of officers for the U.S. Navy and Marine Corps.

> "The Cornell NROTC unit is incredibly close. Midshipmen across all classes are supportive of one another, and are eager to offer help in classes they've taken previously. Overall, mentorship is something we all take seriously, and midshipmen are able to create bonds through academics in addition to unit events."
>
> —MIDSHIPMAN 1ST CLASS NYUL, Cornell University NROTC

After World War II, Cornell's V-12 organization transitioned to NROTC and has trained and commissioned naval officers ever since. When asked what makes their unit special, a Marine Corps–Option midshipman there responded as we've recorded (Midshipman 1st Class Nyul).

While the Big Red NROTC unit has of course decreased in size since World War II—today approximately fifty midshipmen participate each year—the quality

The Cornell University campus. *U.S. Navy photo by Eva Pahl*

of officers trained and commissioned has remained steady. Cornell University NROTC remains one of the most highly regarded programs in the country, a testament to the world-class opportunities available to students in the NROTC program. Cornell hosts an annual drill competition that brings together hundreds of midshipmen and cadets from across the country. Conducting and training for such competitive events in military precision and smartness as the Cornell University Invitational Drill Competition (CUIDC) promotes a culture of resolution, energy, and teamwork.

> "Each fall, Cornell's NROTC program plans and hosts the annual Cornell University Invitational Drill Competition (CUIDC) and Military Excellence Competition (MEC). The special part of this drill competition is that it is almost entirely planned and run by the midshipmen in the unit. This provides a special opportunity for all midshipmen to experience new leadership and management roles that both challenge them, and help them grow into better leaders."
>
> —MIDSHIPMAN 3RD CLASS BROWNING, Cornell University NROTC

Throughout the family of NROTC schools, the camaraderie and support of one's fellow midshipmen is one of the best aspects of the program, foreshadowing the remarkable relationships that will develop through shared military service after commissioning. Recognizing the strength of these bonds, many schools, including

Cornell University NROTC midshipmen attend lab in the Memorial Room of Willard Straight Hall on the campus of Cornell University. *U.S. Navy photo by Eva Pahl*

Cornell University NROTC midshipmen pose for a picture at Taughannock Falls, New York. *U.S. Navy photo by Eva Pahl*

Cornell, set aside special spaces for midshipmen. For example, Cornell's Barton Hall houses all of the University's ROTC units, along with classrooms, staff offices, a weight room, computer facilities, a study area, and lounges.

For more information on Cornell University and its NROTC program, please visit its website at https://navy.cornell.edu/.

"I grew up in the birthplace of the Navy, Beverly, Massachusetts, where George Washington's first ship, the *Hannah,* was commissioned in 1775. I worked on commercial lobstering boats and learned to sail through my middle and high school years. In 1984, USS *John F. Kennedy* (CV 67) visited Boston and one of the local lobstermen, a retired LCDR, arranged a tour for a group of us aboard the ship. During this visit, I learned about NROTC scholarships enabling attendance at traditional universities followed by a commission in the Navy.

"During my first college fair, fortunately, the team from the Officer Recruiting Office was in attendance and provided me more information about the program (recognizing the Internet didn't exist at this time . . .). I applied to the program and was accepted with a three-year scholarship. My next step was selecting the university to attend from the six options I was accepted to.

"After some handwringing and figuring what the best school would be, I elected to attend Cornell University in Ithaca, New York. Quite frankly, I didn't truly understand what the value of an Ivy League education would be; however, my acceptance and scholarship provided the opportunity to attend. I finished up one more summer of lobstering and racing sailboats prior to heading to Ithaca and Cayuga Lake for continued education and experiences.

"My fellow Cornell NROTC members and I arrived about ten days prior to freshman orientation and went through our indoctrination period. This experience taught us the basics of adapting to being in the battalion, Navy customs and courtesies, and basic military drill. At the end of the ten days, we were ready to integrate with the bulk of our Cornell brethren to balance our military requirements with traditional student life.

"Through my freshman year, I integrated with all elements of campus life. We took our naval science classes, drill, and PT around our standard academic load. Additionally, I got a job at the student union at a dining hall and became a student leader amongst my co-workers. We also integrated into our NROTC sailing program with both an offshore sailboat, a 51-foot Morgan Ketch and dinghies of Lasers, 420s and Flying Juniors. My boating experience was recognized by the staff and my peers and I taught an offshore sailing class for the battalion.

"Through sophomore year, I continued in all academic, battalion, and campus life processes while moving to an off-campus apartment. Living with five roommates who were not affiliated with NROTC provided exceptional understanding of why attending an Ivy League school was valuable to me, as these friends remain strong today and are leaders in their individual fields. Today, these friends are a Cornell professor, a world-renowned ophthalmologist, partners at prominent consulting and law firms, and a bond trader. The experience of living with them is one which would not have been as viable without the NROTC program.

"My summer training periods were exceptional and provided me opportunities to learn about the surface fleet and continue to enjoy ocean sailing. My second-class cruise was aboard a CONUS-based cruiser followed by a Sail Training cruise up the east coast. My first-class cruise was the first five weeks of a deployment from Norfolk to Europe. Our ship participated in the fiftieth commemoration of D-Day at anchor off the coast of France with POTUS embarked onboard the *George Washington* a mile or two away. We finished the cruise with visits to Greece and Rome. Once complete with my Navy summer training, I flew to Alaska where I worked for six weeks on a commercial salmon boat before returning to Cornell.

"As my final year of Cornell and NROTC continued, I submitted my ship preferences and was assigned to an FFG out of Norfolk. Our commissioning ceremony was exceptional, as I was able to be sworn in by my uncle, an Army JAG, who was also in attendance for my promotion to CAPT some twenty-one years later. Following commissioning, my future SWO classmates and I headed off to Newport, Rhode Island, to start our path to our ships and eventual assignment as division officers.

"On arrival on my first ship, the amount of time aboard boats, sailboats, and ships inside and outside of the NROTC program served me very well for my progress as a division officer. I qualified as an Officer of the Deck in 5½ months and stood OOD for our entire 6-month deployment to the Mediterranean. We visited seventeen ports during the six months on deployment and I continued to develop my thirst and love for being overseas and operating forward.

"Since Cornell and the NROTC program started me on the path in the Navy, I have served in every area of the world. I have served on seven ships and afloat staffs, participating in offensive operations through Tomahawk strikes and Special Operations Forces (SOF) operations across the littoral boundaries. I have been stationed in Bahrain, Argentina, Japan, Germany, and Italy. I have been in seventy-seven countries through both professional and personal travel. I have had the privilege of commanding at sea four times and have had the opportunity to lead and work with incredible Sailors all around the world."

—CAPT Joseph Femino, USN, Commander, Task Force 64, Cornell University NROTC Class of 1995

Prairie View A&M University–Prairie View, Texas

Prairie View A&M University is a public, historically black university located in Prairie View, Texas, a small city northwest of Houston. Prairie View A&M is affiliated with the Texas A&M University System, and its NROTC program is part of the Houston Consortium, made up of Rice University, the University of Houston, Texas Southern University, and Houston Baptist University. Prairie View A&M has been affiliated with the NROTC program since the late 1960s and was the first historically black college or university to have its own unit.

Original members of Prairie View A&M's NROTC pose for a group photo with Commandant of the Marine Corps Gen Robert B. Neller (*center*) and other distinguished guests after an event hosted by the National Museum of the United States Navy. *U.S. Navy photo by Jonah Farwell*

Prairie View A&M couples the academic and cultural experience of an HBCU with the opportunity to train for and earn a commission in either the U.S. Navy or Marine Corps. The naval officer corps benefits from the broad range of educational, cultural, and experiential diversity present throughout the many schools across the country affiliated with the NROTC program, and Prairie View A&M represents an important aspect of that diversity.

We've reprinted remarks of a senior Prairie View A&M midshipman highlighting the importance of the opportunity to serve a higher purpose (Midshipman 1st Class King).

Prairie View A&M NROTC enhances its midshipmen's leadership training and opportunities by hosting the annual Prairie View A&M Orienteering Meet, an athletic and military competition for Junior (that is, high school–level) ROTC units. Over two dozen Junior ROTC units represent their schools in competition with one another and interact with and learn from Prairie View A&M NROTC midshipmen. A senior Prairie View A&M midshipman particularly emphasizes Orienteering as a significant event each year (Midshipman 1st Class Rasay).

A primary objective of the NROTC program at all affiliate schools is the training and development of young leaders of character. When asked about their favorite aspect of the NROTC program, a senior Prairie View A&M midshipman responded as we've reprinted (Midshipman 1st Class Gutierrez).

Although Prairie View A&M is not the biggest NROTC unit in the country, its association with the Houston Consortium gives it the advantages of a small, tight-knit unit and of access to the resources of a larger network. One freshman midshipman stresses the benefits of a smaller community as a strong point of Prairie View A&M NROTC (Midshipman 4th Class Ramirez).

Prairie View A&M is one of several historically black college and universities affiliated with the NROTC program. They include, among others, Howard University, Spelman College, Morehouse College, Hampton University, and Savannah State University. All qualified students, regardless of race or gender, can qualify for Minority Serving Institution scholarships

> "The NROTC program is outstanding for all the opportunities it offers for someone young and looking to become educated as well as providing the sense of being part of something that matters."
>
> —MIDSHIPMAN 1ST CLASS KING,
> Prairie View A&M University NROTC

> "A major annual event at PVAMU is PV Orienteering. We host multiple Junior ROTC Units to compete and have fun at our university as they partake in physical competitions and mental ones as well. It is a great opportunity to give back to the Junior ROTC Units."
>
> —MIDSHIPMAN 1ST CLASS RASAY,
> Prairie View A&M University NROTC

Prairie View A&M University midshipmen encourage participants in the annual Orienteering Meet. *U.S. Navy photo by Jonah Farwell*

if they attend an HBCU. Additional information on this scholarship option can be found in chapters 3 and 5. For a complete listing of HBCUs, please see appendix I or visit the online listing of NROTC schools at http://www.nrotc.navy.mil.

Additional information on Prairie View A&M University NROTC can be found at its website, http://www.pvamu.edu/nrotc/.

Conclusion

A clear advantage of the NROTC program as compared to other commissioning paths is the variety of schools available at which students can both pursue their undergraduate degrees and develop professionally by completing the naval science curriculum and summer training. The five schools highlighted in this chapter are only a small sample of these fine schools, each with a distinct culture, climate, and tradition, among which may be the best fit for you as you seek to develop and mature into a leader

"I enjoy watching the growth and development of individuals, and I knew being a part of the NROTC program I would be able to enhance that growth by being a leader to those around me. I also take great pride in the military and wanted to serve my country."

—MIDSHIPMAN 1ST CLASS GUTIERREZ,
Prairie View A&M University NROTC

"The very tight bond the unit shares—the size of the unit is fairly small, which lets the students interact very closely with the whole unit to form bonds between one another."

—MIDSHIPMAN 4TH CLASS RAMIREZ,
Prairie View A&M University NROTC

and young professional. We encourage you to reach out directly to schools you may be interested in, ask any questions you have, and set up a visit to and tour of the school and NROTC facilities.

In the next chapter, our focus will shift to the professional mentorship and counseling that form an integral part of midshipman professional development and training in NROTC.

Prairie View A&M University midshipmen march on the field before a football game against Texas A&M University. *U.S. Navy photo by Jonah Farwell*

"I can honestly say that I wouldn't be here without this program. I am from a small country town in Arkansas with about 10,000 people. The NROTC program gave me an opportunity to get outside of my comfort zone and attend a school just forty minutes from downtown Houston. I never considered Prairie View A&M University, but it has turned into one of the best decisions I have ever made. I always knew I would be on a college campus somewhere, but I never thought or dreamed that I would eventually end up in the United States Military, the Naval Service in particular. The NROTC program and commissioning into the Navy has given me a platform to be able to give back to my community and be a provider for my family. I have also been able to travel throughout the world and experience things that most people never get the opportunity to do. When I boarded my first ship, the USS *Vandegrift,* one of the department heads was a Prairie View graduate. It's a great feeling to know that officers from my unit are excelling in their respective military careers and that I am one of the midshipmen we are adding to those ranks (through the midshipmen I am helping to train as an instructor at my alma mater)."

—LT Chambers, USN, Prairie View A&M University NROTC Class of 2013

12 Performance Evaluation, Counseling, and Mentorship

THROUGHOUT YOUR TIME in the NROTC program, you will be monitored, assessed, and evaluated on both your current performance and your potential to serve as a commissioned officer in the U.S. Navy or Marine Corps. While this may seem intimidating, the profession of arms requires that only the most capable be privileged with the opportunity to lead Sailors and Marines. To help you develop into your full potential, the NROTC program maintains a robust professional counseling system that complements the formal performance evaluation system.

In this chapter we will discuss the processes and procedures involved within the NROTC program's professional counseling and performance evaluation systems. Both are key factors in the professional development of NROTC midshipmen. First, we will discuss mentorship and then its context in the NROTC program's performance evaluation system.

Mentorship

When it comes to developing midshipmen from civilians into young men and women of character and competence ready to serve as naval officers, no aspect of the NROTC program is more important than effective mentorship. Mentorship counseling takes many forms, from short, informal discussions after class with your naval science instructor to midshipmen lunches with the commanding officer to mandatory formal beginning- and end-of-semester interviews with your class advisor. All of these represent opportunities to have meaningful, substantive conversations with active-duty naval officers committed to helping you develop into the best leader you can be.

Mentorship sessions may be the only substantive one-on-one opportunities you have to ask your class advisor serious questions about your demonstrated performance and what will be expected of you when you hit the fleet. It is also an invaluable occasion for honest, frank assessment of your performance within the NROTC unit and for a clear-eyed look at areas for improvement in your academics and aptitude. (For the purposes of the NROTC program, "aptitude" refers to all areas of performance not directly associated with academics.) Finally, effective counseling is an important skill for naval officers—once commissioned, you will be both counseling and formally evaluating your own subordinates—so this introduction to what makes a counseling session effective is an important building block of your professional development.

NROTC Mentorship Counseling

You will meet with your class advisor for at least two formal counseling sessions each semester. The first, an initial interview at the beginning of the semester, is intended to verify your progress toward meeting program requirements, assess your previous academic and aptitude performance, discuss necessary personal matters, and provide counsel concerning your billet (see chapter 2) in the midshipmen battalion. You will also be presenting your academic schedule for the semester, along with written goals regarding your academic and aptitude performance. An effective initial interview starts each semester off on a strong foundation. After the first semester, the initial interviews will also serve as "close-out" reviews of your performance during the previous semesters. You will also be presented with a formal evaluation of your performance during the previous semester—a "fitness report," to be discussed more fully below.

Later in the semester, typically after midterms, you will have a progress counseling session to update the initial semester interview. This session serves to update your class advisor on your academic and aptitude progress thus far. It is, however, always best practice to notify your class advisor early on of any academic struggles. Your NROTC unit staff members cannot assist you unless they know there is a problem—and in most cases the only way they can know is for you to tell them.

Based on your performance, your class advisor may require additional counseling sessions to

> "I really appreciate the mentorship program; it helped me adapt to NROTC life and feel like I have people who are here for me."
>
> —MIDSHIPMAN 4TH CLASS BELVIN, University of San Diego NROTC

monitor your progress and provide guidance. These should not be viewed as punishments but rather as assistance in maintaining your focus and as opportunities to receive additional resources. A key takeaway from these mentorship counseling sessions is that you and your advisor are working together to develop and execute a strategy to help you meet program requirements. The strategy's elements may be additional tutoring sessions, study groups, or work with a more senior midshipman who has performed well in your weak areas. Proper mentorship counseling can be a valuable tool in helping you succeed in the NROTC program.

Tips for Successful Counseling

For many young midshipmen counseling is intimidating, particularly if they are having "hiccups" in their academic or aptitude performance. It may be helpful to keep in mind that everyone in the NROTC program wants you to succeed and develop into a capable individual who will make a fine naval officer. Toward that end, to help make your counseling sessions as effective as possible, we recommend the following.

First, be humble—but confident, too. You would not be in the NROTC program, earning a scholarship or a student at your fine institution if you had not excelled as a high school student. Whether success in high school "came easy" or required extensive study and effort, college presents new academic challenges, particularly in the pace of teaching and complexity of material. At the end of the semester there are no asterisks next to grades revealing how many teaching assistant sessions or recitations you attended, only the final grades. If you do not perform in college to the standard of excellence you were used to in high school, you may feel embarrassed asking for help. Be assured, you will suffer much more anguish if you fail a required course and must go through the disciplinary process and retake the class. Have some humility, and some determination, and let your class advisor know as soon as your grades begin to go south. Many courses in college have only a few, heavily weighted grades; in such cases a single poor test can foredoom your final mark. The adage that bad news does not get better with age is germane. You will be in much better standing with your advisor if you have maintained open and honest communications and he or she hears from you before your academic advisor calls.

Remember, academic performance tends to be consistent. Consider that your entire undergraduate career is only eight semesters in length. While you may hope to recover from a poor freshman year with 4.0 marks the rest of the way, the statistical probability is that your GPA will not differ significantly from what it is after your sophomore fall semester. The same holds true in individual classes: your grade on the first midterm is a pretty good indicator of how you will do in the course. Sure, some students bump their grades up after initial scares, but to do that requires extensive additional study.

Second, remember that formal counseling sessions are primarily designed to assist you in meeting program requirements. Your class advisor should help you in setting academic performance goals, course sequences, and professional development milestones. After the initial session, your class advisor will recommend adjustments to your goals as needed but otherwise hold you accountable to them. In addition to academic requirements, your class advisor will monitor your physical fitness performance and recommend to the PNS any necessary remediation. Combining your academic transcripts and physical fitness performance records, the class advisor will build your official student file (both paper and electronic), which for now is your official service record.

A Good Counseling Session

First, be proactive in scheduling your counseling session with your class advisor. They will reach out to their midshipmen and post a schedule either online or on a sign-up sheet near their office. Sign up soon after the calendar is posted, and if you will be unable to meet the scheduled time, communicate as soon as you know it. If this is the case, you should express your regret and suggest an alternative. Be mindful that your class advisor may have professional or personal obligations outside of normal working hours. Meeting at 1800 may be convenient for you, but your class advisor may need to pick up a child from day care or otherwise be unable to accommodate you. The scheduled time should allow you to report a few minutes early without undue hurry: it is very poor form to leave a senior officer waiting for you. If the time slots your class advisor has put out are difficult for you, discuss the matter promptly to find a mutually acceptable solution.

It may be useful to think of the counseling session as a miniature job performance evaluation. You should be thinking about asking the following questions:

Am I on track to graduate on time? If not, why?
Am I physically and medically ready to commission?

How am I performing within the NROTC unit?

What specifically can I do better to improve my performance?

If I were your division officer, what would you want me to improve?

What do you think my weaknesses are?

It may be helpful to write down these or related questions before the meeting with your class advisor, as a reference. The dynamics of the counseling session will depend on your respective personalities and communication styles, but if the conversation seems to lag you can revitalize it with an appropriate question.

As a prospective naval officer, your integrity and honest self-assessment are vital. The great Chinese military strategist Sun Tzu wrote, "If you know your enemies and know yourself, you will not be put at risk even in a hundred battles." In this context, the "enemies" are your required coursework and NROTC obligations. One of your class advisor's chief responsibilities is to help you confront and defeat them. You can only benefit from being open and honest with your class advisor at the earliest signs of professional or academic trouble.

To prepare properly for a mentoring session, look ahead at the coming semester course load and make an honest assessment of the grades you expect to earn in the various courses. If this is your freshman fall semester, there's nothing wrong with shooting for a 4.0 GPA (while realizing that the historical statistics are not in your favor). After your initial semester, use your performance in similar previous semesters and your comfort with various types of material as bases from which to predict your grades. Do not concern yourself with the exact grade you will earn—quite frankly, there is no way to know ahead of time how you will fare with a given professor or subject. Of much more utility is being honest with yourself about which of the expected courses in the coming semester will require more of your attention if you are to do well.

When originally mapping your degree plan, it may be useful to speak with more senior students who have done well to ask about challenging courses. As a midshipman, you are held to both semester and overall GPA requirements. Consequences for poor performance are exacerbated if the low grades are concentrated in a single semester. It is prudent to spread the more difficult courses across your curriculum to reduce the risk of catastrophic semesters. This may not be possible, depending on the nature of your degree requirements, but it cannot hurt to ask your institution's academic advisor how flexible you can be in sequencing your courses. Once you have a degree plan that takes systematic account of less- and more-difficult semesters, you can map out practices to help you execute that plan well.

In the fleet, you will quickly be introduced to a process called Operational Risk Management (ORM). To be brief, ORM is a systematic process of, first, assessing potential trouble areas or dangers in a mission, then implementing sufficient controls to eliminate or mitigate those hazards. A similar line of thinking can be of use here. It stands to reason that study and tutoring habits during your easier semesters can be different from those in the semesters you expect to be more challenging. Time (in your case, to commissioning) is a finite resource, so you must actively arrange and schedule the additional study or tutoring time necessary during the semesters that need them. These extra study periods may require cutting out other commitments from your weekly schedule to free up the needed time. All this requires maturity and forethought—do not fall into the trap of assuming you can "figure it all out" at the last minute.

A helpful analogy is maneuvering a ship at sea. Navy ships are in many cases very large and have correspondingly large forces of inertia that must be overcome to get them moving in a desired direction. A standard rule of thumb in ship-handling is that a large rudder angle eased off as necessary is better than ordering very little rudder and then "bumping it up" to get a desired effect. A similar logic holds for your course of study and preparation. It is a much better plan to schedule additional study hours or tutoring sessions, or both, early in your courses to help lay a foundation for success than to play catch-up after a poor midterm. Your class advisor will be much more impressed if you bring to your mentoring sessions deliberate, proactive plans to support outstanding academic performance than if you report halfway through the semester that you are failing your Calculus II course but will be sure to start attending weekly tutoring sessions. Use a lot of rudder early!

A final point concerning academic preparedness for counseling sessions: you should not let a poor midterm be the first indication that you are not keeping up. A poor midterm is often recoverable, but at the very least you will have dropped your final course grade. Prior to the first midterm, ask your professor or teaching assistant to provide practice problems or other assessment tools to get a fix on how you are doing. This way, you will be able to report your status within a course to your class advisor confidently, even before you have a midterm grade on the books.

In listening to feedback, try to be dispassionate and receptive. If your performance has not been up to standards, you should not take your class advisor's counseling as a personal attack. Your advisor wants you to succeed and is obliged to let you know forthrightly where you stand within the program. In a profession that can literally be life and death, substandard performance can be disastrous for the mission, your people, or yourself. To succeed, you must be able to recognize and seek to improve substandard performance in yourself and others. This is an aspect of a principle called "Forceful Watchteam Backup," and it is vital in complex military teams such as warships, submarines, or Marine platoons. Such a team falls apart if members are unable to deliver effectively or receive constructive criticism for failure to meet an established standard. If a session is difficult for you in this way, once emotions have cooled it would be prudent to discuss with your class advisor how to receive calmly what may seem like bluntly negative feedback.

As discussed in chapter 8, your class advisor may require that your institution's academic advisor agree with and endorse your degree plan, with respect to completeness and timeliness of graduation. If this is the case, schedule the appropriate consultation ahead of time so as to make your review more effective and identify where there is potential danger of falling off track.

Informal and Miscellaneous Counseling

In addition to the required formal counseling sessions held during the semester, your class advisor should set aside "office hours" for informal counseling or study sessions. These should not be "bull" sessions just to pass the time, but if you have a minor question or a professional or NROTC-related matter on your mind, you should feel comfortable approaching your advisor at those times (or any other NROTC staff member).

Your class advisor should specify what extraordinary circumstances they would like to be notified of immediately. In general, the sooner the better. For personal or family issues, you must notify your NROTC leadership if you will be unable to attend required courses or mandatory ROTC events. If the matter is sensitive, you are not obliged to detail the specifics of your circumstance, at least initially, but you do need to let your NROTC chain of command know the circumstance exists and be prepared to discuss the whole story with the XO or CO if they deem necessary.

"Special counseling" is something stipulated by administrative or disciplinary procedures. Although imposed as result of poor performance, its purpose is to assist you in meeting program requirements. As your ability to continue in the program may depend on their judgment of your situation, it is absolutely in your best interest to be mature and professional in these counseling sessions. It is even more critical than normal that you report on time. Weekly or more frequent checkups may be required. You may have to document having completed required study hours and attended tutoring sessions, as well as your quiz/test grades, and present the records to your class advisor—who in turn will be updating the XO and CO.

> "The NROTC unit active-duty staff and older midshipmen are all great mentors and counselors. They do a great job of connecting with each individual midshipman and helping us to succeed in the program."
>
> —MIDSHIPMAN 4TH CLASS SMART, University of California, Berkeley NROTC

The NROTC Performance Evaluation System

NROTC midshipmen are formally evaluated using the standard U.S. Navy Fitness Report and Counseling Record—the "FITREP." Midshipmen's fitness reports serve as official assessments of their performance in all aspects of the NROTC program. The standard form, created and used to evaluate fleet officers, is adapted to suit the unique context of NROTC. In addition, midshipmen's FITREP marks contribute to their national rankings for designator assignment (i.e., officer corps communities), ship selection, aviation order of merit, or at the negative extreme, disenrollment processing. The remarks section of the FITREP should detail areas of strength as well as offer guidance as to how to improve one's performance. Last, the FITREP will numerically rank all midshipmen within a graduating class in terms of relative performance. The Professor of Naval Science is the "signing authority" (and thus takes personal responsibility) for all midshipmen FITREPs.

A Navy FITREP is primarily a listing of performance traits, such as Professional Expertise, Military Bearing/Character, or Teamwork. Within each trait, a midshipman's performance is graded against performance criteria along a 1.0 to 5.0 scale. A 1.0 mark means performance below established standards, and 5.0 is awarded for greatly exceeding them. These "trait" marks are averaged to produce a midshipman's FITREP performance "trait average." This trait average will serve as your official aptitude score within the Officer Programs Management Information System (OPMIS) database.

Because the FITREP is a Navy-wide tool that NROTC has adapted, it has aspects, such as promotion recommendations, screening recommendations, etc., that are more relevant to its original audience. Further, NROTC regulations formally link certain trait marks to particular accomplishments; for example, the highest mark in Professional Expertise is tied to earning a GPA higher than or equal to 3.75 in naval science courses during the previous semester. Your class advisor should explain these aspects of the FITREP during your mentoring session as a matter of professional development, but they are beyond the scope of this book.

An additional professional development aspect of the standard Navy FITREP is that midshipmen will themselves use it to evaluate subordinate and peer midshipmen in the battalion. Midshipmen will draft and forward FITREPs on midshipmen assigned to them. Personnel evaluation and administration are integral parts of your future responsibilities as a naval officer; these battalion reports help introduce you to them. For Marine-Option midshipmen, this professional development is unfortunately moot, as the Marine Corps fields a completely different fleet performance evaluation system (for which, check *The Marine Officer's Guide*).

Conclusion

Counseling and performance evaluations are integral components of the professional development program in NROTC. Whether formal, informal, or special counseling, serious conversations with NROTC leaders can be invaluable growth opportunities for future naval officers. It's so easy to receive counseling when things are all smooth sailing; a true mark of character is to remain engaged and receptive to constructive feedback in proverbial rough weather. Your success in NROTC and preparedness for a commission are the primary goals of your NROTC staff. Being prepared and proactive will help them help you to grow into the best naval officer you can be.

13 Summer Training by Year

FOR MOST MIDSHIPMEN, the experience of "summer cruise" is the most important factor in determining service-assignment preferences (discussed in detail below and in chapter 14). Regardless of how determined you are to serve in a certain community or military occupational specialty, summer cruise provides an invaluable opportunity to experience real-world operations and get a little salt on your collar before commissioning and becoming responsible for leading fleet Sailors or Marines.

Summer training is an integral part of the NROTC experience and is designed both to help midshipmen make informed decisions regarding their service-assignment preference inputs and fulfill statutory requirements for commissioning naval officers. Cruises are conducted during the summer term (late May to the first half of August), so as to not conflict with university academic schedules. An NROTC National Scholarship student will notionally (i.e., ideally) participate in three summer cruise training periods, between freshman and sophomore years, sophomore and junior years, and junior and senior years. These are referred to as, respectively, "third-," "second-," and "first-class" cruises.

Scholarship and Advanced Standing midshipmen who are not on leaves of absence and meet physical readiness standards are eligible for summer training. College Program midshipmen are generally not.

Now that you are equipped with an understanding of the purpose of summer training cruises within the NROTC program, we will delve deeper into what you can expect during each one. Each summer cruise has a specific training purpose in addition to the general objective of giving NROTC midshipmen experience with operational Navy and Marine Corps units. Speaking of Marine-Option midshipmen:

attending and graduating from Marine Corps Officer Candidate's School (OCS) will be your most important summer training, and it is distinct from other summer cruise experiences. A comprehensive look at OCS is beyond the scope of this book, but we recommend *The Marine Officer's Guide,* from the Naval Institute Press.

We will discuss the summer cruises in the order they typically occur for students entering the NROTC program as college freshmen. However, by law, only the first-class cruise or graduation from Marine OCS is required for

"Summer cruise is by far one of the most helpful and fun things we do. I completed CORTRAMID this past year and the experiences I had on CORTRAMID were incredible, exposing me to all different naval communities as well as doing things that none of my friends outside NROTC would ever dream of doing."

—MIDSHIPMAN 3RD CLASS LORICK, Auburn University NROTC

commissioning. While the intent is for all scholarship midshipmen to participate in a cruise each summer, the availability of operational units, capacity and funding, or other factors may reduce the numbers of cruise spots open. Ideally, this will not be the case for you—many midshipmen find summer cruises the most memorable and enjoyable moments of their time in NROTC.

Midshipmen tour the control room of the *Los Angeles*–class fast attack submarine USS *Columbia* (SSN 771) in Pearl Harbor, Hawaii, during their summer cruise. *U.S. Navy photo by Daniel Hinton*

Career Orientation Training for Midshipmen

For NROTC midshipmen, the first summer cruise is an introduction to the war-fighting communities to which they might go after what is known as "service assignment." The third-class cruise, formally known as Career Orientation Training for Midshipmen (CORTRAMID), is conducted after a midshipmen's freshman spring semester. The third-class cruise is unique among NROTC summer events in that it is mandatory for both Navy- and Marine-Option midshipmen. CORTRAMID comprises four consecutive weeklong training periods: one week each with a surface ship, submarine, aviation squadron, and the Marines. Each summer there are East and West Coast CORTRAMID training periods that begin on various dates; midshipmen will typically attend the CORTRAMID training closest to their homes of record. For example, a University of California, Los Angeles student from Atlanta, Georgia, would likely attend CORTRAMID East, while a Yale University student from Los Angeles, California, would likely attend CORTRAMID West. This is not a hard-and-fast rule, and you may be able to arrange a specific CORTRAMID to accommodate other summer commitments or opportunities, such as internships, study abroad, summer jobs, etc.

CORTRAMID East is headquartered at Naval Station Norfolk in Norfolk, Virginia, CORTRAMID West at Naval Base San Diego in San Diego, California. Your travel arrangements to either Norfolk or San Diego will be arranged by your NROTC unit's summer cruise coordinator before you leave school for the summer. You can expect to arrive the weekend before the Monday morning when CORTRAMID will begin. Each CORTRAMID will be hosting hundreds of midshipmen, broken into small groups that rotate through the four weeks of training.

For surface week, the fleet's preference is for midshipmen to get under way with an operational warship homeported in Norfolk or San Diego to observe training evolutions and experience life afloat. Potential platforms include Aegis guided-missile cruisers and destroyers, amphibious assault ships, and littoral combat ships. If midshipmen cannot be embarked (that is, on board ship) for their entire week, they will participate in shiphandling simulators ashore, visit the Surface Warfare Officers School, the Basic Division Officer Course "schoolhouse," tour surface ships of various types on the waterfront, and converse with senior Surface Warfare Officers.

The next week, midshipmen will, ideally, embark a nuclear-powered attack or ballistic-missile submarines. Particular emphasis is placed on giving midshipmen time under way on a submarine to allow them to observe the unique operating environment and "lifestyle" of the submarine force. In addition, midshipmen will tour other submarines, participate in combat training and damage control "wet-training" simulators (mock-up ship compartments that actually and realistically flood) and attend discussions with senior submarine officers. For those destined to be assigned as officers to other communities, this may be the only opportunity to experience life hundreds of feet below the surface of the ocean.

Next, aviation week is an irreplaceable opportunity, particularly for midshipmen who do not intend to become naval aviators upon commissioning, to experience even briefly the rigorous training and operational routine of a Navy or Marine Corps aviation squadron. If at all possible, you will be afforded an opportunity to fly in a genuine fleet or training aircraft, possibly even take the controls. You may also be given familiarization flights on various types of aircraft and chances to "try your hand" in some of the outstanding flight simulators used to train fleet aviators. In addition, midshipmen are introduced to the basic organization of an operational aviation squadron and to the roles and responsibilities of junior officers serving in it. For many, even those who end up in other communities, the opportunities to experience the adrenaline rush of takeoff, aerial maneuvers, and landing make aviation week their favorite.

All midshipmen spend the last week of CORTRAMID with the Marines. The week, typically the most physically demanding, serves as an introduction to the training environment of a Marine Corps unit as well as to the tactical knowledge and leadership abilities required of junior Marine officers. During Marine week, midshipmen fire individual and crew-served weapons, such as the M-16 rifle

> "I loved my cruise aboard USS *Howard* (DDG 83)! It was the most interaction I was able to get with enlisted sailors prior to commissioning. I loved the open sea, the hum of the ship under way, and the smell of saltwater. I feel that Surface Navy Destroyer is the traditional Navy, the old school Navy, the workhorse of the Navy!"
>
> —MIDSHIPMAN 1ST CLASS KING, Prairie View A&M University NROTC

> "My most memorable experience was on my 1/C Cruise this past summer when I was on a submarine transiting from Guam to Yokosuka. I had been in Guam for about five days prior and got to explore the island with the sailors and officers of the USS *Asheville,* eating some of the best food, and swimming in the best beaches. However, as amazing as that was, I truly valued the training experience I received on board the USS *Michigan,* allowing me to see firsthand the life of a submariner. Standing watch with my running mate every night was something I will never forget."
>
> —MIDSHIPMAN 1ST CLASS CLOW, Georgetown University, The George Washington University NROTC

and the M240 Squad Assault Weapon machine gun, respectively. Additionally, midshipmen will be introduced to matters particular to Marine Corps aviation. Again, many midshipmen, even those with no desire whatsoever for career in the Marine Corps, particularly enjoy the shared memorable experiences and camaraderie engendered by Marine week.

CORTRAMID is a defining experience for many midshipmen and is a priceless opportunity to explore the different warfighting communities that you might join upon completing the NROTC program and commissioning as an ensign or second lieutenant. Here is an opportunity, after your freshman year of college and your first year in NROTC, perhaps to handle the most sophisticated warships, dive a nuclear-powered submarine, take the controls of a powerful aircraft, or fire deadly weapons. Contrast these opportunities with an internship performing low-level administrative tasks in a law firm or office.

A final note, and a reminder: you are not committed to the U.S. Navy or Marine Corps until after you return to your NROTC unit at the start of your sophomore year of college and sign your official service contract. The NROTC program

An NROTC midshipman rappels down a wall during Career Orientation Training for Midshipmen (CORTRAMID) Marine week at Camp Lejeune, North Carolina. *U.S. Marine Corps photo by Ashley D. Gomez*

purposefully sequences CORTRAMID prior to your having to decide whether or not to commit to the five years of active-duty service to which you would be obligated in return for your NROTC scholarship. If after your first year of NROTC and your experience during COR-TRAMID you decide that service in the U.S. Navy or Marine Corps is not for you, you are absolutely free to decline to continue, with no strings attached or scholarship money to repay.

Second- and First-Class Summer Cruises

We will now examine the second- and first-class cruises. These cruises are different for each NROTC option. we will discuss first Navy-Option, then Marine-Option, and finally Nurse-Option midshipmen summer cruises.

NAVY-OPTION MIDSHIPMEN

Second-Class Cruise: Sea Trials and the Junior Enlisted Cruise. The second-class cruise occurs between the sophomore and junior academic years. The standard second-class cruise occurs on board an operational surface ship or submarine, even for midshipmen intending to serve in naval aviation or Special Warfare. In addition, the newly established Sea Trials program will be required for all Navy-Option midshipmen. Sea Trials, held at Naval Station Newport in Newport, Rhode Island, is a ten-day program consisting of various shiphandling, damage control, wet trainer, firearms, and other training necessary in the development of naval officers. As this program is, at this writing, in its infancy, the curriculum may change—but it will certainly promote your professional development.

"At the time I went on CORTRAMID, I wasn't confident about my ability to pursue aviation as a service selection. I thought I couldn't qualify for flight school or that if I got in, it would be impossible for me because I'm a liberal arts major. When I had my T-34 flight, I told my pilot all of these things, and he couldn't have been more supportive or confident that someone like me could get through it with great success. He could see how badly I wanted to fly when I didn't even see it myself, and his words gave me the push to commit myself and believe I was fully capable of something I thought was so daunting."

—MIDSHIPMAN 2ND CLASS LOVEJOY, University of Notre Dame NROTC

"My most memorable summer cruise experience was during Marine Week during CORTRAMID, when they gave all the midshipmen a ride in the MV-22s. I was the 'stick chief,' which just meant that I was in charge of taking accountability for all the midshipmen that were going to be on my flight. This meant that I counted each person as they got on, then I got on last. This put me on the last seat by the open rear bay door as they did touch-and-go drills, and where I fell in love with flying. I now am awaiting commissioning with my approved flight contract."

—MIDSHIPMAN 1ST CLASS REITSMA, University of Michigan NROTC

During the cruise you may be assigned to a deployed ship or submarine, but most midshipmen will join ships in the primary fleet concentration areas in the United States. (Opportunities for aviation or Special Warfare exposure are much more plentiful during the first-class cruise.) The primary objective of second-class cruise is to build upon CORTRAMID's brief introduction to life on board a ship or a submarine and to increase awareness and appreciation among midshipmen of the demands of life afloat.

This is the "enlisted cruise" for NROTC Navy-Option midshipmen, where the primary goal is to be introduced to the basic duties and responsibilities, living and eating conditions, and warfighting tasks of the Navy's enlisted Sailors. As future naval officers, you will soon be charged with leading Sailors both in peace and war—you must have a basic understanding of how they live and work afloat. Second-class cruise affords future officers their best opportunity to serve directly alongside the enlisted personnel who perform maintenance and upkeep and stand watches. As hierarchical military organizations, both the Navy and Marine Corps clearly distinguish the roles and responsibilities of officers and enlisted service members. Once commissioned, you cannot expect similar opportunities to involve yourself as closely in the day-to-day work and experience of Sailors.

During the second-class cruise you will be assigned an enlisted "running mate," a high-performing Sailor selected by the command to help introduce you to and indoctrinate you on the integral role of Sailors in the fleet. You will sleep ("berth") and eat ("mess") with the enlisted personnel and work at the tasks—including manual labor and administration, as well as watchstanding and maintenance— that they typically perform. You will be integrated directly into a normal shipboard division, attending "Morning Quarters" and learning as much as you can about the division's assigned area. Your enlisted running mate is an invaluable resource on the lives and challenges of enlisted personnel on board ship—take the opportunity to ask as many questions as possible. While it is natural for many midshipmen to shy away, not to be perceived as a pest, the reality is that Sailors are typically very proud of their work and appreciate a future junior officer's genuine interest in them. If you make your enthusiasm and desire to learn apparent, your running mate may well go above and beyond to make your summer cruise experience as informative as possible.

If your ship or submarine's schedule includes time in port, you should expect to participate in the ship's routine just as a Sailor would. You will be assigned to a

COMMISSIONING FROM THE DECKPLATES

"Joining the ROTC as a prior enlisted Sailor is an experience unto itself. The pressure of having Naval experience creates a level of expectation that, if either underappreciated or overvalued, results in a commissioned officer that is uniquely experienced to lead but unable to mentally and emotionally transition into this new level of accountability and responsibility.

"Prior to enlisting, I had received notification that I was approved for an ROTC scholarship. I opted to enlist instead. After serving on my ship for a few years—USS *Dwight D. Eisenhower* (CVN 69), Combat Systems, Radar Division—I began to feel like I could do my division officer's job and wondered if I was under-achieving. So, I applied for the STA-21 program and was selected. I chose to attend Norfolk State University as a 'cross-town' school under Old Dominion University's Hampton Roads NROTC Consortium.

"Life in the ROTC was what you'd expect: a group of students training to get a sense of what the pressures of performing and leading would be like in the fleet. Prior enlisteds are referred to as Officer Candidates (OCs), not Midshipmen (MIDNs), to capture the difference in overall military experience. OCs are routinely placed in leadership positions early to create an atmosphere of mentoring for the MIDNs, who know nothing of Navy policy, processes, or procedures. It's important that Professors of Naval Science properly manage access to leadership opportunities from semester to semester because leadership billets within the company and battalion (if cross-town schools are involved) carry point values that affect rankings for community selection.

"The battalion had roles and functions like the hierarchal organization structure on a ship: CO, XO, Senior Enlisted Leader (usually a Gunnery Sergeant who was ROTC Staff) and then officers that acted as principal assistants. There were officers for Operations, Administration, and others. For example, our battalion's Administration Officer used the Navy's Fitness Report system to conduct evaluations on our company OCs and MIDNs. This was great practice for conducting interviews when discussing performance for the previous reporting period, processing groups of reports with rankings, and the administration of completing all documentation on time. Plus, the experience of face to face counseling of people that were your peer in age or experience, having, due to positional authority, to deal with the emotions of discussing areas of improvement with subordinates."

—LCDR Desmond Walker, USN, Norfolk State University,
Old Dominion University NROTC Class of 2005

"duty section," a group of officers and Sailors who stand watches, ensure security, and carry out necessary cleaning and maintenance when the rest of the crew is free to depart for "liberty" (that is, to leave the command for a brief but specified period, typically until the next morning) at the end of the workday. For most ships, this means that every sixth day (sometimes more often) you would remain on board for twenty-four hours until your duty section is relieved by the next. During your time on duty, your fundamental responsibility is learning about enlisted watches, both on the quarterdeck and in the engineering plant. The Navy prides itself on maintaining "forward presence from the sea," but individual ships spend more time in port than under way; an appreciation for the challenges encountered pierside is just as valuable as experience of life under way.

For underway periods, your second-class cruise training will include assignment to a "work center," a group of Sailors organized to maintain or operate, or both, functionally related systems or equipment, such as communications gear or weapons. Typically, you will join your running mate's work center to observe and, as possible, participate in its routine. Most Sailors, in addition to their work center responsibilities, stand various underway watches which assist in the operation of their vessels. You will stand watch with your running mate but also rotate through the watch stations, whether "topside," on the bridge, in the Combat Information Center, or in the engineering plant. Last, you will help man a "General Quarters" (GQ) station for battle drills and experience them and other such training events from the perspective of a Sailor.

Second-class cruise is an incredible chance to experience the life and responsibilities of the largest component of the U.S. Navy's personnel—its Sailors. With a sincere desire to learn, an open mind, and the humility to dive right into some hands-on work, you will, we are sure, have an outstanding second-class cruise.

First-Class Cruise: Junior Officer Cruise. Required prior to earning your commission, the first-class cruise typically occurs between the junior and senior academic years. During the first-class cruise, midshipmen interested in serving in a conventional warfare community (surface, submarine, or aviation) are integrated into the "wardrooms" (that is, here, the officers—chapter 14 goes deeper into this elastic term) of a ship, submarine, or squadron. Midshipmen, in concert with their running mates (junior officers, this time), will assume duties and responsibilities appropriate to junior officers. Midshipmen will be berthed in officer staterooms as available or, if necessary, in "Chief Petty Officers' Country" or separate enlisted berthing areas.

> "After sophomore year, I was attached to USS *Hartford* (SSN 768). I met the boat in Tromso, Norway, north of the Arctic Circle. Before we submerged, the midshipmen were told to climb to the sail. Watching the American flag snapping at the periscope mast in the Arctic wind was highly motivating. We were doing about 20 knots surfaced, with no surface contacts in sight, and I was reminded why I want to join the submarine force: operate forward, with little support, and accomplish missions vital to national security."
>
> —MIDSHIPMAN 1ST CLASS SCARLETT, University of California, Berkeley NROTC

A midshipman stands watch as the conning officer on the bridge of the amphibious assault ship USS *America* (LHA 6). *U.S. Navy photo by Kristina Young*

Otherwise, a first-class cruise on board a surface ship or submarine is similar to the second-class cruise, except from a junior officer's perspective. You will be integrated into a division, be assigned inport and underway watches, and see the roles and daily responsibilities of a junior officer. An effective midshipman training program on a ship or submarine will include a series of standardized qualification "standards" similar to those that junior officers work to complete. These both serve as checklists of places to see and things to do but also introduce midshipmen to the basics of formal qualifications (in watch stations, systems, etc.) that will be the framework within which they build their own professional foundations upon commissioning.

For those midshipmen interested in serving in naval aviation upon commissioning, the first-class cruise is an opportunity to be integrated into an operational fleet squadron. Midshipmen, prior to going on an aviation cruise, must complete flight physicals to ensure they are able to fly safely in naval aircraft. Once assigned to a squadron, they will be assigned junior officers as running mates, develop

NAVY BLUE CHIP PROGRAM

"Throughout my Naval career I have held that the most important determinant of an enjoyable and rewarding work experience is the one factor throughout the detailing process in which you have no input: whom you work with. When requesting the next assignment you can prioritize location, job type, and ship type. There is never any real consideration of who works there and how well they work together. The combination of midshipman summer cruise and the Blue Chip Program creates one of the very few opportunities to experience and pick a team. Midshipmen engage in life on a ship and participate in their unique team dynamic. Over that month-long cruise, strengths and weaknesses of the crew are exposed. A midshipman can explore how their skills would impact that team. One other interesting aspect is that academic class rank is not a clear indicator of professional success. ADM John S. McCain Jr. graduated from the United States Navy Academy at #424 out of 441. Even one of the namesakes of the ship I command, CAPT Henry Mustin, graduated one spot above the 'anchor.' Getting midshipmen into the fleet on cruises allows them to demonstrate their potential and be identified early. The NFL draft–style ship selection process for commissioning officers usually results in high demand locations or new ships filling their quota with only the highest academically ranked graduates. The Blue Chip Program enables commanding officers across all locations and ship types to recruit talent that would not otherwise have been sent to them because of an individual's ranking at graduation. When a commanding officer offers and a midshipman accepts a blue chip, the team wins."

—CDR Ryan Leary, USN, Commanding Officer, USS *Mustin* (DDG 89),
Pennsylvania State University NROTC Class of 2000

an understanding of a junior officer's nonflying duties, and be afforded as many opportunities as practicable to fly in the squadron's fleet aircraft or use its training simulators.

Last, midshipmen interested in serving in either the SEAL or EOD communities must complete a first-class cruise "screener" in order to be eligible for assignment to those services.

The first-class SEAL cruise, in Coronado, California, is an introduction to the physical strength and stamina, mental toughness, and leadership abilities required of a junior officer SEAL candidate at Basic Underwater Demolition/SEAL (BUD/S) training. This training is *not* a mini-BUD/S or "Hell Week" (as the final days of competition for acceptance into the SEAL community are known), but it does allow SEAL instructors to screen rising first-class midshipmen for the traits and abilities desired for SEAL trainees. Upon completion of the cruise, you will be invited—or not—to select "SEAL" as your top service-assignment preference. Making SEAL your first choice is just that: the service-assignment board makes the decision, and you must await the results of that board in the late fall.

Midshipmen interested in serving in the EOD community will be assigned to an operational EOD unit to observe the activities of junior EOD officers and participate in the unit's training and daily routine. Senior officers in your assigned EOD unit will assess your potential, and you will be notified of their determination on completion of your cruise, prior to service assignment.

Take advantage of the short time you will have afloat, with your squadron, or with SEAL or EOD officers to prepare yourself for the real responsibilities you will have immediately upon commissioning. You will be formally listing your service-assignment preferences as soon as you return to your NROTC unit in the fall: first-class cruise is the final training event before you do that. If, in earlier years, you are making up your mind between two potential career paths as your first preference, we recommend that you complete your first-class cruise on your second-choice option, as long as you did not do so during your second-class cruise too. Consider midshipmen trying to choose between surface warfare and submarines. Surface warfare is their first choice, but they spent their second-class (enlisted) cruise on board a guided-missile destroyer. A first-class cruise on a submarine would ensure they have adequate exposure to life submerged. You may have a long career ahead; you—and the fleet—will be best served by informed decisions about service-assignment preferences.

> "The 1st class SEAL cruise was quite a challenge. The experience really tested my limits, but I learned a lot about my strengths and weaknesses both mentally and physically."
>
> —MIDSHIPMAN 1ST CLASS BROOKS, University of Virginia NROTC

MARINE CORPS–OPTION MIDSHIPMEN

Now we will explore the summer cruise experiences for Marine-Option NROTC midshipmen. For their third-class cruise, they participate in CORTRAMID with their Navy-Option peers. After the first summer, however, their path diverges. Much of Marine Corps–specific training throughout NROTC is preparation for OCS, which all Marine Corps midshipmen must complete prior to commissioning as Marine officers.

For the junior-year cruise, Marine-Option midshipmen are assigned to an operational Marine expeditionary unit (MEU) embarked, or preparing to embark, on board a U.S. Navy amphibious ship. MEUs and the amphibious ships that carry them are forward-deployed forces ready to respond to national tasking or "contingency" operations (such as disaster relief). Once embarked, you will observe life afloat and the roles and responsibilities of Marine junior officers. If your MEU is

"I enjoyed my first class cruise best of all during my time in NROTC. I had the unique opportunity to complete my cruise aboard the nuclear powered aircraft carrier USS *Harry S. Truman* (CVN 75) while she was on a Middle Eastern deployment. I had had the opportunity to embark and get under way on naval vessels during prior cruises, but had yet to travel overseas. I left my home in South Carolina on a flight to Washington, D.C., where the other midshipmen and I assigned on the cruise quickly recognized each other. We flew from Washington to Kuwait City (about a 12-hour flight) where we caught a connecting flight to Bahrain. We spent one night in Bahrain before boarding a C-2 Carrier Onboard Delivery (COD) flight to the *Truman*. The experience of landing on a carrier under way was exhilarating!

"For the next three weeks I learned from my running mate, a junior officer assigned to the Reactor Controls Division. It was obvious that serving in the Reactor Department, which propelled and powered one of America's capital ships, required extraordinary effort and teamwork. It was an enlightening experience that I am grateful to have had.

"In addition to observing the propulsion plant, I had the opportunity to stand bridge watches and to observe real aircraft carrier flight operations. Our staterooms were directly underneath the flight deck, and as a carrier is an around-the-clock operation, the shock and noise of jets landing and taking off quickly became routine background noise.

"A port visit to Dubai capped off my wonderful experience during the cruise as my peers and I explored the desert metropolis. While not every cruise is guaranteed to be as action packed as mine, no matter where you are assigned, rest assured that opportunities to learn about the operational Navy will abound!"

—LIEUTENANT CORDIAL

deployed, you may have an opportunity to participate in training exercises ashore; in any case, you can develop an appreciation for the physical ability and leadership qualities required of a Marine junior officer.

In lieu of a first-class cruise, Marine-Option midshipmen attend Officer Candidate School in Quantico, Virginia. All NROTC Marine-Option midshipmen must successfully complete OCS in order to be eligible to be commissioned after earning their undergraduate degrees. OCS is a demanding ten-week course designed to ensure that prospective Marine junior officers have the requisite leadership potential, physical capability, and character to lead Marines in battle. Make no mistake, OCS is a challenging training period, and attrition from the course is expected. Successful candidates have trained continuously during their time in NROTC, particularly in mental toughness and decision making under stress.

NURSE CORPS–OPTION MIDSHIPMEN

Nurse-Option midshipmen have their own summer cruise sequence in preparation for their service in the Navy Nurse Corps. Nurse-Option midshipmen will not attend CORTRAMID after their freshman year. Instead, they will be assigned to the medical department of an aircraft carrier or amphibious assault ship, either as a third- or second-class cruise. This affords Nurse-Option midshipmen the opportunity to experience a deployed medical or surgical team. For their first-class cruises, Nurse-Option midshipmen will be assigned to a naval medical facility to gain experience in a hospital environment and for professional preparation prior to commissioning in the Navy Nurse Corps.

Conclusion

In this chapter, we have detailed by year the summer cruise experiences that can be expected in NROTC's Navy Option, Marine Option, and Nurse Option. Summer cruise is one of the best aspects of commissioning through the NROTC program. Peers who commission directly through Navy or Marine OCS will not have the opportunity for formal training with operational units prior to listing their preferences for service assignment. Participate fully and enthusiastically wherever you are assigned during your summer cruises. Doing so will best prepare you for commissioning and also enable you to make an informed decision regarding the community in which you wish to serve.

14 Summer Cruise

FOR MOST COLLEGE UNDERGRADUATES, summer breaks present an opportunity to secure internships or paid junior positions at companies they may be interested in working for on graduation. Civilian students, even if they succeed, may find the experience stressful and ultimately not relevant to their careers. NROTC students will have their own internship-like experiences during summer cruise. These summer training periods are designed, as you saw in the last chapter, to give NROTC students exposure to the practical side of their naval science curricula and some experience with operational fleet forces. In this chapter, having laid out the purposes structure of the summer NROTC program, we will go deeper, with general advice to ensure a successful summer cruise and to avoid some common mistakes.

The Importance of Summer Cruises

BEFORE LEAVING SCHOOL FOR SUMMER CRUISE

Your NROTC unit's summer cruise coordinator will brief the battalion during the spring semester on all aspects of summer cruises and will also provide a checklist of items you must bring in your seabag. In addition, Naval Service Training Command N9 maintains an online *Midshipmen Summer Training Manual* with up-to-date information concerning the administration and conduct of NROTC midshipmen summer training (https://www.public.navy.mil/netc/nstc/NSTC_Directives/NSTC_Manuals/NSTC%20M-1533.5D%20-%20Midshipman%20Summer%20Training%20Manual%20(Feb%2019).pdf).

Before leaving your NROTC unit for the summer, be sure that you understand what administrative documents are required and that you have them. It depends on

A midshipman fires a .50-caliber machine gun during a weapons exercise on board the guided-missile cruiser USS *Monterey* (CG 61). *U.S. Navy photo by Nathan T. Beard*

"As an NROTC midshipman, I have been given the opportunity to have some amazing experiences over my summer cruises and do things that very few people ever get the chance to do."

—MIDSHIPMAN 2ND CLASS THOLEN,
University of Notre Dame NROTC

your cruise date, but you will probably travel to where your summer cruise begins from your home of record. Work with your summer cruise coordinator to make sure that such details as preferred airport are worked out before tickets are booked. You should have several print copies of your orders—the official (and critically important) document placing you on active duty and authorizing you to proceed to a ship or station. All transportation expenses should be paid up front by the government, but you should have physically with you the travel claim forms by which you will claim reimbursement for other legitimate travel costs. You should save receipts associated with your travel; you will need them to complete the required paperwork once your summer cruise is over.

General Advice for Afloat Summer Cruises

Whether you are embarking on board a ship or submarine or joining a training or operational aviation squadron, make the most out of your summer cruise. Your non-NROTC peers are unlikely to have such opportunities—to conn sophisticated warships, dive nuclear submarines, or take the controls of a fighter jet—so take advantage of them. Toward that end, however, you must do your best to fit into the ship or unit you join and comply with its standards and culture.

The rank of "midshipman" is well defined officially and administratively, but culturally, "on the deck plates," it is somewhat ambiguous. As an officer in training, you do not merit the customs and courtesies of those holding commissions, but neither are you a Sailor. In a setting where one's professional identity and social status are so heavily influenced by rank and position, you may find it awkward to situate yourself. Based on our experience of having been midshipmen, of training midshipmen, and of embarking midshipmen on our ships for summer cruises, we recommend the following general guidelines.

First, be humble. By far the least attractive quality in a midshipman would be self-importance, a "vibe" of indifference. When you get to the fleet as a new ensign, the only thing your Sailors will care about is how effective a leader you are, not that you went to an Ivy League school, that you were on the varsity baseball team, or that you won a prestigious academic grant for undergraduate research. Now, as a midshipman on cruise, your responsibility is to learn as much as you can about the operational Navy so that you can make an informed choice of community in which you would like to serve.

Second, demonstrate interest and ask questions. Particularly on your second-class, or "enlisted," cruise (as you recall from the last chapter), displaying a sincere desire to learn about your enlisted running mate's job will do wonders. Nearly all Sailors are proud of, even passionate about, the roles they play in making their ships work and enjoy "showing off" their talents and skills, as well as their spaces, equipment, and systems. You'll find the same during CORTRAMID and your first-class cruises as well.

When interacting with enlisted personnel, be professional, courteous, and cordial—but not excessively friendly. When greeting a Sailor, offer your hand and introduce yourself: "Good afternoon, Petty Officer Smith, I'm Midshipman Cordial. Do you mind if I spend some time with you to learn about this watch station?" You will be closest in age to the junior Sailors, so you may find them easiest to converse with, but you must maintain an appropriate professionalism in your interactions.

Next, for those on board ship and out of ideas on where to visit, we recommend spending time with either the sounding and security watch or the lookouts. The sounding and security watch is typically a junior fireman (a "nonrated"—i.e., not yet a petty officer—engineer) who is responsible for constantly touring all of the ship's engineering spaces and reporting any abnormalities to the engineering officer on watch. You will increase your spatial awareness of the ship and also visit some of the harder-to-reach places not typically on tour routes. Depending on the class of ship, at least one lookout (often more)—with no other duties while on station—is maintained around the clock whenever a ship is under way. This Sailor is responsible for vigilantly scanning the horizon and notifying the officer of the deck (OOD) when warships, other vessels, or anything else that might be significant comes in sight. In remote waters, this critical watch, typically stood by a junior seaman (a nonrated Sailor in training for—to oversimplify—something other than an engineering rating) can become rather lonely. You are sure to get an unvarnished account of the quality of life of seamen on board that ship and a perspective on the experiences of the junior Sailors you will one day lead.

Be sure to not spend all your time in your "rack" (bunk) or the wardroom (here, the officers' mess). Even in ships with effective midshipmen training programs, there will inevitably be downtime, when you are not on a tour, observing an evolution, or standing a watch. Many of your peers will retreat to the comfort of their "staterooms" (in which all officers live except the commanding officer, who has a "cabin," sometimes two) or congregate on the mess decks (the crew's mess) or wardroom to socialize. We encourage you instead to take these opportunities to visit parts of the ship you have not seen before. Sailors are standing watch all about the ship around the clock and might enjoy an opportunity to share their experiences, when permitted (not in the pilothouse, for instance).

You can see, given the importance of striking up conversations with watchstanders, that there will be a dangerous temptation to fraternize with Sailors during your summer cruise. In general, a good rule of thumb is that social interactions with enlisted personnel outside of official settings are unprofessional. For example, the wardroom and chiefs' mess may compete in a friendly putt-putt golf tournament as a way of improving morale and working relationships. Such an event is entirely appropriate for midshipmen. However, if one of the chiefs invites you to the "after party" where you would be the only midshipman present, it would be prudent to decline, graciously. The safest bet for off-ship socialization is to stick with your midshipmen peers or the division officers. During port visits, by all means take advantage of the unique opportunities that summer cruise offers to

A midshipman prepares to take off for an orientation flight during summer cruise.
U.S. Navy photo by Nathan T. Beard

explore new cities, but remember that you are on cruise primarily for professional reasons. Do not squander your future with a single night or bad decision.

The Wardroom

Before going further, be aware that this section most directly applies to surface ships and submarines, though similar principles apply to spaces distinctly associated with officers in an aviation squadron or Marine battalion. Midshipmen on cruise are there to learn about future career options and to develop professionally—not to socialize unduly during working hours or disturb officers in what may be their only refuge in your command.

That said, the wardroom means both the physical location on the ship or submarine where officers eat their meals, conduct meetings, and socialize and is also a collective term for the group of officers themselves. (For an aviation squadron afloat, the "ready room," where preflight briefings and routine meetings are held, is the site of off-duty-hours socializing and relaxation. Standards for ready room conduct are similar to, but maybe more relaxed than, those of a wardroom.) You may hear something akin to, "The wardroom on USS *Awesome* is outstanding!" Typically this means that the ship's officers are excellent, not that the physical space is somehow remarkable. As a future junior officer, you will one day be a member of your ship's wardroom or squadron ready room; part of the value in summer cruise training is that it can ease your eventual incorporation into that aspect of your new environment. However, you aren't a member of the wardroom yet—it is not simply an afloat equivalent of your dorm's social areas. The wardroom is a setting probably unique to warships, sometimes with its own formal organization and duties, and with seemingly arcane traditions and its own ideals of acceptable social behavior. Midshipmen are well advised not to offend.

To establish a proper mindset, recognize that the wardroom is a space set aside in which officers eat, relax, and socialize while afloat; the rest of the crew enter only on business. Typically, only the captain and executive officer are assigned their own living quarters, so privacy is a scarce commodity on board ship. As stateroom mates may be on different watch rotations and thus sleeping at different times, officers wishing to read, converse, or simply take a brief break will use the wardroom instead. Accordingly, treat the wardroom with respect and remember that you are a visitor. While the ship's officers should make every effort to be friendly and forthcoming, the reality is that many of them—on demanding watch schedules, involved in exercise or real-world operations, etc.—may not have a lot of extra time to chat with you. Recognizing, then, the special status of the wardroom, here are some simple tips.

First, understand the ship's policy concerning midshipmen's access to the wardroom. As a rule, it is prudent to knock and ask for permission unless told not to. Midshipmen on their first-class cruises are generally afforded open access to the wardroom, as they are being purposefully incorporated into the wardroom for training purposes. However, midshipmen on their second-class ("enlisted") or CORTRAMID summers should not assume permission to enter the wardroom but should knock and ask first. If the wardroom is unoccupied, simply enter.

Second, as a rule, do not enter the wardroom unless you are in uniform. It is inappropriate to enter the wardroom in PT gear. Always remove your cover upon entering the wardroom, and never put it on a table. There should be hooks outside the entrance to the wardroom where you can place your cover. However, be wary of hooks designated for certain officers, such as the CO, XO, and department heads. If there are no hooks available, simply hold your cover in your hands or place it in your lap.

Third, maintain an appropriate sense of decorum and professionalism. The wardroom is not a library or study lounge, but boisterous conversation, horseplay, or overly loud music or movies are all out of place. The wardroom is absolutely not the midshipmen "hang-out spot," and nothing will rankle the collective wardroom against a group of midshipmen more than chronically seeing them in the wardroom when they should be "out and about" the ship, submarine, or squadron, seeking to learn more about their profession.

Fourth, wardroom meals are formal events and should be treated as such. Arrive a few minutes before the scheduled time, and do not sit until the senior officer invites everyone to do so. (If your duties, such as standing watch, oblige you to be late to the meal, you must ask permission from the senior officer prior to taking your seat.) Be aware that seats will be reserved for the CO, XO, and possibly department heads, so politely ask a junior officer to make sure you do not sit in one. On the other hand, the CO or XO may desire that midshipmen seating be rotated, to put them close to a series of more senior officers.

Centuries of naval experience dictate that junior members of the wardroom should listen more than they speak. The senior officers present should recognize their responsibility to generate pleasant conversation; feel free to add to the gaiety as appropriate but not to pester seniors with questions. If you are unfamiliar with your neighbors at table, be sure to introduce yourself. To break the ice, you might ask your neighbors about their "billets" (assigned duties) on the ship, where they are from, etc.

Next, conversations on potentially controversial topics, such as politics, religion, or romantic affairs, are out of place in the wardroom. This is generally well understood among serving officers, but if a senior officer broaches such a subject you should seek to change it or, if they persist, simply respond, "I'm sorry, sir. My lieutenant back at the NROTC unit told me that I was not to discuss politics in the wardroom. Is this true?" This should serve to remind offending officers of their error; if they persist, politely excuse yourself and let your midshipman training officer (the ship's officer in charge of the midshipmen) know of the issue.

If visiting the wardroom between meals, clean up after yourself. Do not leave empty coffee cups or snack wrappers on the table for someone else to tidy up. During meals, food service attendants (FSAs) typically perform such duties for the wardroom, but observe the actions of others to ensure you follow local etiquette. Be sure to treat all FSAs with appropriate consideration and respect.

When you are done eating, do not linger, as wardrooms often are unable to seat all the officers. You are by no means required to rush your meals, but when you are finished, simply ask the senior remaining officer to be excused—for example, "Excuse me, sir/ma'am (or) OPS/CHENG" (as the operations officer and engineer officer, the "chief engineer," may, respectively, want to be addressed).

Unless you are eating, always rise when the captain (or commodore or a flag officer, if your ship is a flagship) enters the wardroom. While not required, it is good form to rise when any senior officer enters as well.

Foreign Exchange (FOREX) Cruises

The U.S. Navy partners with allied and partner navies in midshipman foreign-exchange cruises for first-class midshipmen and equivalents. These cruises provide opportunities for intercultural social and professional experiences, enhance professional relationships with partner navies, and broaden the international understanding of the U.S. Navy's officer corps. Foreign exchange cruises are available only to scholarship Navy-Option midshipmen.

> "I had the incredible opportunity to complete my second-class cruise in South Korea on a Foreign Exchange (FOREX) this past summer. Working with the Korean Navy and Korean midshipmen was an experience that I believe was a once-in-a-lifetime opportunity."
>
> —MIDSHIPMAN 1ST CLASS RASAY,
> Prairie View A&M University NROTC

A Sailor on board the coastal patrol ship USS *Monsoon* (PC 4) fires an M4 assault rifle as part of a demonstration for a group of NROTC midshipmen. *U.S. Navy photo by Daniel N. Woods*

Approximately fifty to seventy midshipmen and junior officer exchanges can be expected each year, mainly with North Atlantic Treaty Organization (NATO) allies. Foreign-exchange cruise availability will be promulgated to the NROTC units during the preceding fall semester, and a competitive selection process will ensue. Be sure to let your class advisor know if you are interested in a foreign-exchange cruise opportunity. There may be administrative requirements to complete prior to being granted a quota.

Additional Tips

There are some further practical matters to consider. First, as mentioned before, make sure you understand fully the transportation plan to your summer cruise duty station. Your NROTC unit summer cruise coordinator will schedule appropriate transportation to and from your cruise destination. If you are meeting a ship or squadron within the continental United States, this is typically straightforward. If, however, you are meeting your ship or squadron overseas, you may have a considerable journey ahead of you. Be sure to have points of contact, phone numbers, and e-mail addresses of people and activities that could help you during each stage of your travel. If there are issues on the way, keep your unit's summer cruise coordinator aware. Rest assured that the government will reimburse you for any additional legitimate travel expenses incurred due to canceled flights, additional lodging, etc.

Be sure you report to summer cruise with a "full seabag"—that is, everything on the packing list provided by your unit's summer cruise coordinator. Do not assume that you will not need certain uniforms, covers, ribbons, etc. While you should seek to pack efficiently, the required list is just the required *minimum*, and failure to

"Do not be like I was. Probably due to my absent-mindedness, I failed to ensure I had a solid transportation plan to my CORTRAMID summer cruise after my freshman year. Being from South Carolina, I was slated to complete CORTRAMID in Norfolk, Va. I recalled my NROTC Unit Summer Cruise Coordinator telling us that we would receive an airplane ticket via e-mail, but as my cruise departure date came closer, I still had not received one. I called my midshipman chain of command who counseled that the ticket would come on time and that I need not 'disturb' our lieutenant. The day before I was due to report, in a panic and wary of calling the lieutenant, I instead secured my own train ticket from the train station in Savannah, Ga., to Norfolk, Va. The overnight trip involved two train transfers, a bus ride, and a taxi cab to the Naval Station. Upon arriving, I was notified that I had missed my scheduled flight and that my lieutenant had been trying to get in contact with me. Lesson learned that I should have contacted my NROTC Unit Summer Cruise Coordinator as soon as I felt uneasy about my travel plans!"

—LIEUTENANT CORDIAL

"Long before the days of the smart phone, I, along with eleven other midshipmen, landed on the Spanish island of Palma de Mallorca to meet up with our assigned ship for summer cruise. One hitch: the ship was not there and neither was anyone there to greet us. One more wrinkle: out of the dozen of us, only two of us spoke any Spanish (and I was one of them—so that wasn't saying much). After realizing we were on our own, we made a few 'executive decisions,' split up into a few cabs, and all headed to the hotel where we would stay until the ship arrived or we received further directions.

"Palma de Mallorca was one of the top European party destinations at the time, so what could go wrong with a dozen twenty-year-old college students showing up with no responsibilities whatsoever? To make a couple of long stories short, we found out there were several ways to entertainingly pass the time in such an exotic locale. We spent three days exploring this island before the ship arrived. We stayed in port for a few more days before pulling out to head to our next of several tropical Mediterranean destinations: Sainte-Maxime, France (on the French Riviera).

"The best part about summer cruise is that no matter where you go, you will meet fellow midshipmen from around the country, trade college/NROTC stories, and then make new ones together during one of the best 'internship' experiences in the world."

—COMMANDER MURPHY

bring necessary items will put you out of pocket to purchase them or leave you sticking out like a sore thumb while your peers are in the proper uniform.

Have sufficient funds with you to cover basic costs associated with travel, food, and lodging. In order to avoid the embarrassment of being unable to do so, inquire with your unit's summer cruise coordinator about an advance on your summer pay. The Navy and Marine Corps offer an 80 percent advance on the total estimated cost of this "temporary additional duty" assignment. However, squandering your travel funds on a fun night out could place you in an even more embarrassing situation. Further, if your cruise proves to be shorter than initially estimated, you will have to refund to the government the difference. Do not, therefore, let the large initial deposit lull you into excessive spending. It is a good idea to budget a set amount with which to enjoy your summer cruise experience, but if you are able, wait until your summer cruise is over and payments and claims are "reconciled" before spending your actual summer cruise pay.

Conclusion

Summer cruise is an incredibly rewarding experience and a highlight for many NROTC midshipmen. In this chapter we provided some general advice on how to make your cruise successful. These valuable training periods may well be your only exposure as a midshipman to operational fleet units—take advantage of this chance to learn and explore before committing yourself to a preference for service assignment. You may find that a community may spark an interest you had not been aware of.

In the following chapter we will explore in more depth the Navy warfighting communities open to Navy-Option midshipmen for assignment.

15 Navy Warfighting Communities

BEFORE DISCUSSING IN DETAIL the service-assignment process from an administrative perspective, this chapter will explore the key aspects of each of the warfighting communities open to you as a Navy-Option NROTC midshipman. Marine Corps–Option midshipmen are assigned a Military Occupational Specialty based on their performance during The Basic School after they commission as second lieutenants. This process will not be covered here, and we again recommend *The Marine Officer's Guide* for a comprehensive look at that process.

As mentioned in previous chapters, only the first-class cruise is a mandatory requirement for earning your commission, and only scholarship midshipmen are afforded opportunities to attend summer cruises the previous years. Thus, some midshipmen about to be commissioned will not have had the benefit of summer cruise experiences as a factor in deciding between communities. This chapter will introduce these communities as a starting point for further study. We encourage you to engage with your NROTC unit staff members for additional information concerning their respective specialties to help you make informed decisions regarding your own service-assignment preferences.

Surface Warfare Officer

A Surface Warfare Officer (SWO, by the way, is pronounced phonetically, like "Swoh," not letter by letter) serves primarily on board surface combatants and amphibious ships when assigned to sea duty. Officers commissioned into the SWO community are designated as SWO trainees and select their first ships by name and location during the NROTC ship-selection process, discussed further in the service-assignment chapter. SWOs serve on board all major naval surface

NAVAL ASTRONAUT

NAVAL AVIATOR

NAVAL AVIATION OBSERVER AND
FLIGHT METEOROLOGIST

NAVAL ASTRONAUT (NFO)

NAVAL FLIGHT OFFICER

NAVAL FLIGHT SURGEON
NAVAL FLIGHT NURSE
(Gold, Without Acorn)

AVIATION WARFARE SPECIALIST

NAVAL AVIATION EXPERIMENTAL
PSYCHOLOGIST
NAVAL AVIATION PHYSIOLOGIST

NAVAL AVIATION SUPPLY

SURFACE WARFARE OFFICER

SURFACE SUPPLY CORPS

AIRCREW

SUBMARINE

SUBMARINE MEDICAL

SUBMARINE COMBAT PATROL

INTEGRATED UNDERSEA
SURVEILLANCE SYSTEM
ENLISTED (Silver)

SUBMARINE SUPPLY

SUBMARINE ENGINEER DUTY

SSBN DETERRENT PATROL

COMMAND AT SEA

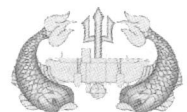

DEEP SUBMERGENCE (Gold)
ENLISTED (Silver)

SPECIAL OPERATIONS

SPECIAL WARFARE [SEAL] (UDT)

SMALL CRAFT

CRAFTMASTER

PARACHUTIST

BASIC PARACHUTIST

DIVING OFFICER (Gold)
MASTER DIVER (Silver)
DIVING MEDICAL
(Gold with Caduceus)
DIVING MEDICAL TECHNICIAN
(Silver with Caduceus)

COMMAND ASHORE
PROJECT MANAGER

EXPLOSIVE ORDNANCE DISPOSAL
SENIOR EOD (Star on bomb)
MASTER EOD (Additional star within
laurel wreath affixed to top of shield)

Some examples of warfare and qualification insignia.

vessels and combatants, including guided-missile destroyers, guided-missile cruisers, amphibious assault ships, amphibious landing docks, amphibious transport docks, patrol craft, minesweepers, and littoral combat ships. The pinnacle of the SWO career path is to serve as commanding officer of a U.S. Navy warship.

SWOs are either "conventional" or "nuclear" officers. Initial at-sea assignment, during which they earn warfare qualification, is identical for both conventional and nuclear officers, but after that "SWO nukes" will attend Nuclear Power and Propulsion training in Charleston, South Carolina, before serving a tour as a member of the nuclear engineering department of a nuclear-powered aircraft carrier.

Surface homeports include Norfolk, Virginia; Mayport, Florida; San Diego, California; Everett, Washington; Pearl Harbor, Hawaii; Yokosuka, Japan; Sasebo, Japan; and Rota, Spain. As you would suspect, these are all cities located on the water, and most are near major metropolitan areas, with all the benefits therein (major airports, vibrant nightlife, good civilian/military mix, etc.). Prior to reporting on board, SWOs will attend initial SWO training, the Basic Division Officer Course (BDOC), and specialty schools to prepare them for their first jobs. If getting to the fleet quickly is a priority for you, then service assignment as a SWO may be an excellent option.

The guided-missile destroyer USS *Milius* (DDG 69) at sea.
U.S. Navy photo by Kenneth Abbate

As you will see during your midshipmen cruises, SWO junior officers perform a variety of operational, administrative, and leadership tasks on board ship. Each SWO will be assigned a division of Sailors to lead. Examples of division officer billets (this list is not all-inclusive) are gunnery officer, main propulsion assistant, antisubmarine officer, and first lieutenant. Division officer assignment puts your leadership skills to the test and is a critical part of your development as an officer. In addition to mastery of your divisional responsibilities, a primary professional goal of the first tour is qualification as a Surface Warfare Officer. This requires that you, as a junior officer, demonstrate your ability to lead a bridge watch under way effectively and operate the ship safely day-to-day at sea, as well as your understanding of how the ship's mission is executed through the employment of its sensors and weapons.

Midshipmen whose service assignment is SWO will incur five-year active-duty obligations in repayment for their scholarships. This equates to approximately two division officer tours. Assuming satisfactory performance during these first two sea tours, SWOs will have at that point the opportunity to choose whether to continue their naval careers or leave the naval service.

A guided-missile cruiser and destroyer steaming in company.
U.S. Navy photo by Michael Russell

"I was commissioned in December 2001, after finishing Naval Reserve Officer Training Corps at San Diego State University. My NROTC Commanding Officer, CAPT Mike Simpson, was an experienced Surface Warfare Officer and infectious leader. I vividly remember him discussing life as a destroyerman and his leadership challenges and opportunities as a young Ensign and I thought 'I want that—I want to be a part of that.' Within six months, by the summer of 2002, I was a division officer in charge of over twenty Sailors on a destroyer on deployment to Asia and the Middle East.

"Life on a destroyer starts out hard, nearly chaotic. I was standing eight hours of deck watches per day. We were doing boarding operations with Naval Special Warfare personnel at night in support of United Nations sanctions. During each watch we would launch and recover helicopters and small boats, maneuvering the ship in tight quarters for winds and seas, while close to fishing boats and oil platforms. We were hailing and querying foreign ships and interacting with foreign navies in an attempt to build a pattern of life in the North Arabian Gulf prior to the start of Operation Iraqi Freedom. I was also learning to manage a division of Sailors and becoming deeply involved in their needs, wants, hopes, dreams, personal lives, and their futures. After months in the steamy North Arabian Gulf, training on the job, I began to put it all together, bringing order to the seemingly endless chaos that is your first year as an officer at sea. The cool operations and technology on the ship are what brought me to be a destroyer Sailor; the relationships I built with my fellow officers and my Sailors are what has kept me coming back.

"A little over a year after commissioning I was a fully qualified SWO who had done a deployment. I had managed the ship in stressful situations, challenging and growing every sensor and facility that I had. I had led Sailors in the most difficult environments at sea and I was proud of my accomplishments. I had driven the ship in and out of ports, alongside oilers, and into anchorages. And I had learned that the trust and faith enlisted Sailors put into us, their division officers, was special. I love being a SWO because I got a chance to lead from day one under tough conditions. I believe that leading Sailors at sea is now what it was for me in 2002 and the same as it was for CAPT Mike Simpson in the 1970s, an absolute blessing. If you are looking for a unique challenge, an opportunity to drive and operate a ship, and to lead Sailors from day one after commissioning, there is no better career than to be a Surface Warfare Officer."

—CDR LEO LEOS, USN,
Commanding Officer, USS *Stockdale* (DDG 106),
University of San Diego NROTC Class of 2001

Submarine Warfare

Midshipmen who meet the high academic and physical requirements involved may be assigned to the Undersea Warfare community—the submarine service—on board the Navy's nuclear-powered attack or guided- or ballistic-missile submarines. Midshipmen assigned to serve as submarine officers will report directly to the Navy Nuclear Power Training Command near Charleston for approximately six months of intense classroom education on the theory and fundamentals of Navy nuclear power. Immediately afterward comes another six-month period, this time practical training in a "prototype," managing a watch team and overseeing the operation of an actual nuclear reactor at a Navy Nuclear Power Training Unit (NPTU) near either Charleston or Ballston Spa, New York.

Initial nuclear-power training is extremely demanding and requires extensive preparation and study. With effective study habits and consistent effort, officers assigned submarine duty should, however, be able to complete it. Officers are then assigned to their first "boats" (as submarines are traditionally called) to begin the process of formally qualifying as Submarine Warfare Officers; when so designated they are awarded their "Dolphins," insignia marking them as submarine officers. At the same time, each will be assigned a division of Sailors to lead, which, as in the surface force, tests leadership skills and contributes vitally to development as an officer.

The U.S. Navy's submarine force is broadly broken into two categories, "fast attack" and "strategic missile" submarines. Nuclear-powered fast attack submarines, known as SSNs, are of the *Los Angeles, Seawolf,* and *Virginia* classes. Fast attack submarines perform a variety of missions, including antisubmarine warfare, antisurface warfare, intelligence collection, surveillance, target acquisition, and reconnaissance. Fast attack submarines are homeported in a variety of locations throughout the world, including Norfolk, Groton (Connecticut), San Diego, Bremerton (Washington), Pearl Harbor (Hawaii), and Apra Harbor (Guam).

Strategic missile submarines, SSBNs, are today all units of the USS *Ohio* class. SSBNs, or "boomers," are armed with multiple Trident nuclear ballistic missiles and are primarily tasked with strategic deterrence. As such, they constitute

A Royal Thai Navy helicopter hovers over the *Los Angeles*–class attack submarine USS *Louisville* (SSN 724) during Guardian Sea 2019, a United States / Thailand exercise. *U.S. Navy photo by Matt Zeismer.*

the most survivable (in wartime) "leg" of the "nuclear triad" of the United States (the other two belong to the U.S. Air Force). Four SSBNs have been converted to guided-missile submarines (SSGNs), having traded their nuclear ballistic missiles for a large magazine of conventional-warhead Tomahawk land-attack missiles. SSGNs perform as high-capacity, stealthy, conventional strike "platforms" in support of attacks on targets ashore. SSBNs and SSGNs are homeported in either Kings Bay, Georgia, or Bangor, Washington.

Midshipmen "service assigned" to submarine warfare are obligated to serve five years, corresponding to initial nuclear-power training and a single three-year division officer tour afloat. Officers who are selected for and complete nuclear-power training are offered competitive financial incentives to continue their service in the nuclear navy.

Naval Aviation

Many young people enter the Navy hoping to fly high above the seas rather than serve on or under them. Naval aviation is a challenging, exciting warfighting community that offers a variety of platforms, mission types, and experiences operating

The *Ohio*-class ballistic-missile submarine USS *Rhode Island* (SSBN 740) Gold crew returns to homeport at Naval Submarine Base Kings Bay, Georgia. *U.S. Navy photo by Brian Tomforde*

advanced aircraft based afloat or ashore. Naval aviation comprises aviators (pilots) and Naval Flight Officers. Pilots are primarily trained to fly naval aircraft, Naval Flight Officers to operate an aircraft's sensor or weapon systems. Initial training is similar for Navy pilot- and NFO-assigned midshipmen.

Initial flight training, known as Primary Flight Training, for all naval aviators is conducted in Pensacola, Florida. Upon completion of Primary Flight Training, prospective naval aviators are assigned to one of several training "pipelines" before beginning the intermediate phase of flight training. It is at this point in your career that you will begin to prepare specifically for the kind of aircraft you will fly: jets, helicopters, maritime patrol, and others. Assignment of student aviators to specific platform types will be based on their performance in initial flight training, their preferences, and the "needs of the Navy" (that is, fleet demand for new aviators). NFOs too will shift to platform-specific training curricula.

Prospective naval aviators, after completing the intermediate phase of flight training in their respective pipelines, then progress to advanced flight training focused on missions associated with their assigned aircraft—such as electronic attack, for a prospective EA-18G Growler pilot. Upon completion of the advanced phase of

Two F-35C Lightning II aircraft from Strike Fighter Squadron (VFA) 125 "Rough Raiders" in formation over the Sierra Nevada range.
U.S. Navy photo by Amber Smalley

aviation training, students are awarded the coveted "Wings of Gold" (of slightly differing designs) officially marking them as either Navy pilots or Naval Flight Officers. Naval aviators will then report to their aircraft's fleet replacement squadron (FRS) for additional aircraft-specific training prior to reporting to their first operational squadron. This last stage is a lengthy one; it may take up to two full years to complete the rigorous training curriculum before finally beginning your first operational tour.

Broadly, naval aircraft are either "fixed-wing" or "rotary-wing." Fixed-wing aircraft include fighter/attack jets, electronic attack jets, maritime patrol aircraft, and surveillance and fighter-direction aircraft. Rotary-wing aircraft include the multimission SH-60 helicopter "family," the heavy-lift CH-53 helicopter, and the multimission MV-22 tiltrotor aircraft. SH-60 and MV-22 aviators will be assigned to squadrons that deploy on combatants; the Navy CH-53 is land-based. Aviators tend to remain in their platform types for their entire careers, although opportunities may exist to change, especially as aging types of aircraft retire and new ones enter the fleet. An example is the transition the Navy is now completing from the P-3 maritime patrol aircraft to the newer P-8 Poseidon.

Sailor signals to an SH-60S Sea Hawk helicopter assigned to the "Island Knights" of Helicopter Sea Combat Squadron (HSC) 25 as it takes off from the flight deck of the amphibious transport dock USS *Green Bay* (LPD 20). *U.S. Navy photo by Anaid Banuelos Rodriguez*

The Navy fields a variety of aircraft, based afloat and ashore. Examples not mentioned previously are the F/A-18A/B/C/D Hornet fighter/attack jet, the F/A-18E/F Super Hornet fighter/attack jet, the E-2 Hawkeye early-warning and surveillance aircraft, the V-22 carrier-onboard-delivery aircraft, and the EP-3 Aries surveillance and reconnaissance aircraft. No matter the platform assigned, you will have the opportunity to rise in rank and position, to serve successively as a division officer, department head, executive officer, squadron commander, and air wing commander. By law, commanding officers of our Navy's capital ships, its nuclear-powered aircraft carriers, are always naval aviators.

Due to the costly nature of flight training, midshipmen assigned as naval aviators incur eight-year commitments, counting from the completion of qualification and designation as naval aviators, whereas Naval Flight Officers are obliged to serve six years, also from initial qualification and designation. Additional financial incentives are available to qualified naval aviators serving at sea and in operational flying status.

Naval Special Warfare

Naval Special Warfare Officers serve in a variety of demanding operational environments in hotspots throughout the world. Each year, a few highly motivated and physically qualified midshipmen will be assigned as prospective Special Warfare

A P-8 Poseidon flies alongside the French Marine Nationale anti-air destroyer FS *Jean Bart* (D 615) while transiting the Strait of Gibraltar. *U.S. Navy photo by Connor D. Loessin*

"When I was in NROTC it seemed most of my class wanted to go naval aviation. In a class of 30 midshipmen only 4 were selected. When I arrived in Pensacola the auditorium was filled to capacity with prospective student naval aviators. Over the next two years the numbers would continually decrease. By the time I got my wings in 2013, I had been through many obstacles. The tests, evaluations, and check flights seemed constant, and continue to this day. The standard of Naval Aviation is high, but the reward at the end is hardly matched by any other service in the Navy. Every day you get do something most Americans wish they could do.

"The skills you learn in ROTC build a strong foundation for your entire Naval career. Naval Aviation teaches you invaluable skills that will make you a better leader and officer. Aviation constantly challenges you to upgrade yourself and be better. This aspect is challenging and it forces a lot of people to give up. However, it's this ethos that makes Naval Aviation one of the strongest air powers in the world."

—LT MATTHEW ZAK, USN,
University of Notre Dame NROTC Class of 2011

Officers and afforded an opportunity to attend Basic Underwater Demolition/ SEAL training in Coronado. After successfully completing BUD/S, prospective SEAL officers go through a nine-month period of training before earning their "Tridents," the warfare device, or insignia, for Special Warfare Officers.

SEAL officers are assigned to any of the small number of SEAL teams, located either in Coronado or at Little Creek, Virginia. Junior officers are assigned to a SEAL platoon and help lead its training, planning, and operations. Midshipmen interested in Naval Special Warfare must perform well academically, physically, and, as noted in earlier chapters, complete a competitive screener in their first-class summer to be eligible. Be aware that there is a high attrition rate in SEAL training—by design. If you don't complete SEAL training, you will be assigned to another warfare community. Prospective candidates must speak with their class advisors as soon as possible to make sure that all special administrative and medical screening requirements are accomplished in time for their service-assignment boards.

Special Warfare Officers incur six-year commitments after initial qualification and designation. As in certain other communities, financial incentives exist to retain the special skills and talents of SEAL officers.

Explosive Ordnance Disposal

Midshipmen may also be designated as Explosive Ordnance Disposal officers. Navy EOD officers serve in a variety of environments but are primarily trained to render safe all types of ordnance, including conventional, nuclear, and improvised explosive devices. Navy EOD officers are specially trained in such operations under or near water and support Navy and joint commands throughout the world.

First Phase Basic Underwater Demolition/SEALs (BUD/S) candidates use teamwork to perform physical training exercises with a 600-pound log at Naval Amphibious Base Coronado, California. *U.S. Navy photo by Shauntae Hinkle-Lymas*

A member of Naval Special Warfare Group 2 conducts dive operations in the Gulf of Mexico. *U.S. Navy photo by Jayme Pastoric*

Initial Navy EOD training is conducted at Panama City, Florida, at the Navy Diving and Salvage Training Center. Follow-on training consists of eleven months at the Explosive Ordnance Disposal Basic School at Eglin Air Force Base in Eglin, Florida. Additional tactical schools to develop such military skills as shooting, rappelling, fast-roping, land navigation, and helicopter "insertion" and "extraction" are located in San Diego and at Fort Benning, Georgia. Candidates who complete the rigorous training pipeline will be officially designated as Explosive Ordnance Disposal Officers and assigned to EOD mobile units, with homeports in Coronado, Point Loma (California), Apra Harbor, Imperial Beach (California), Little Creek, and Rota.

Midshipmen assigned to become EOD officers obligate themselves to serve four years from their graduation dates from EOD school. "Special pays" (that is, allowances in addition to "basic pay") are offered to EOD-qualified officers performing explosive ordnance disposal.

Technicians assigned to Explosive Ordnance Disposal Mobile Unit (EODMU) 5 dive in Apra Harbor, Guam. *U.S. Navy photo by Arthurgwain L. Marquez*

"With an amazing, tight-knit student body and a location in the beautiful suburbs outside Philadelphia, Villanova University brought a hometown feel to the college experience without the feeling of being just another 'student' lost in the mix. Villanova offered a truly unique college life supported by a small and diverse student body, amazing amenities, nationally ranked sports and education programs, and historic campus facilities that made this university feel like the right fit from day one. Its relatively small campus size, as compared to other public and private universities, welcomed and encouraged social interaction with peers and faculty that have yielded durable relationships that form the core of this great institution.

"With a gamut of educational offerings, coupled with outreach programs spanning from local community involvement to global NGO opportunities, Villanova provided a path for students to chase their passions and grow individually while maintaining a sense of belonging to the Villanova student community. Having visited numerous universities throughout my travels, I wouldn't trade my Villanova experience for anything!

"Today, Villanova's superb and nationally recognized education and reputation demands an equally 'impressive' price tag. Unfortunately, this has become a significant barrier to entry for many desiring continued or higher education. Being fortunate enough to qualify for a four-year NROTC scholarship, Villanova University became for me an attainable opportunity, and one that provided access to a one-of-a-kind experience. The Villanova NROTC program combined the typical 'college life' with Naval Service, as you are a member of the Navy Reserve, a midshipman, upon acceptance of the NROTC scholarship. Despite the additional course load per semester, NROTC provided another path to get involved in university events, taught invaluable traits and skills desired in any profession, and forged unique kinships with folks from all paths of life. Midshipmen summer cruises, conducted during summer breaks, provided opportunities to travel the world and experiences unique to the military service. Steeped in tradition, the Villanova NROTC program has been part of the university's culture since World War II. Free education at one of the nation's premier universities, and the opportunity to serve as a naval officer upon graduation, where can you go wrong?!?"

—CDR ROBERT MARSH, USN,
Commanding Officer, Mobile Diving Salvage Unit Two,
Villanova University NROTC Class of 2000

Conclusion

In this chapter, we discussed the warfighting communities open to Navy-Option midshipmen preparing for the service-assignment process. No matter the designator assigned, naval officers within all communities serve in rewarding, fulfilling positions and directly accomplish or assist in achieving national objectives. All communities offer opportunities for long, rewarding, and worthwhile careers of service to our nation. Again, midshipmen or prospective midshipmen should seek the counsel and advice of officers in communities that interest them for further information and detail.

We will now cover the administrative process of service assignment for those midshipmen entering their first-class, or senior, year in the NROTC program.

16 Navy-Option Service Assignment

AFTER COMMISSIONING ITSELF, the most anticipated event of a midshipman's career is service assignment. Both the Navy and Marine Corps are variegated services, containing distinctly different warfighting communities that work together and complement one another. While all graduates of the NROTC program will have the honor to serve in the naval services, there are big differences professionally and culturally between a Marine Corps infantry officer, a Navy F/A-18 pilot, and a Navy Surface Warfare Officer. Service assignment is the process through which Navy-Option midshipmen are assigned warfare "designators" and introduced into their respective communities. Because Marines are assigned their Military Occupational Specialty (MOS) after commissioning during The Basic School and Navy Nurse midshipmen are already designated at this point, their processes will not be covered. In this chapter, we will look in detail at the NROTC service-assignment process.

Some students enter the NROTC program with the goal of serving in a particular community, while others simply desire to serve in the Navy, Marine Corps, or even in the military in general. For some, attending a Blue Angels air show as a child may prompt dreams of being a naval aviator. For others, tales of a family member about their experiences at sea may lead to the goal of being a deck officer on board a surface combatant. The service-assignment process can be the means of turning those dreams into reality.

It must be stressed right here, however, that the process is one of service "assignment," not "selection." The Navy duly considers individual preferences and attempts to accommodate them, but ultimately midshipmen are assigned to the warfighting communities for which they are best qualified, within the framework, as always, of the needs of the Navy. Officers of the U.S. Navy are *naval* officers first and foremost: community designators are secondary. We encourage you to consider your willingness to serve in the community you would least desire before obligating yourself to the NROTC program. If you join the NROTC program with the intent of being, for example, a naval aviator *and nothing else* and do not think you could stand serving on a submarine, the NROTC program may not be the place for you. Once committed to the program you will be—as we are or have been—called to serve the Navy and Marine Corps team where we best can, which may mean subordinating our desires for the good of the service.

With that understanding, we will cover first the general process and then the specifics for each community.

General Service-Assignment Procedures

Each fall a service-assignment board at Naval Service Training Command allocates first-class midshipmen to Navy warfighting communities. That board, composed of active-duty naval officers and supporting staff, arrange in rank order the records of all graduating midshipmen and make decisions on individuals based on performance, preferences, and needs of the service. The data they see are pulled from official student records, so midshipmen should make sure that their vital information (such as GPA, PRT scores, physical qualification, and medical status) is completely accurate in the database. As discussed in chapter 12, your class advisor should go over this information with you during each semester counseling session, if not more often. If corrections are needed, follow up with your advisor to see that they are made: no one will care more about your service assignment than you do.

Each year you will be asked unofficially about your service-assignment preferences. At the conclusion of your first-class cruise, you will make your final inputs. Midshipmen must put their top three unrestricted-line community choices for which they are physically qualified. Midshipmen must also indicate preferences in the restricted line (such as intelligence, supply, information warfare), on the chance they are deemed "not physically qualified" (NPQ) for their desired URL community.

Each warfighting community has an officer "community manager" at the Bureau of Naval Personnel (BUPERS), who deals with matters of community accessions, career flow, etc. On the basis of community "career paths" (the ideal sequence of duty, experience, training, education, and responsibility at various levels of seniority), active-duty officer retention (i.e., percentages of officers who opt to remain in service when their obligations end), economic factors, and so on, community managers anticipate their communities' "demand signals" for officers. We noted earlier that those estimations formed the basis for the number of scholarships offered to your class four years ago, but specific community needs may have changed in the interim. The number of people (to simplify things) each community needs each year is calculated and broadcast to NROTC program management.

That means that each year there are only so many spots available in each community. Although in practical terms this is very unlikely to happen, consider that it would be impossible for every single midshipman to "service assign" as naval aviators—even if the Chief of Naval Air Training had that many open flight-school "seats," competing needs would necessitate sending numerous midshipmen to the surface and submarine communities. Naval Service Training Command is responsible for best matching available talent with the needs of the Navy.

Across the nation each year, midshipmen in their final years are assigned merit scores by which all students of their class will be ranked. Factors in the formula used are the tiers of midshipmen's majors, GPAs, PRT scores, and Professor of Naval Science "points." For better or worse, grade point average is weighted most heavily, followed by major tier, followed by points assigned by the PNS at your unit, followed by PRT score.

Throughout your college years, you give yourself the best chance of being assigned to the service of your preference by doing well academically. Tier 1 and Tier 2 majors enjoy a competitive edge over Tier 3 majors. Major-tier status affects a grade-point-average multiplier in the formula for merit score. A 4.0 Tier 1–major GPA is worth more points than a 4.0 GPA in Tier 3. Grade point average is the largest component of the composite score and luckily is the area over which the individual midshipman has the most influence. In these calculations, completed during the fall semester of a midshipman's senior year, only the first three years' grades are considered. This may be a good thing or bad thing, depending on your academic performance during your first few semesters. At most, we're talking about only six academic semesters, so a single poor semester can have a markedly negative influence on your overall GPA heading into service assignment.

The next factor is PRT scores—more points are awarded for doing better on the PRT. This element constitutes, however, a relatively small portion of the overall score. An outstanding performance on the PRT will not compensate for failure to do well academically, but it is a safe bet that the very top of the national ranking list will be filled with students who excelled both in the classroom and on the PT field. Only your most recent PRT scores will be used for the purposes of your merit ranking, typically those of your spring semester, junior year. While you should always strive to do your best, your performance on your senior year PRT will essentially only document your continued physical suitability for commissioning.

Professor of Naval Science points are added to complete the inputs to the computed score. NROTC unit COs rank their midshipman holistically on the basis of overall performance and potential for leadership and service. Essentially, these are "free" points (though actually you earn them every day in NROTC) that can elevate a student's standing. They reflect subjective ranking, drawing on the class advisor's recommendations, by the PNS of the first-class midshipmen of the unit. They are not affected by any attempt to "play" the precise calculation by NSTC—which does not distribute to units the formula it will use to generate the merit ranking list. There is, however, nothing wrong in asking your class advisor or the PNS where you are ranked within your NROTC unit's class; they may not notify you otherwise.

The results of this calculation will be a score and a ranking. This will be opaque to you, as you will not know your nationwide class ranking, but in general, the better you perform in class, the better you perform in the NROTC unit, and to a lesser degree the better you do on your PRT, the better the odds that you will be assigned to your desired community. Certain warfare communities add their own requirements to the process, which will be detailed in the following sections.

Naval Aviation

If you desire to become a Navy pilot or Naval Flight Officer, you will have to meet additional physical and academic standards. If you are interested, discuss the matter with your class advisor as soon as possible; the medical and physical examinations required can take a long time, particularly if you are not close to an appropriate military medical facility. All prospective naval aviators (both pilots and NFOs) must complete a series of flight-specific screenings overseen by the Navy

An F/A-18F Super Hornet from the "Jolly Rogers" of Strike Fighter Squadron (VFA) 103 launches from the flight deck of the *Nimitz*-class aircraft carrier USS *Abraham Lincoln* (CVN 72). *U.S. Navy photo by Amber Smalley*

Medicine Operational Training Center. Additional information can be found at its website, https://www.med.navy.mil/sites/nmotc/nami/arwg/Pages/Aeromedical ReferenceandWaiverGuide.aspx.

The other major additional prerequisite is the Aviation Selection Test Battery (ASTB), in which you need to earn qualifying scores in both the Academic Qualifications Rating (AQR) and either Pilot Flight Aptitude Rating (PFAR) or Flight Officer Aptitude Rating (FOFAR). Scores for the ASTB are on a 1-to-9 scale, 9 being the highest. The ASTB tests general educational skills but also such flight-oriented characteristics as hand-eye coordination and visual orientation. Midshipmen may take the ASTB up to three times but must wait at least a month between subsequent exams. The most recent, not the overall highest, test score will be used. The NROTC unit staff aviator will be able to assist you in studying for the ASTB by providing guides and practice problems. A generally successful strategy is to take your first ASTB exam in the fall of your junior year; that gives you a fair amount of time to study but also allows for any repetitions necessary to get the score you need.

After commissioning, new officers assigned to naval aviation will report to introductory flight training in Pensacola, as discussed earlier, to begin the long process, lasting approximately two years, of earning their "wings."

Surface Warfare

Prospective Surface Warfare Officers, both conventional and nuclear, do not face any special administrative hurdles before service assignment, but afterward, uniquely, they must begin a "ship selection" process to determine their first assignments. For all midshipmen "service assigned" as SWOs, a new ranking, 1 through x, is generated; it is the order in which they will select from available shipboard assignments. For perhaps the only times in their Navy careers, midshipmen will be able to choose the exact ship (or the type) they would like to serve on and homeports they would like to live in (again, among the "openings" that exist at the time). Surface ships are homeported at a number of locations, both within the continental United States (in CONUS) and forward deployed overseas (i.e., outside of the United States, or OCONUS).

> "The decision to apply for and accept an NROTC scholarship to the University of Notre Dame set the course for an adventure that has seen me travel the world, oftentimes on the roof of a large, floating and well-armed airport. Having served alongside officers from every commissioning source, I feel extremely fortunate for my experience in NROTC where I was challenged in every aspect of development. The foundation for success that is laid by the NROTC program, and its uniqueness in the collegiate environment, allowed me to reach terrific heights (sometimes over 50,000 ft!). Many of these emotions were captured during a F/A-18 flyover I performed before a Notre Dame vs. Navy football game in 2013, and a view that combined all the best things that my time at NROTC Notre Dame created."
>
> —CDR JOHN HILTZ, USN, former Navy Blue Angels pilot, University of Notre Dame NROTC Class of 2002

Midshipmen who have performed exceptionally well during their first-class cruises might not be subject to formal ship selection: in what is known as the "Blue Chip" program, commanding officers of the ships on board which they cruised can invite them to accept assignment to their ships, this time as officers. Midshipmen can either accept or decline, but this would be an opportunity to guarantee their homeport assignments without having to worry about all "slots" there being taken before the list works down to them.

The office in BUPERS, known as PERS-41, responsible for SWO personnel management livestreams the multiday NROTC ship-selection process across major social media and web platforms; you, your friends, family, and loved ones, and naval enthusiasts can share in the experience of ship selection. The list is updated in real time as ships are selected. Some "spots," particularly attractive overseas assignments, are competitive and quickly fall off the board, but each year's iteration is unique. Simply because of how the surface fleet is distributed, most midshipman will go to ships in either Norfolk (Virginia) or San Diego.

Regardless of where they are on the list and the ships they select, all new SWOs find comparable and immediate professional and leadership opportunities there, and potentially the beginnings of long careers of service at sea. Nevertheless, midshipmen often "stress" about ship selection. Most want to get immediately to the fleet and contribute to real-world operations. These midshipmen are eager to go on deployments and quickly earn their SWO qualifications. That's all fine, but the stress is unnecessary. The most important factor in whether you find yourself reporting to that blessed "happy ship" is the officers and crew. A list of available ships' names and homeports cannot possibly tell you this. Further, given the high turnover on board ships, the reality is that a ship's culture is subject to (at least) incremental change. There's usually no way to know beforehand, even if you have insider knowledge from friends or peers on the waterfront. For you as a junior officer, practical but intangible matters like the leadership quality of your department head can have a huge effect on quality of your life personally; your peers elsewhere on the same ship may experience something different.

Under current fleet operational practice, each ship completes a "notionally" (i.e., that's the planning assumption) seven-month overseas deployment in each three-year scheduling cycle. Prior to deployment, prolonged maintenance and training periods aim to put the ship in the best condition and highest state of readiness possible. Actual ship schedules are classified, and you are unlikely to have ready access to the special Internet networks necessary to see them, but in general we recommend, to the extent that you have a choice, reporting to your ship at the end of the maintenance phase and beginning of predeployment training.

Your time commitment on your first ship doesn't begin until after the Basic Division Officer Course. The best timing (again, if you can influence it) would be to attend BDOC either en route to your first ship or shortly after you report on board. Be sure to check with your unit SWO, as career-path timing "milestones" are subject to change.

Submarine Warfare

Midshipmen interested in serving on nuclear-powered submarines must demonstrate outstanding academic achievement and volunteer to serve in the "Silent Service." The NROTC program is one of the primary "accession sources" for officers of the nuclear Navy, and developing successful candidates for submarine service is a prime objective of many NROTC units, particularly at schools with noted engineering and science programs. In addition to the normal service-assignment process, prospective submarine officers must undergo a rigorous set of interviews and pass an additional series of medical screenings.

All U.S. Navy submarines today being nuclear powered, all prospective submarine officers must be acceptable to the Navy Nuclear Power Program (NNPP). Engineers from Naval Reactors (or NR, the Navy Department / Energy Department office responsible for the safety and reliability of Navy nuclear propulsion) rigorously screen and personally interview all applicants. Final acceptance into the NNPP is decided after a personal interview with the head of NR, a four-star admiral. Success at the NR interviews requires extensive study and preparation. Midshipmen interested are eligible to interview with NR after having completed calculus and physics requirements and meeting radiological medical requirements. It is in your best interest and that of the Navy, if you are interested, to apply for an interview as early as possible.

The *Ohio*-class ballistic-missile submarine USS *Louisiana* (SSBN 743) transits the Hood Canal as it returns home from a strategic deterrent patrol. *U.S. Navy photo by Michael Smith*

When you do, an interview date will be set at the Washington Navy Yard, in Washington, D.C. At least two months prior to the interview, midshipmen applying for the NNPP must meet at least weekly with their units' nuclear power officers to practice oral interviews. In addition, the applicant must schedule at least one practice session with a staff officer/educator other than the unit's NPO. Last, prior to heading to the NR interview, the applicant must undergo a "final check" interview with the unit's commanding officer, whose responsibility is to ensure that only prepared candidates are interviewed.

NR's oral interviews are a legacy of the "father of the nuclear Navy," ADM Hyman G. Rickover (1900–1986), who gave his personal assurance that the nuclear Navy would be absolutely safe. They examine applicants' knowledge of undergraduate-level physics and calculus and their ability to work through appropriate problems. Interviewers are much more interested in the application of reasonable methods than simply getting the right answer.

Newly commissioned officers assigned submarines will begin their naval careers at the Nuclear Power Training Command, as we have described. After successfully completing the curriculum, which takes approximately a year, prospective submariners are assigned to boats on the basis of their performance and the needs of the service.

Special Warfare

Midshipmen interested in serving either as Explosive Ordnance Disposal or Special Warfare Officers must meet a few additional requirements to be eligible for assignment. Competition is fierce for a small number of "entry-level openings," and successful applicants will have performed very well in the NROTC program and earned strong PNS recommendations. If you are interested in serving in either community, work with your class advisor to help develop a strategy to make you as competitive as possible. Remember, you *must* complete an EOD or SEAL first-class summer cruise as a sort of "screener" to be eligible for either community. This must be coordinated well ahead of your senior summer, so be sure to make your desires known to your NROTC unit early.

Interested midshipmen must complete the community-specific physical screening test and have the result documented. Official fitness tests must be observed by a serving EOD or SEAL officer, as appropriate. Your class advisor can assist you in coordinating and scheduling this event. Physical fitness tests for these communities are more demanding than the PFA. You will need to be in outstanding physical condition to be competitive for either the EOD or SEAL community.

In addition, only midshipmen ranking in the top 25 percent of their NROTC classes who list EOD or SEAL as their top choices are considered. (Midshipmen may list EOD as a second choice, but only if SEAL is their first.) Applicants must submit a letter of recommendation from their commanding officer and a personal essay that details their desire and potential to serve as either an EOD or SEAL officer, making particular mention of their work histories, athletic achievements, extracurricular activities, and leadership experience. Again, the final component is the strong written recommendation of your commanding officer.

After commissioning, prospective SEAL officers will attend Basic Underwater Demolition/SEAL training in Coronado, and prospective EOD officers go for their initial training in Pensacola.

Service-Assignment Placement

Once the service-assignment board has completed its deliberations and sorted all midshipmen into warfighting communities, a list of these decisions will be sent to NROTC COs. How service assignments are made known to midshipmen will be up to the COs, but typically they either call the midshipmen personally or meet with each in a private setting to give them the good news. Some COs publicly announce the results at a battalion-wide event, such as the weekly Leadership Lab.

SEAL/EOD PHYSICAL SCREENING TEST MINIMUMS

500-yard swim: 12:30
Push-ups: 50 (2 minutes)
Curl-ups: 50 (2 minutes)
Pull-ups: 6 (2 minutes)
1.5-mile run: 12:30

COMPETITIVE SEAL/EOD PHYSICAL SCREENING TEST SCORES

(Taken from the official Naval Special Warfare website, https://www.sealswcc.com/)
500-yard swim: 8:25
Push-ups: 98 (2 minutes)
Curl-ups: 91 (2 minutes)
Pull-ups: 21 (2 minutes)
1.5-mile run: 8:59
(Higher scores significantly increase chances of selection!)

"Applying for Naval Special Warfare would have been exceptionally challenging without the assistance of skilled NROTC advisors who led me through every obstacle. I told my freshman advisor during our first counseling session that I wanted to screen for a chance to become a Naval Special Warfare officer. He told me to maintain a high GPA, outstanding physical fitness scores, and to proactively bolster my application to set myself apart from other students in the selection pool. Sophomore year I was lucky enough to have an experienced SEAL officer as my NROTC advisor and he continued to build me up so that I would stand out at the selection board. He helped me apply for a summer foreign language program called Project GO available only to ROTC students, and he facilitated transportation to a SEAL weekend training session hosted by Notre Dame NROTC. An outstanding service-assignment package ranked me among the top 35 NROTC candidates nationwide who applied for SEAL Officer Assessment and Selection (SOAS). SOAS serves as a candidate's first-class summer cruise. It is a three-week-long event where prospective SEAL officer candidates are challenged and evaluated during physical, intellectual, and leadership obstacles side by side with candidates from the Naval Academy and from Officer Candidate School. Completion of SOAS and adequate performance at interviews was my final step to selection and a chance to go to BUD/S and become a Naval Special Warfare officer."

—ENS JOHN COMBS, USN,
Auburn University NROTC Class of 2018

After service assignment, placement in your first duty station depends on the community. For submariners, naval aviators, and Special Warfare Officers the first assignment will be at a training command; when you transfer to it is a matter of course quotas and timing. Initial training for Surface Warfare Officers can occur either en route to or shortly after arrival at their first ships, as we've seen, so they can usually depart quickly for the fleet.

The precise timing varies slightly from year to year, but you can expect to know which community you have been assigned to by Thanksgiving. Ship selection and reporting dates to first duty stations will not be known until sometime in the spring semester. Your NROTC unit staff will be eager to share this information with you, so try to be patient!

Conclusion

Service assignment is an exciting time for NROTC midshipmen and the last major step prior to graduation, commissioning, and beginning a career as a naval officer. While the service-assignment process is—and rightly—primarily concerned with the needs of the Navy, you should feel confident that if you do well in school and in NROTC and meet the physical or medical requirements, you have a good chance of going to the community of your choice. Ultimately, however, whether you do or not, assignment into any Navy warfighting community is a great honor, to be responded to with gratitude and determination to succeed as a naval officer.

With service assignment "past and opening" (a phrase you'll especially appreciate after your first-class cruise), we will cover aspects of graduation and commissioning in the next chapter, the last of the book that is focused primarily on the prospective or current NROTC midshipman.

17 Commissioning and Reporting to Your First Duty Station

CONGRATULATIONS! You have finally made it! The commissioning ceremony, where you will be awarded a commission as a naval officer, is the culmination of all your hard work and dedication as an undergraduate and a member of the NROTC program. Having completed both your school's undergraduate degree and the NROTC program's requirements, you are officially joining the ranks of the most capable and professional naval services in the history of the world. You should be justly proud of all the work, study, practice, and commitment that it took you to get here. Also, take a moment to think about the support provided to you by your family, other loved ones, and unit staff. No one in the naval services stands watch alone.

The commissioning ceremony is a celebration of your accomplishments in the NROTC program, but more than that, it is a humbling public demonstration of your and your classmates' voluntary service to our nation. From the moment you raise your right hand and commit yourself to support and defend the Constitution of the United States, you are formally entrusted by the people of the United States to do your utmost in the defense of our nation, even potentially at the expense of your life. You are no longer just a student, midshipman, or young person with potential—you are an active-duty naval officer on whom the nation is depending to do your best and lead the young men and women entrusted to you to success in battle. Let the significance of such responsibility sink in.

In this chapter, we will cover some important administrative aspects of commissioning, what a typical commission ceremony is like, the post-commissioning "stash" period (in case you have one), basic pay, leave, and benefits, and a brief description of the steps involved in reporting to your first duty station.

A comprehensive discussion of the many issues of concern to a newly commissioned officer is beyond the scope of this book. For that, we recommend the Naval Institute Press book *Newly Commissioned Naval Officer's Guide.*

Commissioning

A commission as an officer in the U.S. military is an appointment to a formal position of authority within the federal government, its authority ultimately derived from that granted to the commander in chief, the president, by the Constitution of the United States. Citizens granted such authority must make a public oath pledging to serve "well and faithfully" their appointed duties. Officers in all services of the U.S. military must take the following oath of office:

THE OATH OF OFFICE

I ____, do solemnly swear (or affirm) that I will support and defend the Constitution of the United States against all enemies, foreign and domestic; that I will bear true faith and allegiance to the same; that I take this obligation freely, without any mental reservation or purpose of evasion; and that I will well and faithfully discharge the duties of the office on which I am about to enter.

So help me God. (Title 5, U.S. Code 3331)

A retired Marine Corps lieutenant general leads graduating midshipmen of the University of Colorado Boulder NROTC unit in the oath of office at a commissioning ceremony. *U.S. Navy photo by Jonah Farwell*

We strongly recommend that you think deeply about and understand fully the oath you will take to become a commissioned officer. It has undergone revision throughout our nation's history, but allegiance to the Constitution and commitment to do one's utmost in the performance of duties have remained consistent. To see the uniqueness of the role of commissioned officers, contrast it with the oath of enlistment, taken by enlisted service members:

THE OATH OF ENLISTMENT

I, _____, do solemnly swear (or affirm) that I will support and defend the Constitution of the United States against all enemies, foreign and domestic; that I will bear true faith and allegiance to the same; and that I will obey the orders of the President of the United States and the orders of the officers appointed over me, according to regulations and the Uniform Code of Military Justice.

So help me God. (Title 10, U.S. Code)

The most conspicuous difference is the obligation of enlisted members to "obey the orders of the president of the United States and the orders of officers appointed over me, according to regulations and the Uniform Code of Military Justice." As long as an order is duly given and legal, enlisted service members are duty-bound to carry it out to the best of their ability. However, if you reexamine the oath of office, you will see that the statement of obedience is absent—meaning that commissioned officers do not have a similar obligation. To be sure, failing to follow a legal and duly given order can have drastic consequences for a military career, but the implication is that commissioned officers are called on to use their own judgment in carrying out orders beyond the formal guidance of regulation and law. While this point may seem arcane, it is appropriate to consider fully as you begin to absorb the immense responsibility and authority entrusted to you as a commissioned officer.

In addition to the public oath, officers appointed to a commission in the naval services must sign the Officer Appointment Acceptance and Oath of Office, NAVPERS Form 1000/4, discussed further below.

During the commissioning ceremony, you will receive your commission as a paper document, signed by the Secretary of the Navy on behalf of the president of the United States, appointing you to your initial rank and officially declaring your status in the armed services of the United States. Historically, commissioned officers would maintain physical copies of their commission on their persons in times of conflict in order to prove, in case of capture, that they were officers. For example, commissioned officers would retain their rights of property and be afforded more favorable living conditions in captivity than those of common Sailors or soldiers. All that is "ancient history," but the document retains its legal importance and should be handled with care and pride.

THE COMMISSIONING CEREMONY

The actual ceremony is straightforward, but its conduct will depend on the school's preferences and graduation schedule. The effective act is the administration—by a commissioned military officer—of the oath of office. The actual process takes only a few minutes, but there is usually pomp and circumstance for the occasion. In many cases a very senior military or civilian defense official is invited to serve as the commissioning officer and make remarks of guidance and counsel to the commissioning class. The ceremony mirrors other "graduation-style" events, with a procession, invocation, remarks, speeches, and finally the commissioning itself.

Because assuming the status of a commissioned naval officer brings profound responsibilities and privileges, certain details become vital. Legally, the validity of your commissioning rests on your handwritten signature on the NAVPERS form we mentioned, signifying acceptance of the oath of office. The signature of the verifying officer, typically the NROTC unit's commanding officer, must also be present. However, it is your public swearing or affirming of the oath of office that carries the *moral* obligation to fulfill it.

As a final note, it is fully allowable for any commissioned officer, active duty or retired, to administer your oath of office. This can be a special moment and memory for midshipmen with active-duty service members in their families. Your father, grandfather, mother, grandmother, aunt, sister, etc., if a commissioned officer either on active duty or "the retired list," may administer your oath in a small private ceremony distinct from your NROTC unit's.

> "Any commissioned officer—active or retired—can administer your oath. You may wish to consider asking a relative or mentor who served as a commissioned officer to swear you in. My father served in World War II as a Navy officer, and he gave me my oath, which is a treasured memory for me."
>
> —VADM PETER DALY, USN (RET.)

COMMISSIONING CAVEATS FOR FIRST-CLASS MIDSHIPMEN

By law, unrestricted-line commissioned officers must possess undergraduate degrees. For that reason, there may be a delay, typically a week or so, between your institution's commencement exercises and commissioning. In that time the Navy will make certain that all eligible midshipmen have entirely completed the requirements for their degrees and obtain any needed verifications from the school's administration. Another consideration involves differences in academic calendars between the host institution and the schools of cross-town affiliate units. Commissioning ceremonies are typically keyed to the host institution's calendar, which could make the wait for "cross-town midshipmen" even longer.

Make sure your senior year ends on a positive note:

- Keep your grades up and make sure your degree-hours requirements are met.
- Communicate *early* with your professors and academic advisor on any questions.
- Maintain close communication with your NROTC unit advisor to make certain you are on track from their perspective.
- Be sure your family understands your timeline. As just explained, and especially if you are commissioning from a unit as a cross-town midshipman, your graduation date and commissioning date may be different—plan accordingly.

Marine Corps midshipman has gold 2nd Lt. bars pinned on by his father and mother during a commissioning ceremony for Texas A&M University NROTC midshipmen. *Official U.S. Navy photo*

Throughout your senior year, you will be wrapping up any final physical or medical screenings. In addition, administrative in-processing for active duty is cumbersome. Compounding this complexity is the inability of many undergraduates to complete their degree requirements by the end of the senior spring semester. As, again, you cannot be commissioned without having earned your undergraduate degree, the compressed time between the end of the semester, award of final grades, and the commissioning ceremony can cause headaches if things do not flow smoothly.

The worst-case scenario arises if your graduation itself is in doubt owing to mediocre academic performance. As stressed in earlier chapters, crystal-clear communication with your class advisor about how you're doing is essential. At this late stage, much coordination with your professors regarding final project or course grades will be required; faculty will be working to the institution's academic calendar milestones, which may not be soon enough to get you commissioned on time. Against the backdrop of family and friends traveling, perhaps across country, to see their loved one graduate and become an officer, there may be tension between you, your professor, and the NROTC unit staff. Keep in mind that the professor of your senior design class, or whatever is at the crux of the matter, may not understand or sympathize with your special, different timeline.

It should help if you have been in communication throughout the semester with your professors, particularly instructors of your problematic courses. Your school may even, like many large institutions, hold merely symbolic commencement ceremonies, not verifying or awarding actual degrees until some months later. In such cases especially, your professors, if you have not been talking to them, may not realize the stress they would cause you, your family, and your NROTC staff by not having your design project, say, at the top of their grading stacks. In particular, if your performance in mandatory classes has put your passing on time in doubt, be open and honest with your faculty advisor about the situation and the stakes. For the average undergraduate it matters little that final grades are input after the formal commencement ceremony; for you, it could mean not participating in the commissioning ceremony.

Tragically, each year senior midshipmen are disenrolled from the program and incur substantial debts to the government for cheating on exams or plagiarizing final projects. If the "senioritis bug" hits you harder than most, or you fail to manage your time effectively so close to the finish line, and you find yourself "in extremis," *under absolutely no circumstances cut corners or compromise your integrity in an attempt to graduate on time.* It is infinitely better to fail a course honestly than seem to pass and then be caught plagiarizing. Modern tools available to professors and student aides make most cheating attempts fool's errands, very likely to be detected. Your final disposition would rest with your CO, but we would not expect much sympathy for a flagrant violation of your integrity just before commissioning. The episode would be "detrimental to your standing in the program"—that is, would likely end it—and leave you to explain to your loved ones, who have been bursting with pride over your approaching commission. Simply failing the class "the right way" would probably mean retaking it that summer or fall or redoing a project on your own time and dime, thereby delaying—*but not destroying*—your prospects of commissioning.

The Post-Commissioning Period

Some newly commissioned Navy officers will be told, for any of a number of reasons, to remain at the NROTC unit before transfer to their first duty stations. (Marine Corps officers typically do not: after commissioning, new second lieutenants return to their homes of record in a non-duty status until their Basic School course starts.) Most colleges graduate their seniors sometime in May; the Navy will allow for some delay in reporting. Once commissioned, naval officers are in a fully active-duty status and receive full pay, allowances, and benefits appropriate to their rank.

Keep in mind that once you take the oath of office and sign accepting your commission and enter on active duty, you are subject to the orders of your commanding and superior officers. You are no longer a college student—your job is to report for duty at the NROTC unit or wherever else you are directed. There is no such thing as a "nine to five" workday for active-duty officers—you are always on call. That said, however, for the most part you can expect a fairly straightforward and routine working schedule. For NROTC unit staff, summer represents a relatively relaxed period; many take leave or time away, and work to be done in the unit decreases. Typical assignments for "stashed" ensigns include assisting around the unit, helping with administrative tasks, such as filing, and completing required training and administration in preparation for your "permanent change of station" (PCS).

Reporting to Your First Duty Station

If you are like most recently commissioned officers, you will be eager to report to your first duty station. Your NROTC unit staff will work with you on the transfer paperwork. The biggest elements of a PCS are moving your household goods and your own travel. For most newly commissioned ensigns, without dependents and living in a small apartment or dormitory room, a loaded car may be all that's needed to transport you and your stuff to the first duty station. You are entitled to be reimbursed for costs associated with moving yourself. However, if you desire not to or are unable to move yourself, the military will cover the costs associated of hiring a professional moving service. This process can be confusing, so be sure to work with your unit staff officers on it.

A final note: if reporting to a nontraining command, it is appropriate to write a short letter of introduction to the commanding officer. Your NROTC unit staff should be familiar with these letters and can help you make a professional, smart first impression. Your orders will contain contact information for the command (or you can easily find it online—commands have their own websites); use it to reach out and be assigned a command sponsor, who will assist you in transferring.

Be sure that your "gaining" (new) command has your contact information while you are traveling, but know that you are the responsibility of your NROTC unit until you actually report to, and are "gained" by, your new duty station. Your NROTC unit administrative staff will stamp, date, and sign your orders, on paper, the day you check out; your new command, when you report and check in, similarly stamp, date, and sign them. In the interim, you should keep both commands informed of any issues you might have in reporting on time.

Conclusion

Commissioning and reporting to your first duty station are exciting events and mark the formal beginning of your career in the naval services. Whether you serve only your initial commitment, retire as a four-star admiral, or anything in between, you are sure to remember the feelings of excitement and nervousness that accompany this transition and new beginning.

This chapter concludes the section of this book that takes the perspective of prospective or current midshipmen. We turn now to your parents, and then return at the end to you, about to make some of the biggest decisions of your life.

18 NROTC for Parents

FOR MANY PARENTS, a son's or daughter's decision to join the military is a cause for pride but also some anxiety. First of all, we thank you for raising a young man or woman patriotic, selfless, and devoted enough to offer the most valuable commodity anyone has, their time and effort, toward the laudable purpose of service to their nation. You should be proud of their character and moral development. We also understand that you may have some practical questions that might not occur to your son or daughter.

In this chapter, we will cover some of the questions parents most frequently have concerning the NROTC program. Your young person will require support and enthusiasm from loved ones to succeed in college and in NROTC. In contrast to much of the rest of this book, which has the prospective or current midshipman in mind, this chapter is specifically focused on the concerns a parent might have.

Before going further, you can find a more comprehensive overview of the U.S. Navy and Marine Corps in many works available online or at your local bookstore. One that we recommend is the recently published *Parent's Guide to the U.S. Navy*, from the Naval Institute Press.

What Your Young Person Is Signing Up For

The NROTC program is a commissioning path by which qualified college graduates are commissioned as officers in the U.S. Navy or Marine Corps. Newly commissioned officers are granted the rank of either a Navy ensign or Marine Corps second lieutenant, both officers of grade O-1. Officers in the U.S. military perform within specialties, as a submarine officer, infantry officer, pilot, etc., and lead

Sailors in the accomplishment of assigned missions. Newly commissioned officers are provided sufficient training, resources, and time to develop their personal abilities and leadership. Officers who perform well can expect to advance in grade and be given greater responsibility. NROTC graduates incur an obligation to the U.S. government of at least eight years, five of which must be served on active duty. Some specialties, such as naval aviation, involve longer obligations, due to the long and expensive training curriculum necessary before their new officers get to the operational fleet.

While the military is an inherently dangerous profession, attention is paid and discipline is exercised, constantly, to ensure that it is no more dangerous than it has to be. No one can guarantee the safety of an individual, but you should feel confident that your young person will be joining the most professional and competent fighting force in the history of the world—a force that highly values its people as a competitive advantage and foundation for operational success.

Finally, the first year of an NROTC scholarship is offered with no strings attached. Students offered the National Scholarship during high school can have their entire first year's tuition paid without incurring *any* obligation for military service after graduation. During each summer, scholarship midshipmen will participate in a "summer cruise" designed to expose them to the operational fleet. The first summer can be thought of as an introductory and orientation period, in which midshipmen spend four weeks learning about various aspects of the Navy and Marine Corps. Only after returning for the fall sophomore semester does a midshipman have to sign an agreement to remain in NROTC in order to continue earning the scholarship; doing so is what incurs the active-duty obligation. If a student finds that the military life or the NROTC program might not be for them, they can simply decline to continue, with no consequence or pushback.

What your young person is signing up for, then, is professional and military training to become a naval officer after earning an undergraduate degree at an affiliated civilian institution. In return for completing required naval science courses, physical training, and professional development events and for agreeing to a period of active-duty service upon graduation and commissioning, the government will provide a full-tuition scholarship and other financial benefits, including a well-paying, career-oriented, guaranteed job upon graduation. It really is a *very* good deal for the motivated, talented, and patriotic young person!

A newly commissioned ensign's shoulder boards are put on by his brother while his mother and sisters look on during a commissioning ceremony on the campus of Oregon State University. *U.S. Navy photo by Jonah Farwell*

NROTC Scholarship and Financial Information

The NROTC scholarship can be an astonishing financial asset for a family with a child entering college. The cost of a college education has exploded over the past twenty years, and an increasing percentage of college graduates are saddled with ever-increasing burdens of student-loan debt. Collectively, outstanding student-loan debt in the United States is becoming a serious issue. Because parents often choose to pay in full or part of the cost of their child's education, you may be just as happy as your son or daughter that they receive a full-tuition scholarship. In this section, we will detail specifics surrounding the NROTC scholarship.

A FAMILY AFFAIR
Why the Naval Reserve Officer Training Corps: A Father's Perspective

"There are frankly many reasons, both practical and patriotic, why I believe every high school student should consider the NROTC program. Most have been clearly covered in this book. But honestly, if it comes down to simple arithmetic, I suppose the decision to participate could default to basic economics. If that is your scenario—I cannot argue—the NROTC program (or any ROTC program for that matter) provides a viable way to fund college with a little more than a 1-to-1-year payback. Not a bad deal by any standard.

"But as a parent for whom economics was not the primary consideration, some-times I am asked why I support my children's desire to enter into the college program and an early professional experience that, at least on the surface, will expose our kids to an unpredictable future, an unknown culture, and frankly, a profession seemingly full of risk. Risk in all its forms: from emotional (long-distance relationships are tough), to professional (no job or position is guaranteed), to physical (beyond general fitness, chances are every military profession comes with an inherent risk of combat, and con-sequently, bodily harm). It's this last one that rightly causes most people significant pause. Indeed, a military commitment comes with its physical and mental training for the toughest job on the planet—the defense of the nation and the potential promulga-tion of stability operations across a planet that tends to the chaotic.

"In full transparency (and as a retired naval officer), I understand this perspective and will never question a parent's concern and/or critical evaluation of these risks. We all would be remiss as parents if we did not. And yes, ships, planes, and submarines—as safe as they are these days, add an additional layer of risk to that of normal American life. Flying an F-18 off a ship is not the same as being an IT supervisor. Yes, arguments are made that statistically they are safer than driving cars, but in the end—they are activities undertaken *in addition to* driving a car—so it is understandable. The fact is, if they choose to enter military service, our kids may be exposed to an additional level of risk that some would consider unnecessary—and for others perhaps unpalatable. Let's face it, you're being asked to support your kid as s/he signs their early futures over to unknown activities in support of governmental service. A service and culture which may be as completely foreign to you as a walk on the moon. One which promises adventure to your kids—but sleepless nights of worry and concern to you as a parent. That is reality and I'm not here to tell you that you'll have nothing to worry about. Indeed, my own mother contends that having two sons in the Navy ensured an overabundance of visitations to church. Further, I think she would tell you that after 30+ years, she was unbelievably relieved when we both finally retired with all our fingers and toes.

"So I get it. That may not sound like an attractive way to spend your parenthood. Likewise, it's hard to have this conversation with your kids. They don't really want to hear about your anxieties any more than I wanted to hear my parents' reminders that we were keeping them up nights. I wore those same shoes 40+ years ago. I, perhaps like your child, was intrigued by the adventure of it all . . . the allure of learning to fly, traveling the world and living a life of excitement. And while my experiences in most cases exceeded these desires, I now appreciate more my parents' concern—their fre-quent calls and letters as they checked after the welfare of a son who they knew well and trusted . . . but who they also knew as a disorganized teenager and a class clown. Who wouldn't worry? But back then, I took it for granted and simply accepted their con-cern as a byproduct of their parenthood . . . they would (and did) learn to deal with it.

"And now? Oh boy. Now I have a daughter and a son in the NROTC program, both echoing all the excitement of their parents at that age. While we are proud of them, my wife and I have new appreciation for the worry of our parents all those years ago. We empathize even more so for the un-indoctrinated parent. Indeed, I/we share all the same sentiments—perhaps even more acutely as we both have firsthand knowledge of the risks and dangers. Admittedly, we have an advantage, for these concerns are all offset by a corresponding knowledge of the rewards, benefits, and self-actualization that accompanies military service.

"And this gets to the heart of the matter and why I was asked to address would-be parents of NROTC Midshipmen and address the question: 'Knowing what I know now, would I do it all again?' (yes, by the way), and perhaps more significantly 'why?'— 'Why should you support your daughter or son in this particular aspiration?'

"At the end of the day I suppose it's because we believe in the concepts of service for others and the absolute necessity we have to rear and nurture good people. As the quotation goes: The only thing necessary for the triumph of evil in this world is for good people to do nothing. A couple of years ago, as I wrestled with whatever extent I should/ would support our eldest daughter in her own aspirations in applying to NROTC or one of the military academies, this sentiment would frequently be my last of the day.

"For my wife and I, it came down to this fundamental question: Would we support our kids in their decisions to seek service to others, in a socially and economically diverse environment and in doing so become good people who may just one day become great leaders? We said yes. Not because we support them in everything they want (we don't), or because we are convinced that military service is an obligation (it's not) or the only way to serve (it isn't by far). But we support them, despite all the risks and the likelihood of future sleepless nights and days of worry as they serve far from home, because it is a tried-and-true way to produce good people, receive an education, and become the leaders of tomorrow. We choose to support them because their desire for service, while it comes with a sense of adventure, is first and foremost an opportunity for them to buy into their own futures as well as the collective future of the country and the globe. After all, it will be their world one day—complete with all its risks, joys, and blemishes—and they certainly should have the opportunity to ensure it is the world they desire."

—CAPT Greg H. Molinari, USN (Ret.), College of the Holy Cross NROTC Class of 1989

NROTC AND THE NAVY—IT'S ALL ABOUT THE FOLLOW-THROUGH

"As a mother of four and a military veteran, I was happy, though not necessarily sur-prised, when my daughter said she wanted to join the Navy and apply for the NROTC program. My husband and I are both graduates of the program, he from Holy Cross, I from Purdue University, and we have had a fantastic and full life in the military. Our eldest, by the nature of when she joined us, consequently has had the longest expe-rience of life in the Navy and hence a fuller understanding of military life. She was born overseas—and for years was known as our 'bella Neopolitana.' In her eighteen years, she has moved seven times and attended nine schools. Rather than regretting the moves, she now maintains friends all over the world.

"So I wasn't surprised by her desire. What I was surprised about was the way the application process has changed since I went through. Back in 1988 I reported to a recruiter and did much of the application in person, or via mail. Nowadays, there is modern technology that in so many ways makes the application process a bit easier. Though some aspects of the application process are timeless. In regard not just to applying to the NROTC program but to any period of service in the military.

"I was never a military careerist—I entered the program sophomore year at Purdue University—while in the midst of the Registered Nursing program. Frankly I was looking for a way to fund college and get a leg up on the job placement process following graduation. I'd be lying if I said I wasn't excited about chances to live in exciting locations near the beach. So I visited the recruiter; the Navy needed nurses, and as one of eleven children, I needed resourcing and a future. It was an easy decision for me.

"But back then I learned of the need to follow through. There was a lot of paperwork involved and I needed to stay on top of it. My future depended on it. I learned early that it was a big bureaucracy and things could fall through the numerous cracks. In 2016, as my daughter initially applied online—I wondered if all that had changed for the better. The short answer is that while it is easier in many ways to pursue a scholarship via modern technology, it's still all about the follow-through.

"In my daughter's case, she was frequently told that she should hear something by such and such a date. Many times those dates came and went and like many of her generation, my daughter trusted the electrons to get it right. Many a time I pressured her to follow up and not risk becoming a statistic of some web server—lost in an administrative buffer somewhere. Like any organization offering grant aid, the Navy is looking for those candidates that show initiative and follow-through. I argued with her; if she could not take the time to worry about her future and follow through, why should she expect the Navy or recruiter to? Fortunately, she listened to Mom—at least this time.

"Once she broke the code and became known to the recruiting office as someone serious about her prospects, things went better. In fact, she got called back for a second interview and being a veteran of the system, I felt that surely it was because her application had been lost in that buffer somewhere. . . .

"Happily, that was not the case. What *was* the case was that the commanding officer of the recruiting district wanted to conduct a personal interview with our daughter. As she sat down, he asked her if she knew why she had been called back to see him. When she did not, he explained he had been impressed with her essays and her commitment and follow-through. Further, if the results of this particular interview went well, she would leave the office with a scholarship in hand. Still not believing that today could be it, I waited in a waiting room much like a doctor's office, wondering what was going on. . . . An hour later, I having learned she had a scholarship, we sat numb, incredulous but also incredibly overjoyed. She had received what is known as an Immediate Scholarship Reservation (ISR)—meaning she would not need to wait for the general board to meet to receive her results. She had her four-year scholarship in hand and could start picking her university.

"Fast-forward six months and it is Senior Night at her high school. The night where students are awarded for their various academic and/or sporting achievements. Our daughter had done well and was excited to receive a couple of acknowledgments. However, to the surprise of absolutely everyone present (her mom in particular), at the end of the ceremony a Navy commander walked into the auditorium in his dress whites and up onto the stage. It was the same Recruiting District Commander that had presented her the ISR. He called my daughter up onto the stage and explained that he had traveled over one hundred miles to pay special recognition to her for her achievements, her patriotism, and willingness to serve. He explained the program, with a few jokes sprinkled here and there, and outlined these scholarships as chances to embark on a career full of adventure (and more than a few push-ups), one which he himself had never stopped loving. In the end, he presented her an enormous check, like the ones you see winners of the Lotto receive, for $116,000.00, as the entire school erupted in applause.

"As I fought back tears, overcome by a tremendous sense of pride and of gratitude to the Commander and the Navy for making her feel so special in such spectacular fashion, I couldn't help but think that some things never change . . . It is still all about the follow-through.

"Now she gets it and hasn't looked back since. Only a sophomore at the University of San Diego, she is already being given positions of leadership and, like the Recruiting Commander who surprised her twice, she is absolutely loving every minute of it."

—Anne M. Molinari, RN, Purdue University NROTC class of 1991

I AM ALL IN

"As a second semester college sophomore about to come up on the halfway point in her NROTC career, I feel nothing but excitement when I consider what my future holds. Every day, as I wake up at the University of San Diego and walk to my classes, I can overlook the SoCal suburbs out to where they meet the Pacific Ocean and further on out to the distant horizon. Some mornings, as I sip some bleary eyed coffee, I can even see a squadron of navy helicopters in the distance or watch ships and submarines pull in past Point Loma. In San Diego, reminders of my potential future career abound, keeping me centered, focused and humble.

"As a student studying Environmental Studies, who is also involved in both Greek life and volunteer services, I feel totally imbedded in my school community and a full college experience. Yet, as I reflect on my undergraduate time thus far, despite my other involvements, I find my strongest personal foundation lies in NROTC. And no, not in the extremely motivated 'Hooyah!' eat-sleep-and-breathe-Navy-blue-and-gold type of way. Rather, I find my foundation in the people who are full of shared determination, morals, and quite frankly, humor.

"As an example, a favorite memory of mine goes back to the first couple of months of my freshman year. On Saturdays, the NROTC midshipmen at USD form up early for drill. I realize Saturday morning obligations might not sound fun, but I found that usually, after we were finished the morning's routine, we would all head over to the dining hall for food and good humor, before proceeding with our various weekend activities. However, on one particular Saturday, a bunch of us decided to do a group trip to Sunset Cliffs, just north of San Diego. About a dozen of my fellow Fourth Class Midshipmen and I carpooled to the most picturesque cliffs in all of San Diego County for an afternoon of freshman fun. Later, as the sun set and the sky changed into the vibrant shades of orange, purple and pink that I have come to expect here in San Diego, we goofed around, reminiscing about who got chewed out that day, what new hike was explored, and checked in with everyone's life. In short, we bonded. When the sun finally disappeared beneath the horizon and silence fell upon the group, I found myself with a sense of peace and belonging. Looking to my left and right, I knew there would be no better group of individuals to study, socialize, and eventually serve with.

"I was more than I excited, I was (and still am) all in."

—MIDN 3/C Kaleigh M. Molinari, University of San Diego Class of 2021, Environmental Studies Major

A FRESHMAN'S EXPERIENCE

"I personally chose to join the Navy as a part of the ROTC program because I thought it would push me to be a better person mentally, morally, as well as physically. Now, halfway through my freshman year, I find that being a midshipman has done just that. For me, the best part of NROTC is forming bonds with my fellow 4/C classmates as well as the upperclass midshipmen. For example, I know there is always someone who I can trust and rely on to provide insight and guidance. Additionally, as an engineering major, I've found amid the chaos of freshman year that the upperclassmen are great mentors, as they have all been through the same classes and programs—and remember the challenges. NROTC has also made me realize that even when I'm in the dorm, at home on break or just hanging out not in uniform, that I am still a part of the Navy and something bigger than myself and I am incredibly proud of that fact. All in all, I have learned that the NROTC program creates an encouraging environment that is full of opportunity for growth in both academics and character."

—MIDN 4/C John F. Molinari, Villanova University Class of 2022, Engineering Major

Midshipman and Mrs. Molinari. *Courtesy of MIDN 4/C John F. Molinari*

An NROTC scholarship provides full tuition for courses required by the NROTC program and by your young person's stated degree program. Each student is accepted into the NROTC program with a declared major, such as electrical engineering, English, or chemistry. Your student will be required to develop a four-year degree plan early in the freshman fall semester, with oversight and approval from both the institution's academic advisor and the NROTC unit class advisor. This degree map is an agreement between the student and the NROTC program. Deviation is understandable, even expected, over the course of a student's undergraduate studies, but changes must be agreed on between the student and the NROTC staff.

Many students change their minds concerning their majors. A point here is that NROTC scholarships are offered partly in consideration of the student's declared major. The Navy seeks to commission approximately 85 percent of each NROTC class with degrees in engineering, a "hard science," or math major. If your child was awarded a scholarship with the stated intent to study mechanical engineering but after a semester or two decides to change to a liberal arts or "soft sciences" major, the approvals of the NROTC unit's commanding officer and the Naval Service Training Command are required. In most cases, there is little issue in a switch from one hard science to a different one, as long as the degree can be completed within the originally allotted four years. We recommend you have conversations with your student before school starts to help them understand the need to stick with and complete a degree program on time.

Importantly, the NROTC scholarship *does not* fund room and board, which may represent significant costs. However, many schools offer partial or full room-and-board scholarships to midshipmen in good standing in their units. Such benefits, however, are *solely* in the purview of the host institution; the government is not in any way involved in a school's decisions to offer, increase, decrease, eliminate, or enhance such assistance. We list below some of the schools that as of this writing provide room-and-board incentives, but be sure to check with your student's prospective NROTC unit staff to get the most current information.

A final practical consideration concerns the actual disbursement of scholarship funds. The armed forces are of course U.S. government entities, and so all funds to support the Navy and Marine Corps must be authorized and appropriated by Congress, typically on an annual basis as part of the federal budget. Only after Congress has done so can scholarship funds be distributed to your student's NROTC unit, which will then pay your student's tuition bill. Rest assured, if

SCHOOLS THAT OFFER VARIOUS ADDITIONAL ROOM-AND-BOARD BENEFITS

NOTE Amounts awarded vary and are subject to change at an academic institution's discretion. Please visit https://www.nrotc.navy.mil/additional_school_benefits.html for an up-to-date listing and explanation of potential benefits offered. As always, contact the NROTC unit directly for additional information.

Baton Rouge Community College	Norwich University
Carnegie Mellon University	University of Notre Dame
The Citadel	Ohio State University
Clark Atlanta University	University of Oklahoma
University of Colorado	Prairie View A&M University
Columbia College	Regent University
Duquesne University	Rensselaer Polytechnic Institute
Florida A&M University	Rice University
George Washington University	University of Rochester
College of the Holy Cross	Rochester Institute of Technology
University of Idaho	University of Saint Thomas
University of Illinois at Chicago	University of San Diego
Illinois Institute of Technology	St. Mary's College
Jacksonville University	Southeastern Louisiana University
University of Kansas	University of Southern California
Louisiana State University	Southern University and A&M College
Loyola University	University of Tampa
Maine Maritime Academy	University of Texas
University of Maine, Orono	Tidewater Community College
Marquette University	Tulane University
University of Memphis	Tuskegee University
Miami University	Union College
University of Minnesota	Vanderbilt University
University of Missouri	Villanova University
University of Nebraska	Westminster College
Norfolk State University	Worcester Polytechnic Institute

your student is in good standing, the federal government will honor its obligations to pay for tuition, regardless of the internal deadlines set by the school. Under no circumstances should you write a check for your student's tuition if they are on scholarship and in good standing with the NROTC program. If you have any questions, be sure to communicate with the NROTC unit and the institution's financial offices to be sure there are no difficulties.

Helping Your Young Person Succeed

The transition from being a high school student living at home with parents to a relatively free young man or woman in college can cause problems. We are sure that you are interested in giving your son or daughter the best opportunity to succeed. Success as a military officer requires a certain level of maturity, one that can only be developed through self-mastery and self-discipline. Sons and daughters cannot bloom into the men or women they need to become if the link between parent and child is not loose enough to allow them opportunity both to succeed on their own and to learn from mistakes. To use a phrase of the moment, "They're just going to have to figure it out."

The academic issues midshipmen most commonly encounter are related to the required calculus and physics courses. Each Navy-Option midshipman must take and pass two semesters of calculus and calculus-based physics to stay in good NROTC standing. Calculus requirements must be satisfied before the end of the sophomore year, physics by the end of the junior year. Failure to meet these timelines means a mandated "leave of absence" or disenrollment from NROTC. Helping your student develop, while still in high school, a solid foundation in these and related subjects by enrolling in advanced placement, international baccalaureate, community college, or other rigorous courses can pay off handsomely when he or she takes calculus and physics as an undergraduate.

Next, midshipmen must maintain healthy body compositions and levels of physical fitness. Encouraging students to participate in varsity, junior varsity, or intramural sports or other athletic clubs while in high school is a great way to help them develop their physical fitness and at the same time their aptitude for leadership and teamwork. Students must be both physically capable and intellectually sharp to succeed in NROTC and as naval officers. Inordinate time playing video games or staring at a phone screen will not prepare your young person well for the rigors of college and the NROTC program.

Also, a job or a sustained volunteering commitment can help your young person develop skills necessary to accomplish goals—such skills as timeliness, meeting deadlines, and working in the framework of an organized team. Although many adults take such matters for granted, the reality is that some young people struggle with these basic skills necessary for success in college, NROTC, and the naval services, if they never had opportunities to develop them in high school. You should not encourage prospective collegians to stretch themselves too thinly among a myriad of extracurriculars, but we do recommend that you promote their involvement in a few, as a matter of balanced development and maturity.

Last, it is quite common for students to experience anxiety or "growing pains" when entering college life, particularly with the added stress of NROTC requirements. To have been awarded an NROTC scholarship, your young person had to have excelled in high school, but they may not quickly achieve the same level of success as a college student. He or she might be led to doubt their ability to thrive in college and in NROTC, and they will look to you for reassurance. We strongly encourage you to recognize and uphold the vital role of family support in a young person's struggle to achieve their potential and to be willing to provide pep talks when needed. A little support from a loving parent can go a very long way toward making a stressful situation manageable.

Choosing the Right School

Another area where parents may have a positive influence on their child's success in college and NROTC is in the choice of a school. Students choose colleges or universities for many reasons—school prestige, legacy status, geographic location, academic programs, etc. Student who earn NROTC scholarships are likely to have many options available and a number of excellent schools to decide among.

We would like to reiterate a factor mentioned previously, that the NROTC program is designed to be completed *in four years.* Unfortunately, many universities have replaced their presumption of graduation in four years in favor of six years. Institutions that proudly declare their six-year graduation rates may not understand or much sympathize with the singular importance for your student of graduating in only four; this tendency can complicate school selection. As an example, the 2018 four-year graduation rate of the College of the Holy Cross is 89 percent. All other things being equal, a midshipman at Holy Cross is much more likely to graduate on time and without "loose ends" than a midshipman at a school with a low four-year graduation rate. We encourage you, when you tour schools, to speak

> "I called my mom halfway through my first semester complaining that I was fed up, NROTC wasn't for me, and that I planned on dropping out. She calmly, but assertively, offered sympathy, but mandated that I stick with the program at least through the end of the first semester. I agreed and, after a few more months in the program, began to flourish, developed friendships with my fellow midshipmen, and recommitted myself to becoming a naval officer. Some twelve years later, I am grateful for her love and support, but also firmness in helping me overcome my anxiety in adapting to college and NROTC. Family and loved ones' support are critical enablers for midshipman success in NROTC."
>
> —LIEUTENANT CORDIAL

with guides and institutional representatives as to the success the school has had graduating its students in four years.

Also, the prestige of school is not necessarily correlated directly with high graduation rates. Attending a top-tier school will not do any good for young people who cannot complete their degrees with grades at the NROTC standard and on time. While it is impossible to forecast accurately how your son or daughter will perform in college, we feel obliged to hammer home the importance of graduating on time and the fact that schools with lower overall four-year graduation rates may present cultural or institutional barriers to your son's or daughter's earning a degree and commission.

Disciplinary and Administrative Procedures and Consequences

Before we conclude, we must briefly touch on what could happen to a student for whom things do not go smoothly with NROTC. Although this is not the happiest topic, we feel it is important that all parties concerned be fully aware of all the possible outcomes of participation in the NROTC program. Having signed an agreement with the federal government to serve for a period of time in repayment of a scholarship, a midshipman is either commissioned as a naval officer or disenrolled from NROTC. If your student's performance is not up to NROTC standards, counseling and both administrative and disciplinary measures exist to help get back on track. We will cover briefly the aspects most impactful for you as a parent.

First, your child's scholarship will continue to be paid unless the NROTC commanding officer (who is also the Professor of Naval Science, or PNS) places your child on a leave of absence (LOA) or on a leave of absence pending disenrollment. LOA is a serious matter and is generally reserved for significantly subpar performance or legitimate medical conditions. Certain infractions, such as failing to complete the calculus requirement by the end of the sophomore year, automatically put midshipmen on LOA status; others are handled at the discretion of the PNS. Major aptitude offenses, such as engaging in criminal activity, testing positive on urinalysis for drug use, or consistently failing to report for assigned NROTC duties or events, are likely to result in immediate placement on LOA while disenrollment is processed. Only the Secretary of the Navy can disenroll a midshipman from the NROTC program, but it is rare for the secretary to override the recommendation of a Professor of Naval Science endorsed by the Naval Service Training Command.

Placement on leave of absence typically occurs after a Performance Review Board (PRB) ascertains the facts and circumstances of a midshipman's subpar performance. The timing of the PRB can complicate tuition funding. Consider a case of seriously deficient grades. Your student has a very poor freshman spring semester, earning a GPA for the semester below 2.0 and failing two classes. As grades typically do not post officially in a school's database until sometime after students return home for the summer, your student will not be present for the PRB proceedings. A proactive NROTC unit may use online video conferencing or group voice-call technology to convene the board remotely, but Professors of Naval Science often prefer to conduct PRBs in person after students return for the fall semester. Suffice it to say here that it can take approximately two weeks from the PRB session to the final decision of the PNS. If the PNS decides to place your student on an LOA, NROTC will not be paying your student's tuition for (typically) the fall semester. If the PNS has postponed the board until your student returned, you may have little time before the institution expects payment for the coming semester. Someone besides the Navy will have to pick up the tab, which in many cases means *you*. Failure to keep a student's financial account in good standing may prevent the student from receiving official grades for past courses or scheduling the next semester's. Obviously, this would be an extremely stressful time, and open, honest communication between the student and parents would be absolutely required.

Unfortunately, but naturally enough, students whose performance is substandard sometimes believe that they will not actually be placed on LOA. Thus, they may be reluctant to inform their parents of their difficulty, telling themselves that they will receive a lighter penalty than suspension of their scholarship. This is a dangerous, and frankly irresponsible, attitude; it may complicate even more than otherwise their tuition for the next semester, leaving a potentially high-interest student loan as the only feasible option. If you anticipate having to fund your student's college tuition in the absence of the NROTC scholarship, we strongly encourage you to establish an expectation that your student will share grades with you at the end of each term. Your son or daughter may rebel against seemingly obtrusive oversight, but if you are agreeing to pay for their college education if they lose the NROTC scholarship, it is perfectly reasonable that they keep you apprised of their standing in the program. To review: midshipmen must pass all classes required for their degree and maintain a semester and cumulative GPA above 2.5 (on a 4.0 scale) to remain in good standing. If your student is not achieving these standards, you should recognize that the PNS may place your son or daughter on LOA and if so that the next semester's tuition will not be paid for by the Navy.

Multiple terms of LOA are rare; repeated failure to meet NROTC standards generally results in disenrollment. When deciding to disenroll a midshipman from NROTC, the Secretary of the Navy will also decide whether or not scholarship money already paid out is to be recouped, and if so, whether such recoupment requires financial repayment or can be satisfied by a period of active enlisted service in a branch of the U.S. military. Considering the exorbitant cost of tuition at many private universities, a student disenrolled from NROTC in the sophomore or junior year might be liable for a hundred thousand or more dollars. This tragic outcome is in fact the case for a small percentage of NROTC students: being involved and proactive in assisting your student succeed can help prevent it for yours.

Again, we congratulate you on your son or daughter's interest in serving their country by attempting to earn a commission through the NROTC program. Parents, as well as other family members and loved ones, who provide consistent love and emotional support can be difference makers as their sons or daughters strive to achieve their potential. A son or daughter heading off to college is very exciting for a family, and we are confident that the NROTC program is ideal for many of the finest young people (like yours!) that our country has to offer. We encourage you to check the resources online listed in appendix IV or to contact your student's NROTC unit with further questions.

19 Conclusion

"I joined the NROTC in search of a tightly knit community of young Americans with a desire to positively impact others. Now, in my final year of the program, I am proud to say that my experience has fully delivered this and given me deeper satisfaction than I ever expected."

—MIDSHIPMAN 1ST CLASS BUCHOLZ,
University of Michigan NROTC

ASK PEOPLE WHO HAVE SERVED in the military—whether they served five years or twenty-five—and they will tell you that their military experience shaped them in positive ways. It is an honor to serve and wear the cloth of the nation. Service takes many forms, and we hope this book has increased your knowledge and understanding so you can make an informed decision about whether NROTC is the right choice for you.

Many of you will have a wide array of possibilities open to you: in-state or out-of-state, service academy or NROTC, the Ivy League or the South Eastern Conference. For some, the rigor, tradition, and prestige of the Naval, Military, or Air Force Academy may be ideal. However, for those seeking the best of both worlds—an outstanding civilian education and effective military training, all underwritten by a full-tuition scholarship at one of over a hundred NROTC-affiliated colleges and universities—the Naval Reserve Officers Training Corps might be the answer. NROTC can facilitate your undergraduate education at one of the best schools in our nation and be a great springboard to a career in the naval service.

Above all else, we recommend, if you are even casually considering NROTC as an option, that you meet with your local naval recruiter or visit a nearby NROTC

An ensign on the bridge of the *Arleigh Burke*–class guided-missile destroyer USS *Porter* (DDG 78) trains a midshipman during a watch as the conning officer. *U.S. Navy photo by Ford Williams*

unit to discuss your interest in the program. Recruiters or staff officers at either location will be able to answer questions and offer insights and resources valuable for an informed decision. Ultimately, it is never a bad idea to submit an application and then choose whether to decline or accept an NROTC scholarship if offered. If your "Plan A" for college does not work out, having backups open for you could be a blessing. This is an incredibly exciting time in your young life, and we hope this guide has helped decide the next step in your journey.

Some of you have already submitted your applications and are anxiously anticipating the results from your college admission applications and the NROTC National Scholarship Board. We wish you the best of luck and are confident that whatever path opens itself to you, you can make, with diligence and determination, your dreams of serving as a naval officer come to fruition. If you are disappointed with the outcome of the National Scholarship Board, by all means consider participating in NROTC as a member of the College Program. Every year students in the College Program earn scholarships; even if you are not selected, you can forge a path to a commission through NROTC.

"I really enjoy the added structure and purpose the NROTC program gives to my college experience. Being a part of this program gives me the motivation to push myself both physically and academically. It also gives my time at college a real purpose. I know that when I graduate I will be able to apply what I have learned and experienced to something that really matters."

—MIDSHIPMAN 2ND CLASS SELTMANN,
University of Washington NROTC

For those of you already accepted by both your institution and NROTC, kudos for having the foresight to read this guide. Improving your professional knowledge by reading will pay dividends throughout your career—whether in the military or in civilian life. Congratulations on winning a very competitive scholarship, and we wish you the best of luck in the program. Your graduation and commissioning may now seem far in the future, but the four undergraduate years will fly by. Very soon you will be entrusted with leading the most valuable resource our great nation possesses—the brave men and women who serve as Sailors and Marines. Use your time wisely to prepare yourself as best you can for the incredible responsibility that will be yours.

For the parents and loved ones of young people considering NROTC, we hope this guide has increased your understanding of the program. Particularly for those who have not served in the military, the flurry of acronyms and jargon can be daunting, and popular misconceptions concerning military service can be obstacles. We hope that now you have some answers and resources that ease any worries about your son's or daughter's desire to serve.

Last, to all other readers, we hope this book has enhanced your understanding of and appreciation for one of the primary commissioning sources for the officer corps of our naval services. Officers commissioned through the NROTC program have ascended to the highest levels of military, government, and civilian leadership—and their experiences in NROTC helped lay a foundation of discipline, commitment, and service that bore them up throughout their careers. Our strong, vibrant NROTC programs at the best academic institutions across our nation sustain the intellectual, cultural, and social diversity of our naval officer corps.

Please take advantage of the online resources in the book's appendices for the most up-to-date information concerning NROTC. We have enjoyed sharing our experience, our appreciation of the NROTC program, and our hopes for its exciting future helping shape our naval officer corps.

"The Navy recognizes, now more than ever, that the most critical warfighting capability for our national security is the intellectual development of our Naval leaders and warriors. It is our greatest competitive advantage, and it begins with every ensign or second lieutenant. So how we prepare these future leaders and warriors is absolutely critical. Accordingly, the Navy and Marine Corps have invested in a rich educational ecosystem, from Officer Candidate School and the Academy to NROTC, each with their own strengths. This eco-system values above all else diversity of thought and experience, and this is the great strength of NROTC that makes it so important to the Naval service.

"The NROTC program includes persistent Naval training immersed in a unique educational experience enriched by diverse scholars and students. Through this experience, you will learn what it means to be a Naval officer, but you will also broaden your world-view through interdisciplinary coursework, cultural immersion, and independent research. This is crucial because mastery of a broad range of intellectual and cultural content lends crucial perspective to any decision making—decision making that is heart and soul of leadership. This perspective is also crucial because it reinforces a lifelong way of thinking, one that, as Thomas Friedman says in his book *The World Is Flat: A Brief History of the Twenty-First Century,* 'In an age when parts or all of many jobs are constantly going to be exposed to digitization, automation, and outsourcing . . . it is not only what you know but how you learn that will set you apart. Because what you know today will be out-of-date sooner than you think.'

"My experience at Notre Dame was all of this and more. Throughout my career, I have benefitted every day from Notre Dame's mission to develop 'disciplined habits of mind, body, and spirit that characterize educated, skilled, and free human beings.' And because of Notre Dame's unique, strong, and lasting relationship with the Navy, and how I grew as a leader from my NROTC experience, I am the Naval Officer I am today: I benefited from *both* the ideas of 'God, Country, Notre Dame,' and 'Honor, Courage, and Commitment.' It was my experience at Notre Dame that set me on the transcendent path to be not just a leader, but a warrior.

"Speaking of warriors, remember what General Patton once said: 'If everybody is thinking alike, then somebody isn't thinking.' Malcolm Forbes calls it 'the art of thinking differently together.' It is this diversity of thought and experience that will be our greatest competitive advantage in era of Great Power Competition. This is why NROTC is the great force multiplier in the intellectual development of our future Naval leaders and warriors. This is why we will prevail."

—ADM CHRISTOPHER GRADY,
Commander, U.S. Fleet Forces Command,
University of Notre Dame NROTC Class of 1984

NROTC Schools and Cross-Town Affiliates by State

Note: RN = (Registered) Nurse Option

ALABAMA
Auburn University
Tuskegee University

ARIZONA
Arizona State University
University of Arizona
    Cross-Town Affiliate:
    —Pima Community College

CALIFORNIA
San Diego State University
    Cross-Town Affiliates:
    —California State University, San Marcos
    —University of California at San Diego
University of California, Berkeley
    Cross-Town Affiliates:
    —California Maritime Academy
    —Stanford University
    —University of California at Davis
University of California, Los Angeles

University of San Diego
  Cross-Town Affiliate:
  —Point Loma Nazarene University
University of Southern California

COLORADO
University of Colorado
  Cross-Town Affiliate:
  —University of Colorado at Denver

CONNECTICUT
Yale University

DISTRICT OF COLUMBIA
George Washington University
  Cross-Town Affiliates:
  —Catholic University of America (RN)
  —Georgetown University (RN)
  —Howard University (RN)

FLORIDA
Embry-Riddle Aeronautical University
Florida A&M University
  Cross-Town Affiliates:
  —Florida State University (RN)
  —Tallahassee Community College
Jacksonville University (RN)
  Cross-Town Affiliates:
  —Florida State College at Jacksonville
  —University of North Florida
University of Florida
University of South Florida
  Cross-Town Affiliate:
  —University of Tampa

GEORGIA

Georgia Institute of Technology
    Cross-Town Affiliates:
    —Georgia State University
    —Kennesaw State University
Morehouse College
    Cross-Town Affiliates:
    —Clark Atlanta University
    —Spelman College
Savannah State University
    Cross-Town Affiliate:
    —Armstrong Atlantic State University

IDAHO

University of Idaho
    Cross-Town Affiliate:
    —Washington State University

ILLINOIS

Illinois Institute of Technology
    Cross-Town Affiliates:
    —Kennedy King College
    —University of Illinois at Chicago
Northwestern University
    Cross-Town Affiliate:
    —Loyola University (RN)
University of Illinois
    Cross-Town Affiliate:
    —Parkland College

INDIANA

Purdue University (RN)
University of Notre Dame
    Cross-Town Affiliate:
    —St. Mary's College

IOWA

Iowa State University

KANSAS

University of Kansas

LOUISIANA

Southern University and A&M College (RN)

Cross-Town Affiliates:

—Baton Rouge Community College

—Louisiana State University

—Southeastern Louisiana University

Tulane University

Cross-Town Affiliates:

—Dillard University

—Loyola University

—University of New Orleans

—Xavier University

MAINE

Maine Maritime Academy

Cross-Town Affiliates:

—Husson University (RN Option only)

—University of Maine at Orono (RN)

MARYLAND

University of Maryland, Baltimore County

University of Maryland, College Park

MASSACHUSETTS

Boston University

Cross-Town Affiliate:

—Boston College (RN)

—Northeastern University (RN Option only)

College of the Holy Cross

Cross-Town Affiliate:
—Brown University
—Worcester Polytechnic Institute
—Worcester State University (RN)
Massachusetts Institute of Technology
Cross-Town Affiliate:
—Harvard University
—Tufts University

MICHIGAN
University of Michigan (RN)
Cross-Town Affiliate:
—Eastern Michigan University

MINNESOTA
University of Minnesota (RN)
Cross-Town Affiliate:
—Macalester College
—University of Saint Thomas

MISSISSIPPI
University of Mississippi

MISSOURI
University of Missouri
Cross-Town Affiliate:
—Columbia College

NEBRASKA
University of Nebraska

NEW JERSEY
Rutgers University, New Brunswick (RN)
Cross-Town Affiliate:
—Princeton University

NEW MEXICO
University of New Mexico
    Cross-Town Affiliate:
    —Central New Mexico Community College

NEW YORK
Cornell University
Rensselaer Polytechnic Institute
    Cross-Town Affiliate:
    —Russell Sage College (RN Option only)
    —Union College
State University of New York Maritime College
    Cross-Town Affiliate:
    —Columbia University (includes Barnard College)
    —Fordham University
    —Molloy College (RN Option only)
University of Rochester
    Cross-Town Affiliates:
    —Rochester Institute of Technology
    —St. John Fisher College
    —State University of New York at Brockport

NORTH CAROLINA
Duke University
North Carolina State University
University of North Carolina

OHIO
Miami University
Ohio State University

OKLAHOMA
University of Oklahoma

OREGON
Oregon State University

PENNSYLVANIA

Carnegie Mellon University
    Cross-Town Affiliates:
    —Duquesne University (RN)
    —University of Pittsburgh (RN)
Pennsylvania State University (RN)
University of Pennsylvania (RN)
    Cross-Town Affiliates:
    —Drexel University (RN)
    —Temple University (RN)
Villanova University (RN)

SOUTH CAROLINA

The Citadel
University of South Carolina
    Cross-Town Affiliates:
    —Allen University
    —Midlands Technical College

TENNESSEE

University of Memphis
    Cross-Town Affiliates:
    —Christian Brothers University
    —Rhodes College
Vanderbilt University
    Cross-Town Affiliates:
    —Belmont University (RN Option only)
    —Tennessee State University

TEXAS

Prairie View A&M University
Rice University
    Cross-Town Affiliates:
    —Texas Southern University
    —University of Houston (University Park Campus)

Texas A&M University
    Cross-Town Affiliate:
    —Texas A&M University at Galveston (Navy Option only)
University of Texas (RN)
    Cross-Town Affiliate:
    —Huston-Tillotson University

UTAH

University of Utah
    Cross-Town Affiliates:
    —Weber State University
    —Westminster College

VERMONT

Norwich University (RN)

VIRGINIA

Hampton University
Norfolk State University
    Cross-Town Affiliate:
    —Tidewater Community College
Old Dominion University
    Cross-Town Affiliate:
    —Regent University
University of Virginia (RN)
Virginia Military Institute
    Cross-Town Affiliate:
    —Mary Baldwin University
Virginia Polytechnic Institute

WASHINGTON

University of Washington
    Cross-Town Affiliate:
    —Seattle University (RN Option only)

WISCONSIN

Marquette University (RN)

Cross-Town Affiliates:

—Milwaukee School of Engineering (RN)

—University of Wisconsin, Milwaukee

University of Wisconsin

NROTC Scholarship Application Checklist

1. *Determine the fall semester in which you are expected to begin undergraduate studies.* For example, a high school senior graduating in spring 2021 would likely begin college in fall 2021. The deadline for all application materials is 31 December of the year before the school year being considered. Using the example of a student entering college in fall 2021, all application materials will be due by midnight on 31 December 2020. Applications will be accepted beginning in spring 2020 for the fall 2021 school year.

2. *Contact either your local NROTC unit or Navy or Marine Corps Officer recruiter to begin the application process.* The Navy's official NROTC website is located at http://www.nrotc.navy.mil/, that for Navy Officer Recruiters at https://www.navy.com/local, and the site for Marine Officer Selection Officers at https://rmi.marines.com/request-information. This process should be completed as soon as you have a desire to seek a commission in the U.S. Navy or Marine Corps, although you are not eligible to begin the application process formally until the spring semester of your junior year of high school.

3. *Prepare for and take both the SAT and ACT college entrance examinations.* Either test is acceptable for the application, and the highest score received on either test will be used in your application. Test scores earned in the two years prior to the application deadline are acceptable; in the case of a fall 2021 student, scores earned from December 2019 to December 2021 will be considered. Registration information for the SAT can be found at https://college readiness.collegeboard.org/sat/register and for the ACT at http://www.act .org/content/act/en/products-and-services/the-act/registration.html.

4. ***Determine your top five school choices.*** As part of your NROTC scholarship application, you will need to select at least five schools for possible placement, with at least one of your first three being a school at which you would qualify for in-state tuition. You should plan on applying to all five of your potential schools, as your scholarship may be assigned at any listed on your application. It is prudent to visit each school, if possible, and to reach out to each of the five schools' NROTC units to express your interest and to ask any questions. Keep in mind that the five schools must be from different NROTC units— not cross-town affiliates of the same unit.

5. ***Ask (1) a guidance counselor/school administrator, (2) a math, science, or English teacher, and (3) another teacher, counselor, coach, or employer for permission to use them as references.*** The individuals you list on your application will be contacted directly by the Navy and asked to fill out a reference form and provide written remarks. It is good form to have a conversation with these individuals before submitting your application.

6. ***Establish an account at the official NROTC application website, https://net focus.netc.navy.mil/nrotc/candidate_app/Login.aspx.*** This is where all application materials will be submitted. Do this at least a few months prior to your application deadline to allow time to overcome any technical complications.

7. ***Complete the required Applicant Physical Assessment and provide the score sheet to your recruiter.*** Information on the test can be found at http://www .nrotc.navy.mil/physical_requirements.html. The test must be administered and signed for by a physical education instructor, athletics coach, active-duty officer, active-duty E-7 or above, or an NJROTC instructor. Prospective midshipmen must meet both body composition (i.e., height and weight) standards and complete their maximum number of crunches, push-ups within two minutes, and one-mile run to the best of their ability. No minimum standards are listed, but maximum scores can be earned by meeting the following standards. Body composition standards are equivalent to active-duty Navy or Marine Corps standards and are found in appendix V or online at https://www.fitness.marines.mil/BCP_Standards/ for the Marine Corps or at

https://www.public.navy.mil/bupers-npc/support/21st_Century_Sailor
/physical/Documents/Guide%204-%20Body%20Composition%20
Assessment%20(BCA).pdf, for the Navy.

	Crunches	Push-Ups	1-Mile Run
Male	95	75	5:20
Female	95	50	6:00

8. *Schedule your officer interview.* Officer interviews for all applicants for the national scholarship must be conducted with an active-duty naval officer. NROTC unit staff members at a nearby NROTC unit are available to conduct your officer interview even if you are not interested in attending school there. If you do not live near an NROTC unit, your officer recruiter will help you arrange your officer interview.

9. *Complete the online application.* Complete the form and required essays online at https://netfocus.netc.navy.mil/nrotc/candidate_app/Login.aspx. The application itself is long and may require a few hours to complete. Take your time and particularly invest effort in your short essays, as they will be the only personal statements you will be able to present to the scholarship selection board.

10. *Have someone else review your application.* It is prudent to have another person you trust look over the application to ensure it is professional, grammatically correct, and accurate. Good people to ask for their review are your officer recruiter, parents, or high school teachers. Your reviewer may help you avoid simple mistakes that would detract from the overall quality of your application.

11. *Submit your application!* Only after careful preparation and deliberate review should you formally submit your application. Adjustments can be made after your application is submitted, but doing so requires coordination with the National Scholarship Board. Again, the deadline for all application materials is the last day of December of the year prior to beginning college.

Note: Medical screenings will occur after a scholarship offer is made. While waivers may be considered by the medical screening board, it is prudent to examine the list of disqualifying conditions at http://www.nrotc.navy.mil/physical _requirements.html.

Professional Core Competencies

Note: The competencies reprinted in this appendix serve as the standard for the training and development of naval officers in the NROTC Program. The original can be found at https://www.public.navy.mil/netc/nstc/NSTC_Directives/NSTC _Manuals/2019%20Officer%20Professional%20Core%20Competencies% 20(PCC)%20Manual.pdf.

I. NAVAL ORIENTATION AND OFFICERSHIP

A basically trained officer must know and understand the fundamentals of Naval Officership as a profession. These fundamentals include but are not limited to the Officer's Oath as related to Navy Core Values, naval customs and traditions, military drill, uniform wear, watchstanding, and basic elements of naval regulations.

A. Comprehend the role of commissioned officers as members of the U.S. Armed Forces and know the obligations and responsibilities assumed by taking the oath of office and accepting a commission including the Constitutional requirement for civilian control.

   1. Comprehend the Naval officer's roles and responsibilities as a member of the profession of arms.

   2. Comprehend the significance of special trust and confidence vested in commissioned officers.

B. Know uniform regulations.

   1. Demonstrate proper uniform wear and military grooming standards.

   2. Demonstrate personnel inspection procedures.

C. Demonstrate marching, formations and basic drill maneuvers.
1. Demonstrate close order drill.
2. Know proper execution of the officer's sword manual.
D. Comprehend the UCMJ, practice of military law, and applications of regulations as they may involve a junior officer in the performance of duties.
1. Comprehend the purpose, scope, and constitutional basis of Navy Regulations and the Uniform Code of Military Justice and relate these regulations to personal conduct in the military service.
2. Comprehend junior officer responsibilities relative to the military justice system including familiarization with:
(a) essential publications relating to military justice.
(b) search and seizure.
(c) apprehension and restraint.
(d) non-judicial punishment.
(e) investigations.
(f) courts martial.
(g) administrative discharges.
(h) extra military instruction.
E. Know the requirements for watchstanding and be able to demonstrate a proper watch relief and the requirements, procedures, and format for keeping logs.
1. Know basic Navy terminology and professional nomenclature.
F. Know the origins and current usage of naval customs and traditions.
1. Demonstrate military courtesies such as saluting, introductions, and forms of address.
2. Know basic shipboard etiquette, flag etiquette and proper display of basic Navy flags and pennants.
3. Demonstrate proper protocol with respect to quarterdeck procedures, wardroom etiquette, and small boat/vehicle etiquette.
4. Know military ceremonial functions including colors, parade formations, and changes of command.
5. Know social customs and basic protocol for formal and informal functions to include receiving lines, dining outs, mess night, and the Navy/USMC birthday ball.

G. Comprehend command relationships and organization.

1. Know command relationships and organization for both operational and administrative environments as prescribed by the SORM.

2. Know the Navy and Marine Corps officer and enlisted rank/pay-grade structures and insignia.

3. Know the officer ranks in the Army, Air Force, and Coast Guard.

4. Know relevant Navy and Marine Corps unrestricted and restricted line communities and applicable warfare insignias.

II. LEADERSHIP AND ETHICS

A basically trained officer must understand the relationship between the Oath of Office and Navy Core Values, have personal values consistent with Navy Core Values, practice sound judgment while enforcing rules and regulations, and be a valued team leader who fosters loyalty up and down the chain of command. The core competencies in this area include but are not limited to critical thinking, effective communication, planning and decision making, basic leadership and management principles, and classical ethics as related to moral decision making.

A. Comprehend the relationship of the Oath of Office to Navy core values.

1. Know and recite the Oath of Office.

2. Comprehend the significance of special trust and confidence vested in commissioned officers as members of the profession of arms.

3. Comprehend the basic elements of the Constitution of the United States.

4. Know the Navy Ethos.

B. Know and comprehend the Navy Leader Development Strategy.

1. Know the Charge of Command.

2. Comprehend the relationship between authority, responsibility, and accountability.

3. Comprehend the leader development elements of experience, education, training, and personal development.

C. Comprehend the professional, moral and ethical responsibilities of the Naval Officer.

1. Comprehend the relationship of integrity, moral courage, and ethical behavior to authority, responsibility, and accountability.

2. Demonstrate, by personal example, the professional attributes and behaviors of a Naval Officer.

3. Know the International Law of Armed Conflict including Rules of Engagement (ROE), conduct of hostilities, rights of individuals, obligations of engaged parties, and the Code of Conduct for members of the U.S. Armed Forces.

D. Demonstrate an understanding how the following influence an officer's ability to effectively lead in an organization:

1. Importance of officers leading by personal example.

2. Prioritization of Constitution, mission, service, command, shipmate and self.

3. Use of authority.

  (a) Definition of a lawful order.

  (b) Process for challenging unlawful orders.

4. Conveyance of clear and concise Commander's Intent.

5. Degree of delegation and decentralization.

6. Officer-enlisted professional relationship.

7. Fostering loyalty up and down the chain of command.

8. Morale and esprit de corps.

9. Supervision and follow-up.

10. Time management and prioritization.

E. Demonstrate an understanding of basic counseling skills.

1. Comprehend the importance of feedback to mission effectiveness.

2. Comprehend motivational techniques which may be useful in leadership situations.

3. Apply counseling skills to performance evaluation debriefings, discipline infractions, career guidance, and personal problems.

F. Know the importance of deliberate planning and the military decision making process.

1. Know the elements and intellectual standards of critical thinking.

2. Know the importance of properly developed mission statements and objectives.

G. Apply leadership skills to achieve objectives.

1. Comprehend the relationship between goal setting and feedback and apply this understanding to measurements, inspections, and reports.

2. Apply techniques and skills to measure organizational effectiveness by establishing qualitative and quantitative performance standards.

3. Comprehend different leadership styles and how they apply to different situations.

4. Comprehend basic principles of human behavior and group dynamics.

5. Comprehend the characteristics of informal and formal groups.

6. Apply leadership and management skills to design work groups based on task requirements, group capability, and available resources.

7. Know the importance of diversity and inclusion when leading an organization.

8. Know the importance of fostering innovation when leading an organization.

H. Demonstrate the ability to communicate effectively.

   1. Demonstrate effective oral and written communication.

   2. Comprehend different forms of naval correspondence.

I. Know the basic elements of the assignment process, career planning (including the requirement for Joint Duty), promotions, milestones and career paths for Navy/USMC.

J. Know the Navy/USMC training and qualification process (PQS, JQR and Warfare qualification).

1. Comprehend the importance of training and qualification to personal/professional development and mission readiness.

2. Know the importance of continuing education, professional reading, and lifelong learning to professional and personal development as a leader and Naval Officer.

3. Know the availability and applicability of the CNO's Professional Reading program to personal development.

III. SEAPOWER AND NAVAL HISTORY

A basically trained officer must understand Seapower as a critical element of national security and prosperity for the United States of America in both peace and war. A basically trained officer must understand the missions and functions of the Navy and the role of naval forces in protecting the global maritime commons, deterring potential adversaries, and fighting/winning our nation's wars when required. The core competencies in this area include but are not limited to maritime strategy, missions and functions of the Navy, geography as related to maritime strategy, the evolution of sea power, and the history of the U.S. Navy and USMC.

A. Comprehend current maritime strategy.
   1. Comprehend the relationship of seapower to national interests and maritime strategy in both peace and war.
   2. Know the impact and significance of geography and Sea Lines of Communication on maritime strategy and naval operations.
   3. Know the missions and functions of the U.S. Navy as described in maritime strategy.
   4. Comprehend the importance of maritime partnerships and coalition operations.
   5. Comprehend the importance of regional and cultural expertise/ awareness to naval forces' ability to successfully plan, operate forward, and engage effectively.
   6. Comprehend the importance of a forward naval presence to maritime strategy through forward stationed and rotationally deployed forces.
   7. Know major aspects of the U.S. position on United Nations Convention on the International Law of the Sea (UNCLOS) regarding territorial seas, contiguous zones, high seas and rights of innocent passage and the impact of UNCLOS on maritime strategy.
   8. Comprehend the concept of "liberty as a mission" as related to port visits, engagement, and theater security cooperation.

B. Comprehend the mission and basic organization of the Navy and Marine Corps:
   1. Know the operational and administrative chains of command within the Department of the Navy.
   2. Know the names and locations of the numbered Fleets and naval component commands.
   3. Know the basic size and composition of the Navy (platforms and personnel).
   4. Know the roles, responsibilities, and organization of the Reserve Component.

C. Know the missions and basic organization of the major components of the other services.

1. Know the current organization of the Department of the Navy and the relationship of Navy organization to Department of Defense, Joint Chiefs of Staff, and the unified and specified commands.

D. Know the basic concepts and philosophies of Joint Warfare.

1. Know basic military staff organization (N, S and J-codes).

E. Know significant events in U.S. naval history.

1. Know the evolution of the Navy and Marine Corps including the origins of the service along with prominent leaders and their contributions.

2. Know the role naval forces have played in the national strategies and policies of the United States in both peacetime and war.

3. Comprehend the historical evolution of sea power and its effects on world history.

    (a) Comprehend the importance of power projection by seaborne forces and cite historical examples.

    (b) Know the significant historical developments of naval weapons systems, platforms, tactics, techniques, and procedures.

4. Know the history of the Reserve Component.

5. Comprehend the importance of innovation on naval warfare.

IV. PROGRAMS AND POLICIES

A basically trained officer must possess a working knowledge of Navy programs and policies. The core competencies in this area include but are not limited to professional administrative responsibilities, personnel management, classified material handling, UCMJ and Navy Regulations, naval correspondence, fitness and wellness programs, and safety and environmental programs.

A. Know basic administrative responsibilities of an officer including:

1. Personnel administrative actions with regard to officer and enlisted service records, performance evaluations, advancement recommendations, promotions, and selection board procedures.

2. Know governing documents for naval correspondence.

3. Know how directives are organized and revised.

4. Know importance of documenting and evaluating training.

B. Know basic requirements and procedures for proper handling and disclosure of classified material, consequences for inadvertent disclosure, and consequences for violation of the espionage laws, including:

1. Maintenance of classified material security, including techniques for avoiding technology transfer.

2. Disclosure (clearance and need to know).

3. Basic security classifications and their corresponding handling requirements.

C. Comprehend all current Navy and Marine Corps commissioning sources as they relate to both peers and subordinates.

D. Comprehend the UCMJ, practice of military law, and applications of regulations as they may involve a junior officer in the performance of duties.

1. Comprehend the purpose, scope, and constitutional basis of Navy Regulations and the Uniform Code of Military Justice and relate these regulations to personal conduct in the military service.

2. Comprehend and demonstrate adherence to the standards of conduct for military personnel.

E. Comprehend current Navy or Marine Corps regulations, policies, and programs relative to the following fitness and wellness issues:

1. Substance and alcohol abuse prevention and detection, including urinalysis testing programs, treatment, and consequences.

2. Physical readiness, nutrition, and weight control.

3. Operational Stress Control.

4. Suicide Prevention.

5. Athletics, recreational, and off-duty safety.

6. Demonstrate personal physical fitness by conforming to Navy or Marine Corps physical fitness testing standards.

7. Demonstrate a fit military appearance by conforming to applicable Navy or Marine Corps body fat percent and/or height-weight standards.

8. Demonstrate fundamental swimming skills through successful completion of Third Class swimmer qualifications.

F. Know Navy safety, energy, and environmental programs.

1. Apply the fundamentals of Operational Risk Management and Time Critical Risk Management.

2. Know Navy energy policy, energy goals, and Fleet energy initiatives.

3. Comprehend the operational, legal, and stewardship importance of compliance with environmental policies and programs both afloat and ashore.

G. Know financial, medical, retirement, and other benefits available to military personnel.

1. Know the basic elements of personal financial management.

2. Know current policies and programs relative to educational opportunities.

H. Know the following Navy programs and policies:

1. Comprehend and apply current equal opportunity policies and programs.

2. Comprehend and apply the official policies on prevention of sexual harassment, fraternization, and hazing.

3. Comprehend the official policies for Sexual Assault Prevention and Response including Bystander Intervention.

4. Know the policies regarding pregnancy, family care plans, EFMP, and family readiness.

5. Know Navy programs and policies on diversity and inclusion.

6. Comprehend the Personally Identifiable Information (PII) program and policies.

7. Know travel regulations and government credit card program.

V. TECHNICAL FOUNDATIONS AND NAVAL WARFARE

A basically trained officer must have fundamental technical knowledge and understand basic principles of naval warfare in order to capably lead our technologically advanced Navy. The core competencies in this area include but are not limited to basic engineering fundamentals, naval systems and weapons systems, basic platform characteristics, and basic fundamentals of naval warfare.

A. Know the basic characteristics and capabilities of the major weapons systems and platforms of the U.S. Naval forces.

1. Know the designations, characteristics, capabilities, and missions of ships, aircraft, and weapon systems of the U.S. Navy, Marine Corps, and Strategic Sealift Command.

B. Comprehend basic engineering concepts.
    1. Know the concepts of work, power, and efficiency and their application to propulsion systems.
    2. Know the basic operation, key components, and safety considerations of propulsion systems.
    3. Know the basic principles of auxiliary systems.
    4. Know the basic principles of electrical power generation, distribution, and electrical safety.
    5. Comprehend the factors and criteria for structural integrity and operational employment in platform design.
    6. Comprehend basic principles of fluid dynamics.
    7. Know the purpose of the Navy Maintenance Material Management (3-M) system and its PMS and MDS subsystems.
C. Comprehend weapons systems, platforms, and environmental factors.
    1. Know the basic threats potential adversaries can employ against Navy platforms.
    2. Know what effects chemical/biological/radiological/nuclear (CBR-N) attacks have on the combat environment.
    3. Know the operating principles and common uses of platform weapon systems.
    4. Comprehend the basic theory and use of radar, sonar, and fire-control systems.
    5. Comprehend the basic theory of electronic warfare systems.
D. Know the importance of energy as a critical combat enabler and understand best practices in energy efficiency.
E. Know how each of the following components of naval warfare contributes to the basic sea control and power projection missions of the Naval service:
    1. air warfare.
    2. undersea warfare (including mine warfare and antisubmarine warfare).
    3. surface warfare.
    4. strike warfare.
    5. amphibious warfare.
    6. electronic warfare.

7. mobile logistics support.

8. special warfare.

9. expeditionary warfare.

10. Cyber/C5I warfare (command, control, communications, computers, combat systems, intelligence).

F. Demonstrate an understanding of naval communications and COMSEC.

1. Demonstrate proper radio-telephone communication.

2. Demonstrate communication security procedures.

3. Comprehend cyber/satellite based communications.

4. Know the different bands of radio communication across the spectrum.

G. Know the significance of intelligence in the application of naval warfare.

H. Understand the need for OPSEC including recognition of the OPSEC threat.

I. Know the purpose of the Navy Doctrine Library System (NDLS) and its hierarchy of publications.

1. Know the Composite Warfare Commander (CWC) concept.

2. Know the concepts and publications that govern Navy command and control, doctrine, and tactics.

J. Know current Anti-Terrorism/ Force Protection (AT/FP) procedures and requirements.

K. Demonstrate proper handling and firing of U.S. service small arms using current safety procedures.

VI. SEAMANSHIP AND NAVIGATION

As every Naval officer must be a capable mariner—a basically trained officer must understand how to safely operate at sea. The core competencies in this area include but are not limited to shipboard damage control, theory and practice of navigation at sea, basic ship handling, steering and sailing rules for preventing collisions at sea, and understanding and calculating relative motion between maneuvering ships.

A. Know terms, nomenclature, and use of shipboard deck equipment and fittings.

B. Comprehend shipboard safety and preparedness.

C. Demonstrate shipboard damage control.
　1. Know the typical shipboard damage control organization and responsibilities of key personnel assigned.
　2. Know how shipboard watertight integrity is obtained through installed shipboard features to increase material conditions of readiness.
　3. Know the procedures, objectives, and priorities in combating progressive deterioration from fire and underwater hull damage.
　　(a) Know classes of fire and agents, equipment, and procedures used to extinguish them.
　　(b) Know the use of equipment, materials, and procedures for countering progressive flooding and structural deterioration.
　4. Know the procedures for donning and doffing damage control breathing equipment.
D. Comprehend the theory and practice of navigation at sea.
　1. Comprehend the longitude/time relationship.
　2. Demonstrate time conversion and time zone determination.
　3. Know the correct procedures to determine the time of sunrise and sunset.
　4. Know the theory and use of electronic navigation systems.
　　(a) Know basic principles of radar navigation.
　　(b) Comprehend operating principles and limitations of GPS and navigation chart datum.
　5. Comprehend the uses of navigational datums and the various chart projections.
　6. Know chart symbology particularly those symbols pertaining to hazards and dangers.
　7. Know how to select the proper charts (both paper and electronic) and how to determine chart accuracy and reliability.
　8. Apply correct plotting procedures when navigating in piloting waters.
　　(a) Apply the six rules of dead reckoning in keeping a plot of ship movements.
　　(b) Know the definitions of the terms: track, speed of advance, speed over ground, PIM, EP, LOP, and relative bearing.

(c) Know turn and danger bearings.

(d) Demonstrate the ability to plot and interpret fixes and running fixes.

9. Know the advantages, disadvantages, and applications of gyro and magnetic compasses.

(a) Apply terrestrial navigation methods to determine compass error.

(b) Apply magnetic variation to a given location.

(c) Know the concept of deviation and the use of the digital flux gate magnetic compass.

10. Know the basic principles of celestial navigation.

11. Know the capabilities and limitations of various instruments used in piloting to determine direction, speed, distance, and depth of water.

12. Know the essential publications and records used in navigation and comprehend their value.

13. Know the characteristics and application of various aids to navigation in piloting and comprehend their importance in safe navigation, including:

(a) buoyage systems—IALA.

(b) lights/daymarkers.

(c) radar beacons/markers.

14. Apply correct procedures in planning and plotting approaches to harbors and anchorages.

15. Comprehend tidal action and know tide classifications and reference planes.

16. Demonstrate the ability to use the Current Triangle to find course and speed made good, set, drift, and compensating course and speed to negate set and drift.

17. Know terms associated with the Terrestrial Coordinate System; equator, prime meridian, great circles, small circles, parallels, meridians, latitude, longitude, and rhumb lines.

18. Comprehend relative motion and demonstrate capability to solve problems associated with relative motion.

(a) Comprehend the theory of relative motion as graphically displayed by the geographic and relative plot.

      (b) Comprehend the significance of bearing drift and apply bearing drift to determine relative motion.

      (c) Demonstrate the ability to compute target angle.

      (d) Comprehend the speed triangle and the relative plot associated with a maneuvering board (MOBOARD).

      (e) Demonstrate the use of a maneuvering board to accurately:

         (1) Determine the CPA and time of CPA of an approaching vessel.

         (2) Determine the true course and true speed of a maneuvering ship.

         (3) Determine course, speed, and time for proceeding to a new station or to intercept another vessel.

         (4) Determine true wind direction and velocity.

         (5) Determine course and speed to produce desired wind.

         (6) Determine an avoidance course of a given target.

  19. Know the Rules of the Road as found in the USCG Navigation Rules—International and Inland.

  20. Know the use of ATP-I Volume II and the International Code of Signals (PUB-102).

E. Know environmental weather factors affecting naval operations.

  1. Know the sources of environmental products/predictions/forecasts available to naval units underway.

  2. Know the impact of hazardous weather conditions on surface and flight operations at sea.

F. Know controllable and non-controllable forces in shiphandling.

  1. Know the effects of controllable forces in shiphandling such as engines, rudders, propellers, lines, anchors, and tugs.

  2. Know the effects of non-controllable forces in shiphandling such as wind, current, depth of water, etc.

  3. Demonstrate the ability to issue standard commands for engines, rudder, and line handling.

G. Know various systems for internal shipboard communications and demonstrate proper sound-powered phone procedures.

H. Know the basic terms and procedures associated with replenishment at sea.

I. Demonstrate the skills required for a Skipper "B" Qualification.

NROTC Online Resources

Official Navy website	www.navy.mil
Official Marine Corps website	www.marines.mil
Navy Officer Recruiting	https://www.navy.com/joining-the-navy/ways-to-join/become-a-commissioned-officer
Marine Corps Recruiting	www.marines.com
NROTC website	www.nrotc.navy.mil
NROTC Application	https://netfocus.netc.navy.mil/nrotc/candidate_app/Login.aspx
Naval Special Warfare website	www.sealswcc.com
Navy Physical Fitness	https://www.public.navy.mil/bupers-npc/support/21st_Century_Sailor/physical/Pages/default2.aspx
Marine Corps Physical Fitness	https://www.fitness.marines.mil/
SAT Registration/Study	https://collegereadiness.collegeboard.org/sat/register
ACT Registration/Study	http://www.act.org/content/act/en/products-and-services/the-act/registration.html

Navy/USMC Physical Readiness Standards

Note: In fall 2020, the U.S. Navy PRT will replace curl-ups with plank holds. As of this writing, standards for plank duration have not been promulgated.

Navy Male & Female Physical Readiness Test (PRT) Charts

Physical Readiness Test (PRT) Chart for Males: 17–19 Years of Age

Performance Level	Points	Curl-Ups	Push-Ups	1.5-Mile Run
Maximum	100	109	92	8:15
Outstanding	90	102	86	9:00
Excellent	75	90	76	9:45
Good	60	62	51	11:00
Satisfactory Medium	50	54	46	12:15
Probationary	45	50	42	12:45

Physical Readiness Test (PRT) Chart for Females: 17–19 Years of Age

Performance Level	Points	Curl-Ups	Push-Ups	1.5-Mile Run
Maximum	100	109	51	9:29
Outstanding	90	102	47	11:30
Excellent	75	90	42	12:30
Good	60	62	24	13:30
Satisfactory Medium	50	54	20	14:45
Probationary	45	50	19	15:00

Physical Readiness Test (PRT) Chart for Males: 20–24 Years of Age

Performance Level	Points	Curl-Ups	Push-Ups	1.5-Mile Run
Maximum	100	105	87	8:30
Outstanding	90	98	81	9:15
Excellent	75	87	71	10:30
Good	60	58	47	12:00
Satisfactory Medium	50	50	42	13:15
Probationary	45	46	37	13:30

Physical Readiness Test (PRT) Chart for Females: 20–24 Years of Age

Performance Level	Points	Curl-Ups	Push-Ups	1.5-Mile Run
Maximum	100	105	48	9:47
Outstanding	90	98	44	11:30
Excellent	75	87	39	13:15
Good	60	58	21	14:15
Satisfactory Medium	50	50	17	15:15
Probationary	45	46	16	15:30

Physical Readiness Test (PRT) Chart for Males: 25–29 Years of Age

Performance Level	Points	Curl-Ups	Push-Ups	1.5-Mile Run
Maximum	100	101	84	8:55
Outstanding	90	95	77	9:38
Excellent	75	84	67	10:52
Good	60	54	44	12:53
Satisfactory Medium	50	47	38	13:45
Probationary	45	43	34	14:00

Physical Readiness Test (PRT) Chart for Females: 25–29 Years of Age

Performance Level	Points	Curl-Ups	Push-Ups	1.5-Mile Run
Maximum	100	101	46	10:17
Outstanding	90	95	43	11:45
Excellent	75	84	37	13:23
Good	60	54	19	14:53
Satisfactory Medium	50	47	15	15:45
Probationary	45	43	13	16:08

Navy Height and Weight Standards Chart

Height (inches)	MALE Maximum Weight Standard (pounds)	FEMALE Maximum Weight Standard (pounds)
57	127	127
58	131	131
59	136	136
60	141	141
61	145	145
62	150	149
63	155	152
64	160	156
65	165	160
66	170	163
67	175	167
68	181	170
69	186	174
70	191	177
71	196	181
72	201	185
73	206	189
74	211	194
75	216	200
76	221	205
77	226	211
78	231	216
79	236	222
80	241	227

Marine Corps Physical Fitness Test (PFT) Standards

Male 3-Mile Run Standards

Age Group	Maximum Time	Minimum Time
17–20	18:00	27:40:00
21–25	18:00	27:40:00
26–30	18:00	28:00:00

Female 3-Mile Run Standards

Age Group	Maximum Time	Minimum Time
17–20	21:00	30:50:00
21–25	21:00	30:50:00
26–30	21:00	31:10:00

Male Pull-Up Standards

Age Group	Maximum Reps	Minimum Reps
17–20	20	4
21–25	23	5
26–30	23	5

Female Pull-Up Standards

Age Group	Maximum Reps	Minimum Reps
17–20	7	1
21–25	11	3
26–30	12	4

Male Crunch Standards

Age Group	Maximum Reps	Minimum Reps
17–20	105	70
21–25	110	70
26–30	115	70

Female Crunch Standards

Age Group	Maximum Reps	Minimum Reps
17–20	100	50
21–25	105	55
26–30	110	60

Marine Corps Height and Weight Standards Chart

Height (inches)	MALE Maximum Weight Standard (pounds)	FEMALE Maximum Weight Standard (pounds)
57	127	120
58	131	124
59	136	129
60	141	133
61	145	137
62	150	142
63	155	146
64	160	151
65	165	156
66	170	161
67	175	166
68	180	171
69	186	176
70	191	181
71	197	186
72	202	191
73	208	197
74	214	202
75	220	208
76	225	213
77	231	219
78	237	225
79	244	230
80	250	236
81	256	242
82	263	248

NROTC Alumni Medal of Honor Recipients/Commissioned Ships

World War II

John Joseph Parle, USN, Creighton University NROTC Class of 1942

George Ham Cannon, USMC, University of Michigan NROTC Class of 1938

Robert E. Galer, USMC, University of Washington NROTC Class of 1935

David M. Shoup, USMC, DePauw University NROTC Class of 1926

John Lucian Smith, USMC, University of Oklahoma NROTC Class of 1936

Vietnam

William McGonagle, USN, University of Southern California NROTC Class of 1947

Terrance C. Graves, USMC, University of Miami NROTC Class of 1967

James E. Livingston, USMC, Auburn University NROTC Class of 1962

United States Navy Ships

USS *Shoup* (DDG 86)

"Dare to Read, Think, Write, and Publish"

By ADM Jim Stavridis, U.S. Navy

BENJAMIN FRANKLIN ONCE SAID, "Either write something worth reading or do something worth writing." But I would say, "Do both!" Live well, write about it, and write it well. Life in today's military certainly takes care of the "worth writing" part of Franklin's advice by providing us a broad, rich array of worthy experiences and ideas, worthy of living, but also worthy of reading, documenting, discussing, and—above all—publishing.

Much as the sea has been the inspiration for many writers—poets, novelists, journalists, even scientists—our military profession itself is a sea of inspiration. It is ever-changing, nearly boundless, often Hollywood-style exciting, and begs to be interpreted, presented, and debated. Indeed, we already have a well-established literary heritage, from purist strategy and tactics to fiction and even science fiction, but each of us has a role to play in continuing and improving on this heritage.

And it has never been easier to get started. All you need are some ideas you care about and pen and paper . . . or more likely, just a keyboard.

Something Worth Writing

All of us who have served have observed or lived something worth writing *and* something that would be good for others to read. We often express these ideas and observations in wardroom discussions, which are critical elements of personal and unit development. But these discussions usually make local impact only and stay within the lifelines of the ship or unit. Publishing your thoughts for others to see, however, extends the reach of your ideas and sparks a larger discussion, a larger professional conversation. In the case of widely read journals—whether service specific like *Proceedings* or the *Marine Corps Gazette*, or broader-reaching joint or international publications like *Foreign Affairs* or the *Harvard Business Review*—your ideas can influence a great many and inspire conversations in numerous wardrooms or even academic centers, boardrooms, and cafés.

But here is the catch: your ideas will not go anywhere unless you have the courage to "hang them out there" for others to see. Publishing can be a daunting task. In our professional lives, we can rationalize and mitigate the risks of holding station alongside an oiler in heavy seas or landing our aircraft on a pitching carrier deck; but for many, the thought of having our ideas read by others pegs the risk meter as unacceptable. Once our thoughts are out there, we feel we have lost control.

Let's face it, sometimes mentors even advise people against publishing, because it is perceived as a "career risk." Don't be afraid—have the moral courage to vet your ideas responsibly and sensibly. In virtually every case of which I am aware, even the most controversial articles (and I've written my share) are respected as attempts to contribute and respected as such.

The key to publishing and mitigating any risk is twofold: finding the appropriate venue and writing as best you can with complete honesty for that audience. Finding a venue is getting easier all the time. There are many print journals, for example, that would eagerly publish your ideas, stories, and articles, especially professional military journals. You don't have to be the CNO or a combatant commander to get them published, although one day you might find yourself in those shoes. After all, just look at three young officers who published in *Proceedings* over the years, names you might recognize: Lieutenants William F. Halsey, Chester Nimitz, and Ernest J. King. What ever happened to those guys?

In fact, *Proceedings*, or any professional journal, would become irrelevant without the youth of the force publishing ideas and taking interest in the greater professional conversation. If you look at the more exciting, thought-provoking, or innovative articles printed today, you more than likely will find young minds behind them—lieutenants, lieutenant commanders, and commanders. And the best ideas often come from unlikely sources and certainly are not the sole dominion of the "brain" or "genius" of the unit.

Options for publishing and testing our ideas are also ever-expanding. The Internet and electronic publications afford us ample opportunity to match our ideas against those of others. Blogs and Internet forums are great arenas for testing the waters, sharpening arguments, and crystallizing thoughts. Perhaps these forums even reduce the perceived risk level of publishing, lowering the "whole Navy will read this" anxiety factor.

To a certain extent this is true, and electronic forums serve a great messaging purpose. But military professionals should be cautioned always to keep the conversation aboveboard and to avoid anonymous posting while keeping classification and good judgment in the forefront of our minds. I'm sure we've all learned the lesson of the e-mail we wish we hadn't sent—the one that got forwarded well beyond the lifelines of the ship—and that returned to haunt us. So use all the media available, but do so within the bounds of command sense, policy, regulation, and especially classification.

Something Worth Reading

Even though we have growing publishing opportunities, that does not mean writing well is getting any easier. As Nathaniel Hawthorne once observed, "Easy reading is damn hard writing." Writing is a skill that needs continuous honing through practice, study, and formal mentorship if possible. Much as physical fitness and technical proficiency require dedicated time and effort, so too does writing. In fact, writing is a key skill for all leaders, regardless of rank, and must be exercised, evaluated, and rewarded when done well.

Of course, we have to keep in mind that not all of our writing will be worth reading. All of us will create some losers—I sure have. Even the best writers have had their flops. The key is to keep writing and publishing anyway. Much as a baseball player who bats .333 (only one in three successes) is having a great season, a writer can also have hits and misses and still be successful. Of course, through bouncing your ideas off your peers and through honest editing, you should be able to turn your thoughts into a well-written argument and better position it for success. Always show a draft article to a few trusted advisers for comments and criticisms before turning it loose like a fawn in the forest for the real world.

When writing a professional article, I think Mark Twain has the best advice. "The time to begin writing an article is when you have finished it to your satisfaction. By that time, you begin to clearly and logically perceive what it is you really want to say." Rewriting is essential. But, on the other hand, do not let the perfect article be the enemy of the very good one. The perfect article does not exist! Trying to make it so will only guarantee you never publish it. By all means re-write, edit, deliberate, think; but ultimately, launch your ideas and see what comes.

Be prepared, however, to face criticism. Despite your best efforts to formulate an idea and write it well, there will be critics. But you should look at criticism as a strength of the system. It means people are reading your work, that they are thinking, and that the environment is set for overall professional development. Besides, your argument, if written well, might persuade, inform, or influence the audience just as you intended.

Taking a good idea beyond the article phase can also be rewarding and make a lasting contribution to our literary legacy. Often an article or series of articles can germinate and grow into a full-length book. And probably the best way to master your subject of interest is to research and write a book about it. In the naval service, we have many published authors whose works still influence new generations of sea-goers.

Of course, our culture has evolved over the years when it comes to writing. Alfred Thayer Mahan is a legend for his strategy classics, but after he wrote his defining opus *The Influence of Sea Power upon History, 1660–1783,* Mahan was admonished by a superior who said in a famously quoted fitness report, "It is not the business of a Naval officer to write books." I disagree. Don't feel you have to write a book, but on the other hand, don't rule out the possibility that eventually you may want to do so. And don't forget that Mahan ended up retiring as an admiral after all. No one remembers the officer who wrote the fitness report; but everyone knows Admiral Mahan, and the *Arleigh Burke* destroyer named for him proudly sails the seas today.

The Marketplace of Ideas

In this rapidly globalizing 21st century, our nation and our military are out competing in a marketplace of ideas. We live in a 24/7 news cycle with near instant reporting and widespread dissemination of stories. It is a teeming, tumultuous, and exhausting marketplace. There has been a tremendous push for military professionals to understand, quantify, and assess our ability to compete in this arena. On all fronts, we must excel at strategic communication—the ability to get our message out to the right audience, at the right time, with the proper effect, and in all media.

Each of us has a clear obligation to contribute to this effort, to be a part of the conversation, to help our ideas compete. Our nation was founded on ideas that just could not be repressed—those of freedom and liberty. In 1776, we launched these ideas into a world ruled by a different system. Our ideas faced stiff competition, and throughout the years we have even suffered wars to defend them—wars like today's struggle against extremists who use terrorism as a weapon, often to suppress freedom of expression. Our second president, John Adams, once wrote that the best way to defend our ideas was through using our minds: "Let us tenderly and kindly cherish, therefore, the means of knowledge. Let us dare to read, think, speak, and write."

So, dare to read and develop your understanding. Carve out the time to think and form new ideas. Dare to speak out and challenge assumptions and accepted wisdom if your view differs from them. Have the courage to write, publish, and be heard. Launch your ideas and be an integral part of the conversation.

Why? Because it makes our nation and our profession stronger. In the end, no one of us is as smart as all of us thinking together.

ADM James Stavridis, USN (Ret.), is a 1976 distinguished graduate of the U.S. Naval Academy who spent over thirty-five years on active service in the Navy. He commanded destroyers and a carrier strike group in combat and served for seven years as a four-star admiral, including nearly four years as the first Navy officer chosen as Supreme Allied Commander for Global Operations at NATO. After retiring from the Navy, he was named the dean of The Fletcher School of Law and Diplomacy at Tufts University in 2013 and served as the U.S. Naval Institute's Chair of the Board of Directors from 2013 to 2019. Currently, he is an operating executive with The Carlyle Group and Chair of the Board of Counselors at McLarty Associates. He has written articles on global security issues for the *New York Times, Washington Post, Atlantic Magazine, Naval War College Review,* and U.S. Naval Institute *Proceedings* and is the author or coauthor of several books, including *Command at Sea,* 6th ed., and *Destroyer Captain.*

From U.S. Naval Institute *Proceedings* 8, no. 134: 16–19.
Reprinted with permission. © 2008 U.S. Naval Institute/www.usni.org.

Index

About the Authors

VADM PETER H. DALY, USN (RET.), is the Chief Executive Officer and Publisher of the U.S. Naval Institute. A career Surface Warfare Officer, he is a graduate of the College of the Holy Cross, where he received his regular commission through the Naval Reserve Officer Training Corps program.

CDR MICAH D. MURPHY, USN, is a Surface Warfare Officer currently serving in his third command tour. He is a native of Wheaton, Illinois, commissioned in 2001 through the University of Notre Dame NROTC, and also holds an MBA from the Kellogg School.

LT BRENDAN E. CORDIAL, USN, is an active-duty U.S. Navy Surface Warfare Officer currently serving as an afloat department head. He is a native of Beaufort, South Carolina, and commissioned in 2011 through the University of Notre Dame NROTC.